Who Died In Deptford?

The Mystery of Christopher Marlowe

Jennifer Clarke

Daybreak Publications

Copyright © November 2019 Jennifer Clarke
All rights reserved.
ISBN: 9781695863019

DEDICATION

To my husband, James Clarke, a playwright and the son of a glover.
.

Also by Jennifer Clarke

Non-fiction
Chekov – a study (unpublished dissertation, Keele, 1972)
Errors in Cohesion in the writing of second language learners and others in the primary school
The Campaign for the Right of the Married Woman to Earn

Plays
The Coral Island -
A horror story for teenagers
Morgue -
A ripping tale

With James W. Clarke:
Shades of Isis –
A nativity story

Poetry
Missives from Periclean Athens
Earthbound
Flags of Renunciation
Tea and Ginger Cake
Playing with Matches
Tales from the Ringing Isle
Noah's Ark
Songs of the Simmerdim
The Animal Town Express

With James Clarke:
The Foxes Triumphant

Other
The Slushpile (editor)
The Aylestone Bulldog Association Newsletter (editor)

CONTENTS

	Acknowledgments	i
	Introduction: Two Bodies, One Face	1
1	Deptford 1593	12
2	Inquest – May 1593	18
3	Who is Marlowe – Who is Shakespeare?	28
4	'Two Houses, both alike in dignity'	35
5	Mind the Gap	66
6	Going to Rheims	85
7	A Holder of Horses	93
8	Parker Scholar	100
9	'The Play's the Thing!'	114
10	Some Groat's Worth of Wit	139
11	Of Thomas Watson, Gangs - and *Romeo and Juliet*	154
12	Vlissingen and the Philosophers' Stone	174
13	Richard Baines – Priest and Spy	201
14	The Strange Arrest of Thomas Kyd	211
15	The Three Musketeers? Robert Poley, Ingram Frizer, Nicholas Skeres – and Eleanor Bull	225
16	John Penry – Like Macavity, He's Not There	233
17	Who Died in Deptford?	248
18	The Burial Place	276
	Conclusion: The Bones Assembled	292
	Appendix I – Some Red Herrings	315
	Appendix II – Juliet and Shakespeare's Gangs	340
	Appendix III – Marlowe's Ancestry	346
	Appendxi IV – List of William Shakeshaftes	348
	Appendix V – Cited Texts	350
	Appendix VI – A Paranoid Society	375
	Time Line	285

References	401
About the author	415

Note on usage in the text

Throughout I have used the name Corpus Christi for Marlowe's Cambridge college, although the contemporary name was Benet's College, after the church nearby, Benet being a contraction of Benedict. I have also referred to the King's School in Canterbury, although during Elizabeth's reign it was called the Queen's School. This usage is to conform with other biographers of Marlowe

ACKNOWLEDGMENTS

I would like to acknowledge the help and support of my husband, James Clarke in the research for this book. Also the following: Thomas O'Rourke, my fellow campanologist, who introduced me to the idea that Marlowe's death was highly suspect through a mutual interest in historical crimes; Lucy Hughes, Archivist at Corpus Christi College, who was most helpful in my journey to find Marlowe; Peter Farey, for allowing me to read his investigation of 'one Morley', a very interesting view of the question whether Marlowe was ever tutor to Arbella Stuart (which I have not used or referred to as it is unpublished); and lastly, Professor Emeritus Alex Murdoch-Physant for his advice on writing and publishing the study.

'Can Christopher Marlowe be a *nom de guerre* assumed for a time by Shakespeare?'

The Monthly Review, August, 1819

Introduction

The Theory: Two Bodies, One Face

'The longer time has elapsed the more things fall into proportion. One sees them in their true relationship to one another.' [1]

The intention of this study is not to write a life of Christopher Marlowe. This is not a biography and therefore the events known of Christopher Marlowe and William Shakespeare have been accepted as accurate as far as they go. What follows is an investigation into whether what we know of Marlowe and Shakespeare suggests that they might have collaborated and whether Christopher Marlowe survived the attack in Deptford.

One of the stumbling blocks to his survival is that there is nowhere Marlowe could go and could support himself even if he was still employed as a spy by the

---

1　　Christie, A. *The Mysterious Mr Quin: At the 'Bells and Motley'*, Mr Quin, p. 78. Harper, 2003.

Elizabethan state. Another stumbling block is the existence of a body, of a man about thirty years old, presented to the coroner on 31 May 1593. Also investigated is whether Shakespeare has any separate existence before the disappearence of Marlowe, outside the bare facts of his life in Stratford-on-Avon. There is no evidence Shakespeare and Marlowe knew each other[2] or that Shakespeare existed in London before 1592, yet they are indelibly associated with each other in people's minds. Indeed, there is a sense that before 1592 Shakespeare and Marlowe have two heads but the appearance of one body - rather like Leonardo's cartoon of the Madonna and St Anne in the National Gallery, London.

***

For over a hundred years there has been controversy over the death of Christopher Marlowe. When the records of the inquest on his body were uncovered in 1925 in the Public Records Office in London by Dr. Leslie Hotson, it became clear that ideas about his death, as previously known, were inaccurate. It also became clear that the evidence of Marlowe's murder rested on the testimony of three very unreliable witnesses, Robert Poley, a secret agent, and Nicholas Skeres and Ingram Frizer (not Francis Frazer, as recorded in the burial record of St. Nicholas' church, Deptford) both confidence tricksters and also employees the one of Marlowe's patron, Thomas Walsingham, and the other of his possible enemy, the Earl of Essex.

---

2   Except for a vague reference in one of Shakespeare's plays - which may not be there to show acquaintance, but merely knowledge of a recent famous event, for the sake of topicality.

The death, previously thought of as a pub brawl, and described as such in some contemporary accounts, was no such thing, it appeared, but an event set up in a contrived meeting in what might be a safe house, and the man who had actually killed Marlowe was later given a pardon by the Queen.

The controversy has not only touched on the death of Marlowe but also on the authorship of the plays of his contemporary, William Shakespeare. There appeared to be so many similarities between the writers, and the evidence for Shakespeare's authorship so thin, that some people began to think that the real author of Shakespeare's plays was Christopher Marlowe, and that far from dying on Deptford Strand, he had survived the attack by Ingram Frizer and somehow escaped to the continent, from where he sent plays back, many set in exotic locations, to an unknown player in London, William Shakespeare. Shakespeare became an actor/manager and had the plays performed (and later published) under his name in order to conceal the fact that Christopher Marlowe, an inconveniently knowledgeable spy, was still alive.

There are three problems with this scenario. The first is that there is good evidence that William Shakespeare wrote the plays ascribed to him, both from the publication of his work during his lifetime, his name being in lists of sharers of the Globe theatre, and in the lists of players, and after his death by elegies naming him the 'swan of Avon' (Ben Jonson in the First Folio) and others attesting that the man buried in Stratford-on-Avon, who was interested in finances and leases, was also a famous playwright.[3] The

---

3   That artists do not write of their work is not new. Not all artists

second is that a body was buried in St. Nicholas church, Deptford, and was identified in the record as Christopher Marlowe, so if this is not Marlowe then who is it? The third problem is that if the second problem is resolved by showing that Marlowe did escape, where did he go, and what – and this is most important – did he live on? He had no profession, and there is no poet or playwright in continental Europe he could have been. He had also been called an atheist by his own countryman, not a description likely to endear him to either Catholic Europe or those countries which were becoming Protestant.

Suggestions that he went to Italy, specifically to the town or area of Bassano, or that he adopted a new identity, have nothing to support them. Suggestions as to his possible new identity, for example that he was a M. le Doux, are not just unproved but proved to be untrue[4]. That he might be a 'Christopher Marlowe' who came to England from Spain around 1601 is clearly impossible as this man is the wrong age to be Marlowe. So, if Christopher Marlowe survived he had to have an occupation which gave him both an income and protection against the charge of atheism.

And there is still the problem of the body at the inquest, identified by three witnesses as Christopher Marlowe. If not Marlowe, then who is it?

---

conform to the romantic idea of genius invented by the Victorians. The sixteenth century was less self-conscious than the eighteenth and nineteenth centuries, and even then, for example, Van Gogh mainly wrote to his brother for money.

4   Farley, P. *Deptford and M. le Doux*, Peter Farey's Marlowe Page. (Farey.P and Caveney, G.)

Apart from the suggestion that the body was that of a local sailor or a passer by, or perhaps a victim of Frizer and Skeres' financial conniving, the main contender put forward for the body is John Penry, hanged virtually in private on 29 May, of whom there is no record of burial.

The sailor picked off the street is an intriguing tale, but full of difficulties. Marlowe was a playwright, and considered to be a gentleman. Any body must show the signs of being a gentleman, and this is unlikely to be the case with the body of a sailor, with, at the very least, hands roughened by working with wet, salt-rimed sheets. There is also the question of clothing – the body would need stripping and re-dressing in clothes likely to be worn by a gentleman playwright. Not impossible, of course, but time consuming. (see Nicholls etc who refutes sailor theory)

Exploring the idea that both Frizer and Skeres were 'coney catchers', that is confidence tricksters, suggests a very likely source of a body is someone they were conning; a young man, perhaps far from home, who was being persuaded to sign a bond [5] and who would not be missed. An intriguing idea but again rather difficult to substantiate. For instance, a young man being conned of his money would probably not have remained all day. He *might* have consented to being called 'Marlowe', on the grounds that Frizer and Skeres were going to put the debt on the playwright, and not him, but that is carrying conspiracy theory a step too far. Ultimately the candidate for the body most favoured ends in being John Penry.

But John Penry also presents problems. The first is that he was hanged. Unless we assume the entire jury was

---

5   As Drew Woodleff did in 1593.

suborned by persons unknown (someone on the Privy Council, Thomas Walsingham, Audrey Walsingham) then sixteen men, upright citizens of Deptford, had to be completely unaware of the signs of hanging on the body, which not only include a stretched neck (possibly concealable) but a blood suffused face, not as easily concealed. As the wound on the body, a knife gash through the top of the eye, is described it is unlikely the jury did not notice signs of strangulation.

In any case someone spent the entire day of 30 May 1593 at Eleanor Bull's house in Deptford, talking, eating, walking in the garden. If it was not Marlowe, then who was it?

So the problem of the body seems intractable.

Given that Poley, Skeres and Frizer were entirely capable of lying about everything, the evidence given at the inquest means very little. The most important thing is the wound to Marlowe's body, a wound that would not have killed immediately, but was a killing wound. As interesting is the pardon given to Frizer and the month long alibi given to Poley by the Privy Council. There is enough in these to suggest something was done that needed to be hidden. It might have been the murder of Christopher Marlowe, it might have been an escape plot. It might have included the murder of someone else.

If it was an escape plot or a murder plot who was the intended victim? Was it Christopher Marlowe, or was it someone else? If it was not Christopher Marlowe, who was at Deptford? And if it was not Marlowe, where did Marlowe go?

The question is, did Christopher Marlowe die at Deptford, or the separatist John Penry? Evidence suggests the possibility of either.

But there is one other candidate for being the corpse at Deptford who is never included in the list of possibilities. It is that mysterious figure William Shakespeare, who appears as if from nowhere as Marlowe disappears. Did the unknown Shakespeare die at Deptford, in place of his fellow playwright, the infamous Christopher Marlowe? But if so, how? And, indeed, why might that happen? What circumstances would put Shakespeare at Deptford rather than Marlowe?

***

If it were possible to show that Marlowe had survived Deptford and his body been replaced by that of Penry, there is yet another question to answer. If Marlowe went abroad why did he continue to write in English and send the work back to London. Players only paid about £8 a play, and Shakespeare writes only thirty-seven, which would net him £296 over twenty years. Marlowe spoke French and probably Italian, as well as being proficient in Latin. Abroad he would write plays and poetry in those languages for local performance, not send back plays in English to be sold for £8 each. There was a market for plays in continental Europe and for Latin plays and poetry in princely courts, universities and among aristocracies. There, and to a growing interest in theatre generally, is where Marlowe would aim his literary endeavours, not London. But we already know that the problem is there is no evidence that anyone who could be Marlowe did this.

But if Marlowe had a profession which would give an income and also a refuge then his escape from England becomes much easier, given that he was a secret agent used to passing the ports, and probably in possession of a passport.

What profession could Marlowe possess that allowed him free travel in continental Europe? The clue may well be in the accusation, in 1587, that he intended going to Rheims. We do not know the origin of this rumour, though we do know that the Privy Council roundly dismissed it, saying that Marlowe had been working for his country. There is one profession which would allow Marlowe to escape to the continent, and that would account for much of his behaviour, his reported blasphemy and atheism, and the lack of any hint of relations with women. That profession is of a Catholic priest, working in England to undermine the English crown. If Marlowe did go to Rheims and returned ordained it would give him privileged access to every recusant household in the country, and would make him an extremely useful secret agent. That he might also be working as a double agent, or passing false information to the church on the continent, is also probable. In this case, his escape from Deptford is explained. He left England as a special agent and arrived, probably in France, but his likely final destination was Spain, as a Catholic priest. As an ordained priest Marlowe would have had sanctuary in Catholic Europe and also been of use to England's spy masters as an agent, his contact in England being William Shakespeare. If Marlowe trained for the priesthood at Rheims and returned as a recusant priest it explains a great deal about his behaviour, and also sheds light upon the enmity he was held in by Richard Baines.

It is therefore, the main argument of this book that Christopher Marlowe was not murdered at Deptford Strand, on 30 May 1593, but that he survived and went abroad. It is also contended that only one man wrote the plays attributed to Christopher Marlowe and William Shakespeare and that the man who wrote them was William Shakespeare. Christopher Marlowe, who was associated with

Shakespeare, escaped abroad when England got too hot for the man known as Christopher Marlowe. He was able to do this, and completely disappear, because he became a Catholic priest in order to spy on traitorous Catholics for the Elizabethan state. Thereafter William Shakespeare continued to write plays and poetry but in the aftermath of Elizabeth I's wish to see Marlowe dead Shakespeare distanced himself from the work attributed to Marlowe, and wrote under his own name, changing his style wherever he could, and moving in completely separate circles from those frequented by Christopher Marlowe.

For we have few records of Shakespeare's friends. Thus, Ben Jonson calls himself Shakespeare's friend, but also called him a play broker (which he probably was - it means someone who buys and sells plays) and clearly considered this a shady and infamous job. He was also quite scathing about his writing in the same poem, The Poet Ape (the title is a term to describe someone who is not a poet). He also criticised Shakespeare's writing on numerous other occasions, citing his lack of geography and his habit of not correcting his playscripts, but writing freely and fast, something he reports actors being impressed by. He apparently visited him (along with Drayton) a few days before Shakespeare died and it was a convivial meeting - but the report of the event – a meeting in a local public house - was written 50 years after the event by the then vicar, who knew none of his protagonists. No well known poet, apart from Jonson, wrote elegiac poems in the First Folio either. But Jonson reports actors speaking about Shakespeare, and Shakespeare had two friends who most definitely had his interests at heart - or at least the will to profit from his fame. They were John Heminges and Henry Condell, to whom Shakespeare left bequests in his will, and who published the

First Folio in 1623. Nevertheless, apart from these four people, all our knowledge of Shakespeare is from his commercial and legal life, the use of his name on plays not by him, which were clearly cashing in on his fame, and his being a partner of Richard Burbage and an actor in the company they ran. But whoever Shakespeare was associating with, they were far removed from any circles Christopher Marlowe had moved in.

***

In support of the theory that Marlowe was not murdered in Deptford and that Shakespeare wrote the main body of his and Marlowe's work, it is suggested that Marlowe and Shakespeare did know each other exceedingly well, perhaps even being lovers. So close were they that they were interchangeable. Marlowe did indeed go to Rheims, where he became a priest but also tangled with Richard Baines (himself a mysterious figure with at least two identities: that of a lawyer's son who studied at Lincoln's Inn for a while, who was hung for the theft of a cup, but also that of a priest in the vicinity of Lincoln), leaving Baines with a life-long enmity for Christopher Marlowe. It is also contended that William Shakespeare took Marlowe's place at Cambridge (and took over the activities expected of a Parker scholar) and got his education there whilst Marlowe was at Rheims, and that once both had graduated they moved to spying on recusants on behalf of Francis Walsingham and Lord Burghley.

Lastly, the record of Marlowe's activities in Vlissengen (Flushing) and in London are reviewed and explained, suggesting that the man known as Christopher Marlowe was not a minor spy but an important government agent, working on projects for Walsingham and Burghley so sensitive, and so damaging to the state if revealed, that he could never be brought to trial for any of his activities, however dubious, even though he was involved in organised crime, and that he was not summoned to the Privy Council in May 1593 as either a witness or a suspect, but as an agent, ready to carry out a dangerous and secret task for Burghley and his son, Robert Cecil.

Chapter One

Deptford, May 1593 - the Traditional Account

At the end of May, 1593, four men attended a 'feast' in Deptford, at an inn run by Eleanor Bull. They spent all day at the inn, using a private room, which was furnished with benches, a table and a day bed, and in the late afternoon they walked in the garden. They were employees, in various capacities, of the late Francis Walsingham, and his cousin, Thomas Walsingham and were also associated with Lord Strange, a cousin and heir of Elizabeth I, and also the Earl of Essex, then a rising star at court. This was not the only connection with the royal court. Eleanor Bull was apparently related to one of the Queen's favourite waiting woman, Mistress Parry, and also to Lord Burghley himself, and was possibly also in the pay of Walsingham or perhaps the Privy Council.

The discussions that took place were perhaps of the problems of the day: Robert Poley, Ingram Frizer and Nicholas Skeres were all, after all, employed by prominent men of the Elizabethan court, all active in the times' convoluted politics. Perhaps they spent their time discussing the Spanish problem – for England was felt to be in danger of being attacked by a new armada. Although the Spanish Armada of 1588 had been defeated by English seamanship (based on the ability to attack and plunder) and God's wind, which blew the great galleons right round the north of Scotland where many were wrecked on the Shetlands and other islands, yet the threat remained from Philip II's Spain[1]. Elizabeth had been excommunicated by the Pope and her realm was open to attack by any Catholic power, for she was considered to be illegitimate, her mother, Anne Boleyn, merely Henry VIII's concubine, and her right to the English throne null. Linked to this discussion was that of the Scottish crown, for by 1593 there was worry about the succession. Elizabeth had no children, and her heirs were diverse, and included her cousin, Ferdinando, Lord Strange, who in actual fact was next in line according to the will of Henry VIII. Poley had travelled several times in Scotland on the work of Lord Burghley and his younger son, Robert Cecil, for determining what would occur when Elizabeth died – an event both expected and dreaded – was important for the governance of the realm. The two problems were linked. Cecil was working towards a solution to the continuing Spanish threat and also favoured the Scottish succession to the throne of England, but some, Essex among them, thought Burghley was being devious and supporting a Spanish solution to the succession problem. James VI of Scotland was the son of the Catholic heir to England, Mary

---

1 Most of the Armada ships got home, so one could say that God's wind preserved them from the attacks by the English ships, thus saving them to serve another day.

Stuart, who had been executed at Fotheringhay in 1587, but he was a Protestant and married to a Protestant born princess, Anne of Denmark [2]. He seemed the best hope for a stable, Protestant England's survival, the other heirs being in non-royal lines descended from Henry VIII's younger sister, Mary. James was the great-grandson of Henry's older sister, Margaret, and James IV, who had been killed at the battle of Flodden leaving his infant son (James V) to succeed him.

Politics, and dangerous politics, might thus the conversation of the day. What had the other man to say of their discussions? There can be no answer to that question, and we must rely for the truth being told by his three companions. The fourth man died at Deptford on a hot day in May, when London was besieged by the plague, and hurried into an unmarked grave at St. Nicholas church. The fourth man was named as Christopher Marlowe, poet, playwright (and spy).

So what had happened at this feast of four colleagues (it is doubtful that they can be called friends)? The party had been by invitation, and Frizer said that he had summoned Marlowe to it. Marlowe was at that time in a difficult situation. He had escaped the stench and plague of London by visiting his patron Thomas Walsingham at his country house but had been summoned from there by order of the Privy Council to answer questions on a charge of atheism made against him by Thomas Kyd. Previously it has been assumed he had been arrested, but if so it was a very odd arrest. He was neither imprisoned nor questioned, but required to attend the Privy Council. On the day in

---

2   She later converted to Catholicism.

question, 30 May, he was still, apparently, under orders each day to attend the Privy Council, but he does not seem to be under any other form of restraint, unlike the man who named him as owner of atheistic writings, Thomas Kyd, who had not only been arrested but tortured. Marlowe was also on bail of twenty pounds for another crime, that of breach of the peace against two constables.

    To discover the origins of the charge of atheism we need to go back to the beginning of May when the playwright Thomas Kyd was arrested on the 12 May and his lodging searched on suspicion of being linked to a series of notices (called bills) threatening refugees from France and Holland, known as the Dutch Church Libels. Heretical writings were found in Kyd's possession. What he had was a description of the Arian heresy – that Jesus Christ was not co-terminous with God the Father – and this statement amounted to treason. Kyd (the son of a scrivener) strenuously denied that the writing was his but said it belonged to Christopher Marlowe with whom he had shared his lodgings two years previously. He said Marlowe's papers must have got mixed up with his and that he had not noticed their inclusion in his bundle. This theory had some verisimilitude since a refutation of the Arian heresy was held at the King's School, Cambridge, attended by Marlowe when he was fifteen, and contained the description found at Kyd's lodging. Marlowe was also reported on several occasions to have made heretical and atheistic remarks to his friends and acquaintances. He was thus already suspected of heresy or atheism. On Kyd's evidence then, a warrant was issued for Marlowe on 18 May and he was fetched from Thomas Walsingham's house. On 20 May Marlowe attended the Privy Council but it was apparently not sitting and so he was ordered to attend every day until he could be seen. He seems not to have returned to Walsingham's house at Scadbury, where he may have met Poley or Frizer who later sent him an invitation to Deptford, so it is not clear where he was lodging. Sometime during the same week a deposition was made by another government agent, Richard Baines (an old foe of Marlowe's from an abortive mission to Flushing), accusing Marlowe of atheism and linking him to important and influential political and social groups. It is not clear whether this deposition was seen by the Privy Council before the meeting in Deptford, but Richard Baines certainly meant to profit by the fall of a colleague – or possibly to cover his own tracks, for Richard Baines had become a Catholic priest in order to the better spy on recusant Catholics.

The visit out to Deptford must have appeared as some sort of holiday, and the participants certainly behaved as though they were at leisure. Eating and drinking, walking in the garden, apparently chatting comfortably. But late in the afternoon a quarrel broke out, according to Poley, Frizer and Skerres. Marlowe was lying on the day bed just behind a bench where Frizer was sitting between Poley and Skerres, so tightly spaced that he could not turn. All four were probably, to a modern eye, drunk. Marlowe, without apparent provocation, pulled Frizer's knife out from his belt and hit Frizer with it, leaving a shallow wound on his head. Frizer managed to twist round and there was a scuffle in which Frizer became possessed of the knife. He stuck it into Marlowe's eye, killing him. While this scuffle took place Poley and Skerres looked on, doing nothing.

The blow to the head and the following scuffle were not unusual events in Elizabethan England. Fights between men in taverns, and in the street, were common. Everyone carried a knife, and gentlemen, and those not so gentle, carried swords. Any fight could be lethal. It paid to be polite, but holding one's temper in check was not necessarily considered to be a virtue. Both Marlowe and his companions had form, being confidence tricksters and in Marlowe's case a brawler. Indeed, Marlowe had been involved in an affray in Septmeber 1592, when he had a fight in Canterbury with a tailor called Corkyne and was only spared gaol because his father stumped up bail of twelve pennies. Several years earlier he had been involved in another attack which resulted in the death of the victim, William Bradley, and landed him in prison. Luckily for him, his was not the killing blow, and he had friends on the Privy Council. This time he was the victim and Poley, Frizer and Skeres united in making sure none of them would be accused of murder. The death was caused in self-defence.

On 30 May a coroner's court was convened with twelve jurors who all viewed Marlowe's body in the room where he had died and saw the wound above his eye. Once they had decided, with the help of the coroner, and the statements from the three witnesses, that this was Christopher Marlowe, gent, and that he had attacked Frizer who had then defended himself, (and could show a wound on his head as proof) the body was hastily buried in an unmarked grave. Tributes from London's theatre world poured in over the next few months, but a new star was rising as Marlowe's died: William Shakespeare of Stratford-on-Avon, poet, playwright, glover's and illegal wool dealer's son, was now becoming well known.

Chapter Two

Inquest, 31 May 1593

The only contemporary evidence for the manner of Christopher Marlowe's death is the coroner's inquest held on 31 May 1593, the day after his death. The court was convened in Deptford and viewed Marlowe's body in situ, at the establishment where he had been stabbed. Only three witnesses were called before a coroner and sixteen jurors, all local men of standing and apparent honesty. They were Nicholas Draper, gentleman, probably the foreman, as he is put first, Wolstan Randall, gentleman, William Curry, Adrian Walker, John Barber, Robert Baldwyn, Giles Feld, George Halfepenny, Henry Awger, James Batt, Henry Bendyn, Thomas Batt senior, John Baldwyn, Alexander Burrage, Edmund Goodcheepe, and Henry Dabyns, and it seems unlikely that they were suborned in any way, presumably having been chosen from the list of eligible men in the Hundred. By some measurements the coroner's court that day was within the purlieus of the Royal Court (within the verge, as the Queen was at Greenwich) but others suggest it is just outside the verge and thus by rights a second coroner should have sat with Coroner Danby. However, it is not certain that the absence of the second coroner makes the inquest illegal. It is possible that Danby was also coroner for Kent (as Honan says) and thus would not need a second coroner with him. Legal or not the evidence that Marlowe died in a brawl over the reckoning is recorded by the court and this is the only contemporary evidence of what happened on 30 May 1593. Three witnesses are mentioned but the testimony of only one is recorded and still existent, that is the evidence of Ingram Frizer. (The church burial record lists the murderer as Frances Frazer - which was originally read as Archer - which, until the discovery of the inquest record in 1925 by Leslie Hotson, led to various elaborate theories about Marlowe's death, including that he had killed Frances Frazer in a crime of passion and taken his place, or gone into hiding in fear of being tried for the murder, until killed by Burbage in 1598).

Ingram Frizer said that he and his companions had arrived at Eleanor Bull's establishment at 10 a.m. and stayed there all day. They ate in a private room and made quiet conversation. Late in the evening, about 6pm, they all went into the garden and strolled about, still talking, then went indoors for supper. It was only after supper that events changed. Marlowe was lying on a day bed or couch in the room and Frizer, Poley and Skerres were sat at the table, on a bench, all together, possibly playing a game. Vaughan, in Goldengrove, states that they were 'playing at tables', that is backgammon, which means only two people were playing and one was watching, but this game does not appear to be mentioned in the coronor's report.

Vaughan says: 'Not inferior to these (Diogenes and Pliny referred to earlier in the text) was one Christopher

Marlow by profession a playmaker, who, as is reported, about 7 years ago wrote a book against the Trinity: but see the effects of God's justice; it so happened, that a Deptford, a little village about three miles distant from London, as he meant to stab with his poniard one named Ingram, that had invited him thither to a feast, and was then playing at tables, he quickly perceiving it, so avoided the thrust, that withal drawing out his dagger for his defence, he stabbed this Marlow into the eye, in such sort, that his brains coming out at the dagger's point, he shortly after died. Thus did God, the true executioner of divine justice, work the end to impious Atheists.'

Thus, Vaughan is quite clear that the company was playing backgammon. Backgammon is a high stakes gambling game so there was possibly betting as well. At some point Marlowe got up and took Frizer's knife out of the back of his belt and struck Frizer with it, twice on the head. Frizer was able to show the thin, shallow wounds of this attack to the court. Frizer said he was stuck tight between Poley and Skeres and it was difficult to defend himself but he managed to turn and grab the knife and struck Marlowe in the head. Marlowe at once died. Vaughan was connected with those who knew Marlowe – his stepmother was sister-in-law to the Duchess of Northumberland, Dorothy Devereux. There is then, a connection between Marlowe and the Earl of Essex (who was Skeres employer) but it is rather tenuous, and his report was not published until seven years after the event.

The coroner's report states that the knife had entered Marlowe's brain by up to two inches along its thickest part. The jury viewed the body and attested that there was such a wound and that the dead man was identified as Christopher Marlowe, gent.

No other testimonies are recorded but Poley, and possibly Skeres, presumably corroborated Frizer's story in order to make convincing a plea of self-defence against Marlowe, who then emerges as the villain of the piece, in that he started the fight. The court records that the fight was over the bill – 'the reckonyinge'. It is not clear why there was such an argument. Marlowe was apparently at Deptford at Frizer's invitation, so one might not expect him, as a guest, to be footing the bill in any way. There may have been testimony by Eleanor Bull and her tapsters as to the events of the day and the identity of the guests, though they apparently did not witness the killing. However it happened, any such testimony is not included in the record.

Once the inquest had come to its conclusion Marlowe's body was buried in the churchyard of St. Nicholas, Deptford, with surprising haste on 1 June. The burial was noted and that Marlowe was killed by Francis Frizer. The grave was unmarked and is now lost.

So far, so good. The coroner and jury were convinced of the truth of events and the evidence and their conclusions were sent to the Royal Court of Chancery where, by 28 June, Frizer was given a pardon for causing the death of Christopher Marlowe in self-defence. But were the events described by Frizer what actually happened? In the ensuing weeks and years accounts of Marlowe's death varied, while his plays and poetry continued to be published for a few years but then went out of fashion. Much later, in the nineteenth century – and before the facts of the inquest were revealed in 1925 – some questioned whether Marlowe had died at all. A street brawl (one of the contemporary hearsay accounts calls it this) appeared an ignominious end to a playwright by the nineteenth century seen as a rival to William Shakespeare. Not only that, but many began to notice similarities in the works of Marlowe and Shakespeare, parallel plots, similar wording, and references to Marlowe's life and death in Shakespeare's plays. Conspiracy theories began to abound, not among those who were academically interested in Renaissance playwrights, but in those who were inclined to the Romantic view of literature. Shakespeare seemed so plodding, so very dull in his life, a glover's son, uneducated beyond grammar school, a man who in retirement bought land and sold wool, a man who wrote a will about property and left his wife the second best bed, a man whose only recorded speech is about enclosures in Stratford. The idea that Shakespeare the merchant's son had not written Shakespeare's plays grew. Various candidates were put forward, Francis Bacon (by his American namesake, Lucy Bacon), the Earl of Oxford, Elizabeth I herself. Or, could it be, that Marlowe had survived the fight at Deptford and that he wrote Shakespeare's plays, sending them from some hideout abroad to be performed at the Globe Theatre jointly owned by Master Burbage and Master Shakespeare, who was allowed to give his names to the works of the disgraced and heretical poet and spy, Christopher Marlowe?

For the difficulty of the inquest on 31 May 1593 is that all the witnesses participating, and the victim himself, were not just employees of Francis Walsingham, until his death, and of Lord Burghley and Sir Robert Cecil. They were spies and government agents employed by the Privy Council to ferret out sedition, and particularly Catholic plots. All four were accustomed to lie and dissemble and to bear false witness. Robert Poley actually said that he would lie rather than incriminate himself. Did he do so on 31 May 1593? And if he did so what was the real cause of the quarrel that ended with Marlowe's death – if indeed there was a quarrel?

***

Marlowe had been asked to attend the Privy Council on 21 May on the word of the playwright, Thomas Kyd, who had been arrested a few days before. Kyd accused Marlowe of atheism, a charge that could result in being burnt at the stake. But Marlowe, unlike Kyd, was not put in prison but left at liberty on bail to appear before the Privy Council when it could hear him. He was at liberty to go where he would as long as he attended the council each morning. Presumably he had attended it on 30 May before setting out for Deptford, since the court was at Greenwich.

The frequently so-called inn at Deptford, run by Eleanor Bull, may have been a safe house for government agents and not a public house of any sort. If so, Marlowe was perhaps expecting to be offered more government work or a plan to evade his present difficulties. What it looks like he should have been expecting is an assassination plot. But whose plot might it have been?

Several candidates for wanting Marlowe's death exist. They include Walter Raleigh, whose scientific meetings had acquired an atheistic bent that Raleigh probably did not want to have exposed to the Privy Council. Marlowe is thought to have known several members of Raleigh's circle, including the scientist Harvey and the poet, Thomas Watson with whom he had been involved in a fatal fight in 1589, with William Bradley. Watson had died by 1593, and it has often been suggested this was as a result of his imprisonment after the affray. Marlowe had received a pardon from the Privy Council for the death of Bradley, rather as Frizer was to do on 28 June. Marlowe also knew the poet Roydon, whom Poley says had gone to Scotland – both Watson and

Roydon were government agents. Other candidates are Burghley and Cecil and other members of the Privy Council - Sir John Puckering was the recipient of Baines' Note, but it is not clear when he actually saw it - perhaps afraid of the taint of atheism that Marlowe's trial could leave on them. They would certainly have been in a position to arrange Marlowe's accidental death in a brawl, and Poley or Frizer quite capable of taking on such a proposition. Other candidates are Thomas Walsingham's wife, afraid of the taint of homosexuality being attached to her husband, and Frizer himself, worried that his patron would be smeared by Marlowe, thus affecting Frizer's own prospects. The Earl of Essex may also have had reason to remove Marlowe, an associate of Elizabeth's previous favourite, Raleigh.

None of these possibilities really work. Raleigh's scientific meetings were known about, and any whiff of atheism would already have come to the authorities' attention because several members of his circle were in government pay. Thomas Walsingham seems to have been sincerely attached to Marlowe but he continued to employ Frizer for many years after Marlowe's death – unlikely if he thought that Frizer had been paid to kill Marlowe by his wife Audrey Sheldon, or anyone else, or if he thought Frizer had killed Marlowe to secure his own advancement. The Privy Council had other means of dealing with Marlowe which would have caused less comment. Marlowe himself does not appear to have thought that he was in any danger – though had it come to trial he might well have defended himself from a charge of atheism by saying it was one of the ploys he was using as part of his government work. He would then have been fighting for his life – but it may never have come to trial, just as Marlowe's previous misdemeanours had not. Even if it had, a defence that he was using atheism to catch atheists would not have damaged members of the Privy Council – they were free to use any means they could to prevent treason, and atheism was treason.

Perhaps, then, the plot was not an assassination plot. But if not, then what was the plan? It seems to have ended with Marlowe's death, in which case it may have gone wrong. Except that the only evidence that the body seen by the coroner was Christopher Marlowe is that given by three liars. There is no other evidence that it was Christopher Marlowe. Did he perhaps survive the attack? If he did, then how was it done and whose body was shown to the coroner and jury? And what happened to Christopher Marlowe – for he disappears permanently from the English scene?

The contention since the nineteenth century by those who believe Marlowe survived is that he went abroad. He could indeed have done so, except that he had been accused of atheism, a crime acceptable nowhere. And to what countries could he have escaped? Most of Europe was Catholic, and the Protestant Netherlands were in the thrall of Catholic Spain. An English Protestant would have had difficulty finding a refuge anywhere in Europe, except possibly Geneva. But suppose Marlowe did escape. What would he live on? Although William Shakespeare apparently made a good living out of writing and performing plays it was a precarious profession, at the mercy of public taste and favour – the knowledge of which would be outside the ken of an exiled Marlowe. Why would Marlowe not stay in London in disguise, a friend, a local tradesman, an actor who is close to Shakespeare if continuing to write for the English theatre is his aim? There is no advantage in going abroad and writing if there is not enough money engendered to share. And there is the difficulty of sending any money abroad. Shakespeare, if Marlowe *was* feeding him plays, spent his money widely too, buying land, a coat of arms, building a house, going into business with Burbage. Where was the surplus to send to Marlowe?

But there was one employer in Europe whose coffers were deep and who had employment to offer in plenty, especially to the right kind of English exile. The Catholic church encouraged the English to defect from Elizabeth I and her ministers. Catholic priests were in and out of the country, and frequently caught. Most of them were English Catholics trained either at Rheims/Douai or at Valladolid in Spain. Being a Catholic priest gave access to knowledge of Catholic families and Catholic plots – and Christopher Marlowe was a spy. One of his accusers, Richard Baines, had trained as a Catholic priest in order to spy on Catholics. Many have thought he failed, but he actually had a long career as a spy, and there is no reason to think others might not also have succeeded. The records concerning the English seminarians at Rheims/Douai are poor. Of the forty English Martyrs recorded there little is known, including their real names. Christopher Marlowe had been chosen as a Parker scholar by John Parker, the legitimate son of an Archbishop. That an archbishop had a legitimate son sounds perfectly respectable now, but in Elizabethan England it marked a departure from canonical custom. Elizabeth I said that she did not know how to address Archbishop Parker's wife – for she did not accept that married clergy were proper. So Archbishop Parker was in the forefront of the Protestant revolution, challenging by his marriage the accepted notion of a celibate clergy – this makes him an extreme Protestant according to the lights of his day. It is likely that those chosen as Parker scholars were expected to hold the same radical views. Marlowe was a spy – and it will be suggested later that this was linked to his Parker scholarship – and what better way to spy on Catholics in this age of fear of Catholic plots than to be a Catholic priest? If Marlowe was a Catholic priest he would have no difficulty, in 1593, in disappearing into Catholic Europe, and would be assured of a livelihood, perhaps training other English seminarians to go back to England. It would also explain the strangely fragmented life he lead, and the apparent lack of major contact with his home in Canterbury after he left it in December 1580, aged sixteen.

Before discussing this possibility it will be useful to look at the lives of his accusers, his killers and his rival playwright, William Shakespeare, as well as what we know of Marlowe himself.

Chapter Three

Who is Marlowe – Who is Shakespeare?

What do we really know about Christopher Marlowe? We think we know that he was the son of a cobbler, and was a playwright, an atheist, a homosexual, a blasphemer, a brawler. We think we know that he shared a room with Thomas Kyd and that they wrote together. We think we know that he was recruited as a spy by Francis Walsingham, Elizabeth I's spymaster, around 1585, whilst at Cambridge. We think we know that he wrote seven plays: *Dido, Queen of Carthage*; *Tamburlaine 1 and 2*; *Edward II*; *The Jew of Malta*; *Doctor Faustus* and *The Massacre at Paris*, some poetry, translated Ovid's *Amores* and some of the work of Lucan and wrote an unfinished long poem, *Hero and Leander*. References literary references suggest he might have written an eighth play apparently about Hannibal [1] though this has not survived in any form whatsoever and the

---

1   This could tentatively have been called *Hannibal of Carthage*, perhaps, on the model of *The Tragedy of Dido Queen of Carthage*.

only real evidence for it is a reference to it in another of Marlowe's plays [2], and a ninth, *The Maiden's Holiday*[3], (his only known comedy, completed or revised by John Day) the only copy of which was destroyed accidentally in the eighteenth century. [4] We think we know he knew William Shakespeare, perhaps wrote with him (some believe part of *Henry VI Part II* – especially the Jack Cade scenes – are Marlowe's)[5] or was a member of the same troupe of actors, working for, but unknown to, Lord Strange, and that both were known to Robert Greene. We think he probably knew Richard Baines, that he was a minor spy, involved in counterfeiting, and that the agents Poley, Skeres and Frizer knew him through their espionage connections. We think we know that Ingram Frizer invited Marlowe to a feast in Deptford. We are sure Marlowe knew Thomas Watson, because they were in a brawl together when a man called

---

2   According to Honan, in *Dr Faustus*.

3   *The Mayden's Holaday* appears as number 13 in John Warburton's list of MS plays destroyed by his cook (he apparently kept them in a cupboard in the kitchen). (Lansdowne MS 807, British Library). The play was also listed in the Stationer's Register for April 1654 as being by Christopher Marlowe and John Day. Day may have finished a play attributed to Marlowe – Day flourished post 1599 and died c.1640.

4   Honan, Park, Christopher Marlowe, Poet and Spy. Honan also explores the suggestion that the play *Timon* **might** be Marlowe's, written around 1580, before he went to Cambridge. Honan suggests there are similarities of style, viocabulary and characterization: the play contains a character very like the nurse in *Dido* (and *Romeo and Juliet*).

5   New Oxford Shakespeare edition of *Henry VI Part 1*, 2 and 3 will give Christopher Marlowe as co-author. Bakeless, J.E. in *Christopher Marlowe,* Jonathan Cape, 1938, p.164, suggests Marlowe and Shakespeare collaborated on *Henry VI.*

Bradley was killed; we suspect he knew the poet Royden, who went to Scotland, and was a frequenter of Walter Raleigh's circle, having acquaintance with many of its members, and that he made atheistic speeches to those persons. We know he knew Thomas Walsingham, because he was staying at his house when we think we know he was arrested on 20 May 1593. Kyd tells us Marlowe intended to go to Scotland like Royden. We think we might know what he looked like. [6]

But we know almost none of this. We actually know that someone called Christopher Marlowe was baptised in Canterbury in February 1564 (OS 1563), and that his father was a shoemaker [7], that he got a place at the King's School in Canterbury, aged just short of fifteen. We know someone called Christopher Marlowe so impressed Archbishop Parker's son, John Parker that he was given a Parker Scholarship lasting six years, at Corpus Christi, Cambridge [8], after only a few months at the King's School. We know that after the brawl with Watson and Bradley two men perhaps associated with the Privy Council put up bail for

---

6   Downie, J.A., Marlowe Fact and Fiction in 'Constructing Christopher Marlowe'.
7   There is a huge difference in wealth and status between a cobbler, who mends shoes, and a shoemaker who makes them. John Marlowe seems to have paid for his son's education at the King's School in Canterbury in shoes, and then appears to have claimed the money back when the headmaster died (Riggs, p.47).
8   Then known as Benet's College, after the church nearby. Six year scholarships were only given to those intending to take holy orders. Marlowe is able to continue his scholarship after taking his B.A., suggesting the college thought he would take holy orders.

Marlowe.[9] We know Thomas Walsingham's friend or employee Christopher Marlowe was taken as a witness from his house on 20 May 1593, to be interviewed by the Privy Council and that he was apparently put on bail without surety (but he was on bail for another breach of the peace). We know that someone was identified as Christopher Marlowe at an inquest in Deptford on 31 May 1593, and that this person was hurriedly interred in St. Nicholas' churchyard, Deptford, with a note in the register that he had been killed by one 'Francis Fraser'. We do not know what he looked like, we do not know his proper name (for he and others spell it in a variety of ways that suggest different pronunciations). This is all we know. Everything else is presumption, assumption, guess, rumour and second-hand reporting. None of it would stand up in a modern court of law.

But one thing we do know is that the person identified as Christopher Marlowe on 31 May 1593, was murdered in Deptford on 30th May 1593, and that at least three witnesses lied to the coroner's court on the following day.

We also know that Marlowe had a contemporary, born in the same year of 1564 (NS). A man who wrote plays and whose work seems to have some similarity with Marlowe's. That man is William Shakespeare, the son of a Stratford-on-Avon glover. So what do we know of Master William Shakespeare, gent? It is much the same as with Marlowe. A child called William Shakespeare was baptised in Stratford-on-Avon in April 1564 (as it happens, St. George's day). A man called William Shakespeare was buried in 1616 (and we believe he died on 23 April but actually that is the date

---

9   This is explored in Chapter Eleven.

of burial) and there is an enigmatic stone over his grave. We know he married Anne Hathaway (although this is misspelled in the register) and had three children, Susannah (who inherited the bulk of her father's fortune) and twins, Judith (who did rather less well out of her father's will) and Hamnet, the only son, who died aged eleven. We must presume Shakespeare was in Stratford-on-Avon around August of 1582, since Susannah was born in May 1583, and also around Easter (1 April) 1584 since the twins were born in February 1585 – although they may have been born early as twins often are. He was certainly present on 27 November 1582 when he married Anne. Apart from these dates we know nothing about William Shakespeare until Greene mentions one 'Shakescene' in his *Groatsworth of Wit* in 1592 [10], which suggests that Shakespeare is in London, probably living in Shoreditch (near Norton Folgate), and is writing plays. After 1593, when Marlowe dies, we know a little more. Shakespeare joins with Burbage in a theatre venture, he presents plays, loses his son in August 1596, buys New Place the following year, applies for a coat of arms, goes to court, appears as a witness in a family dispute in 1604 and writes a play (*All's Well that Ends Well*) based in part on the case, leaves London permanently in 1613 and dies in 1616 and that in the following years thirty-seven plays written by him, as well as sonnets and the poems *Venus and Adonis* and *The Rape of Lucrece* among others, are published and remain in print and performed for the next four hundred years, even to the present day. We think we know what he looks like, because Ben Jonson tells us the

---

10   But not everyone agrees that it is Shakespeare that is meant by Greene.

memorial at Stratford is a good likeness; and intrigued by the words on his tomb.

Again, we know little of this for fact. There is no record, apart from his marriage and the births of three children, of Shakespeare's activities between his baptism and 1592-3. The only evidence we have about Shakespeare's life involves financial dealings – the buying and selling of land, enclosure, becoming a gentleman by applying and getting a coat of arms for his father and his dealings as a play broker, playwright and sharer in the Globe. We believe he may have collaborated, probably with Beaumont and Fletcher, producing plays such as *The Two Noble Kinsmen* and *Thomas Moore* (Hand H) and perhaps also *Arden of Faversham* (though the title of this play is itself odd: Faversham may have been the place the Marlowe family originated, and Arden is Shakespeare's mother's maiden name which is used in his play *As You Like It* as a name for the forest where the action takes place [11]), and we may guess he worked with others because collaboration was frequent in playwriting circles in the sixteenth century: what was not borrowed or co-written was often plagiarised. It has been speculated that Christopher Marlowe, versions of whose lines appear in some of Shakespeare's plays, tolerated such borrowings from someone he probably knew, and that Shakespeare referred to his friend in later plays (in *As You Like It*, for example, where there is a reference to Marlowe's *The Passionate Shepherd to His Love.* though in 1599, rather oddly, this poem was published as being

---

11 See Appendix I. The real Forest of Arden is near Stratford-on-Avon.

Shakespeare's [12]). Very little of this rests on any evidence at all. No-one ever remarks that Shakespeare and Marlowe were acquainted, not even Thomas Kyd who claims he lived with Marlowe.

What we do know is that between 29 May and 1 June 1593, two men who had been involved in charges of sedition and atheism and who may both have visited Scotland, apparently died – but there was only one body definitely buried.

---

12   Though this might be explained by Shakespeare's activities as a play broker.

Chapter Four

Two Houses Both Alike in Dignity
What We Actually Know About the Backgrounds of Christopher Marlowe and William Shakespeare

So, it turns out that we actually know little about either Marlowe or Shakespeare. This chapter's intent is to elaborate on what is actually know about them, and what can be guessed or presumed.

Christopher Marlowe (1564(1563 OS)-1593) is known now as one of England's most famous playwrights, second only to William Shakespeare in current fame. His plays were written from sometime in the mid 1580s until his apparent death in 1593. The subjects were classical but also drew on European and Near Eastern history as known to the Elizabethans. He also translated the love poetry of Ovid, a favourite poet for Elizabethans and also some of the works of Lucan, wrote *The Passionate Shepherd*, and began but did not complete the long poem *Hero and Leander* (which was later completed by Chapman). Seven plays survive: *Dido, Queen of Carthage, Tambulaine the Great, Parts I and II,*

The Jew of Malta, Dr. Faustus, Edward II and in corrupt form *The Massacre at Paris*, and he possibly wrote two other plays.[1] All the surviving plays are intellectual in content, deriving from Marlowe's classical reading and reading of history, both subjects which he studied at Cambridge, either as part of the syllabus or from his own inclination and interest. They contain little comedy but have many scenes of love, politics and sometimes violent death.

Christopher Marlowe sprang from the level of society the sixteenth century knew as the middling sort. In this he was of exactly the same stock as his contemporary, William Shakespeare. Christopher Marlowe's father, John Marlowe, was in Canterbury in 1559, apprenticed to Gerard Richardson, a shoemaker. Marlowe probably came from a long line of tradesman. Boas lists the first recorded Marlowe appearing in 1414.[2] In 1521 one Richard Marley, a freeman of Canterbury and a tanner, and the son of a John Marley, tanner, died leaving his estate to his son, Christopher. Christopher died in 1540, leaving a pregnant widow, Joan, and a son, John, whom several researchers have assumed was the playwright Christopher Marlowe's father. However, this is unlikely as John Marlowe was probably born in Ospringe near Faversham.[3] This John,

---

1   As listed in Chapter Three, one about Hannibal, and a comedy titled *The Maiden's Holiday*, neitherof which have survived. Some researchers, e.g. Park Honan, consider that *Timon* (a play about Drake's circumnavigation) might have been written by Marlowe whilst he was at school. Some authorities also attribute *Edward III* to Marlowe.

2   See Appendix III, giving Boas's full list, and comments on likelihood these are Marlowe's ancestors.

3   Marlowe Society citing William Urry, *Christopher Marlowe and Canterbury* (Faber and Faber, 1988) - see discussion on pp 12-13.

who became a shoemaker, married Catherine Arthur, daughter of William Arthur of Dover (we know little of her family but they do not appear to have been prosperous and she seems at some point to have been a servant). Their second, and eldest surviving, child, was Christopher, baptised on 26th February 1564 (1563 OS) – he had an elder sister named Joan or Mary, who died in infancy, aged about six, (another, nameless, daughter was buried in 1568). John Marlowe was literate as is shown by his acting as a witness to wills and as a bondsman for marriage licences until his death in January 1605, however, it seems he could write no more than his signature (he is witness to wills) and a few words, but it was not uncommon to be able to read but not to write very well in the sixteenth century; ability to read the Scriptures was thought to be of great importance, for a Protestant was responsible for pursuing his own salvation, but being able to write was much less important. He and his wife, Catherine, had nine children of which six survived including four daughters. The family was prosperous and well to do in Canterbury society. They lived in four different parishes in the city and John became an official of the council. Marlowe's sister Joan (or Jane) married John Moore in 1582 aged twelve or thirteen (she was born in 1569) and died in childbirth within the year. Even in the sixteenth century this is young for marriage and childbirth (the average age of marriage is supposed to have been twenty-five [4], based on parish registers of marriage). It may

---

4   But averages cover a range of ages – if 25 is the mean, then many people married earlier or later.

be that names got mixed up and is this the elder daughter who supposedly died. [5]

Thus, Marlowe and his family are well documented for middling sort Elizabethans. Even so we have little knowledge of his whereabouts between 1580 and 1587, and know little of his life before he went to the King's School [6], and we can also only assume he attended a 'petty grammar school'. [7] Nominally he was at Cambridge from 10 December 1580, but is frequently absent and at least once someone else takes his place in the Buttery accounts.

Marlowe was born and baptised in Canterbury. He was in some ways more fortunate – or his family luckier – than Shakespeare. His father, John Marlowe, was a shoemaker and became an officer of the council; Christopher won a place, at the late age of fourteen, to the King's School, from where he went to Corpus Christi, Cambridge on a scholarship founded by Archbishop Parker. He went to Cambridge in December 1580, in his seventeenth year. When he arrived at Cambridge he was not immediately recognised and registered as a Parker scholar. This did not happen until the following term, in March 1581. His attendance at Cambridge can be traced in the Buttery Books, and he was often absent. In 1587 the university refused to give him his MA because of his absence and rumours that he intended going to Rheims (implying he

---

5   If the story is correct it sounds very like the genesis of the story of Romeo and Juliet – Juliet was 'not fourteen'. Joan's birth and marriage are examined more closely in Appendix II.

6   Then known as the Queen's School. Marlowe is entered on 14th January 1578 (NS), a few weeks before his 15th birthday.

7   Honan, P. *Christopher Marlowe, Poet and Spy,* p. 31. Kuriyama, ibid, p.11.

intended to become a Catholic priest, a treasonous objective at this time) but the Privy Council ordered them to confer the degree as (to paraphrase) it was not Her Majesty's wish that those who had been diligent in her service should suffer because others were ignorant of that service. The implication, and accepted explanation, of this is that Christopher Marlowe had been recruited at Cambridge as a government spy and this explains his frequent absences from the university.

Christopher Marlowe must have been an exceptional scholar at the King's School to be given a Parker scholarship. He must also have been a notable Protestant for such scholarships would be unlikely to go to persons of unsatisfactory religion, that is, with Catholic leanings. Archbishop Parker [8] was himself a scholarly man, who set up a college at Stoke by Clare which included provision for poor scholars. He became Warden of Corpus Christi College and set its finances on a secure footing. His description of the land and income of the Cambridge colleges persuaded Henry VIII to leave them intact, rather than allowing laymen to take over the university's land. Parker was an evangelical, following the ideas of Martin Bucer, the reformer and a possible Zwingian[9] and Thomas Cramner, Henry VIII's Archbishop of Canterbury, martyred under Mary I, all promulgating the idea that preaching was more important than ceremony, and the primacy of scripture over ecclesiastical authority. In 1547 he did something entirely radical. He married Margaret Harleston of

---

8   Encyclopedia Britannica, 11th Ed. Vol XX. Cambridge: Cambridge University Press, 1910. 829.
9   Encyclopedia Britannica, 11th Ed. Vol IV. Cambridge: Cambridge University Press, 1910. 713.

Mattishall in Norfolk (with whom he had been living) in June of 1547, two years before legislation in 1549 legalised clerical marriage. This puts Matthew Parker in the forefront of the Protestant revolution, especially when taken with his insistence on the importance of preaching and of inner piety. Despite his difficulties with the Reformation, which included the destruction of the college at Stoke by Clare because of the Chantries Act of 1547, Parker was clearly in tune with it although he went to Cambridge in 1520 without any hint of being a reformer. He was a Norfolkman but apparently not influenced the ideas of the Lollards. He almost certainly met the new ideas that informed his future life, at Cambridge where theological debate was rife and there were secret cells of Lutheranism. After the reign of Mary I Catholicism, although not illegal, had a bad press in England. Mary had martyred over 300 Protestants, by burning at the stake and although her husband, Philip II of Spain, had discouraged his wife's efforts he was following a similar path in order to root out heresy. There was not only suspicion of Catholics in England, there was outright fear that if the old religion returned and a move was made to stamp out heresy, and Catholic Europe and particularly Spain was allowed back the Inquisition would follow it – and in this light must be seen the likely psychological consequences to Parker of his colleague and friend, the reformer Matthew Bucer's body being exhumed and burnt in 1557 as a that of a heretic. Additionally Parker was himself present at the execution of Thomas Bilney [10] of Trinity College, who advocated the primacy of faith over the penitential regimes of medieval Christianity. Parker later

---

10   *The Death of Thomas Bilney,* J. H. Merle d'Aubigné

attested that Tilney had not recanted of his radical ideas – and it would seem, nor had Parker. That rooting out Catholics might be of interest to Parker is possible. He had himself come under reforming influence at Cambridge, and so knew that young men, away from home, were easily led into new ways – or errors. What more natural, once he had the means, than to set up a group of 'spies' at his own college to keep an eye on vulnerable young men and report back to the authorities?

By the time that Marlowe would have entered Corpus Christi on his Parker scholarship and Catholic ideas were infiltrating the university in place of Lutheran ones, many Cambridge graduates were making the journey to Rheims in order to be trained as priests who would carry the Catholic mission back to England. Archbishop Parker had died in 1575 but the scholarship system continued to be administered by his elder son, John Parker. There was, in the paranoid years after Elizabeth's excommunication and the Pope's declaration of her illegitimacy, a greater need to discover who the Catholics in the university were. What method would be easier to do this than to have spy on their fellows, students provided for by the very Protestant Archbishop Parker's scholarship? As Warden of Corpus Christi, and Vice-Chancellor of the University, Archbishop Parker was universally respected. He was in the forefront of the establishment of the English church, and a married priest. The choice of Protestant boys to keep an eye on their fellow students would be a simple matter, especially if each Parker scholar thought he was unique. And Marlowe is described as having Catholic friends and accused of going to Rheims, which suggests that the university authorities had noted his propensity for religious dispute and interest in those with questionable Catholic religious sympathies.

Marlowe was probably recruited as a spy in Canterbury and his religious opinions may have been instrumental in his being able to take up a place at the King's School at such an advanced age (the cut off for scholars was fifteen, and Marlowe therefore only just got in at fourteen and some months). Once at Cambridge he clearly came to the notice of others interested in spying on Catholics and was again recruited, this time to spy for Elizabeth on treasonous matters taking him away from the university in the service of the Privy Council.

And there is a problem with Marlowe. To get to Corpus Christi he must have been a diligent and good scholar, a hard-working young man expected to do well at his studies – for Parker scholarships were given out on that basis, whatever other role their beneficiaries were intended to play. But Christopher Marlowe does poorly at Cambridge, coming 199 out of 231 of all university scholars and 8 out of 12 among the scholars at Corpus Christi. [11] One might have expected a Parker scholar to do better! A second problem is his constant absence and the persistent rumour that he had gone to Rheims to be ordained as a Catholic priest. Why would such a rumour become current at Cambridge? Marlowe was on a Protestant scholarship which had the intention of educating young men to be ordained. Why should there be any rumour that Marlowe was Catholic? Clearly he had Catholic connections at Cambridge but he was likely spying on them, not fraternising.

Several biographers either say or imply that the provision of becoming a priest was onerous to Marlowe,

---

11   Bakeless, ibid, p.76.

who was temperamentally unsuited to holy orders. Others have pointed out that Marlowe's propensity to violence has been exaggerated. He is recorded as having taken part in an affray on 18 September 1589, together with Thomas Watson (another man associated with espionage) and that William Bradley, the man set upon, was killed by Watson. [12] He is also recorded as having a fight with William Corkyne in Mercy Lane, Canterbury on 15 September 1592, attacking him with a sword and dagger. Corkyne was a tailor, so one wonders if this quarrel was over a bill, but there is no inkling of the cause of the affray. Marlowe was also on bail for £20 at the end of 1592 for an affray in Shoreditch. [13]. He appeared before Owen Hopton, the magistrate who had appeared in the Bradley-Watson affray, and was bound over to keep the peace.

In the translation given of the original Latin by Park Honan: 'There has appeared before me, Owen Hopton, knight, Christopher Marle of London, gentleman, and he acknowledges that he owes our lady the Queen twenty pounds of good and lawful English money, on the condition that he will personally appear [14] at the next general sessions of the Peace' (October 1592 were the next general sessions).

Christopher Marle was bound over to keep the peace, especially in regard to the men he seems to have accosted: constable Allen Nicholls, and sub-constable Nicholas Elliot, of Holywell Street.

---

12   Nicholls, C. *The Reckoning*, pp. 211-212.
13   Honan, P, ibid p. 288. In Hogg Lane.
14   If Marlowe failed to appear in October the £20 would be levied by taking his goods, lands and tenements to be then given to the state. Honan, ibid.

These are the only recorded incidents, ending with a court appearance and in the second instance with John Marlowe, Marlowe's father, having to stand bail. Neither of the early affrays ended in any real punishment, and, although Thomas Watson appears to have spent until the February 1590 in Newgate, waiting for his pardon, it is unclear whether he was actually detained there. It was Sir Roger Manwood who presided at the sessions in December 1589 and Marlowe was given bail, a verdict of self-defence having been offered. Manwood was a Canterbury man and also notably corrupt, but there is no reason to suppose he knew Christopher Marlowe personally (although Marlow wrote a short Latin elegy in honour of Manwood, on his death in 1592). Marlowe's other connections are more likely to have secured his release.

The only other affray mentioned in connection with Christopher Marlowe is the fight at Deptford where he is named as the instigator of the quarrel. In an age when men readily took to sword or dagger to resolve a quarrel, three incidents over a number of years, and a fourth being very doubtful indeed, might be considered no particlular indication of a violent man given to sudden anger any more than anyone else. However, despite the paucity of evidence, there is a sense that Marlowe *was* a brawler, and given the times he lived in, his age at death, and looking at the plays he is credited with writing, he probably conformed to the habits of his contemporaries. More evocative of Marlowe, some might say, is his performance when witnessing a will with his father and brother-in-law (Joan's widower) in August 1585, when he is described as reading the will in a clear voice, [15] but reading well is no indication of character. Whether Marlowe habitually fought or not, he *was* arraigned for doing so three times, and his companions at Deptford were believed when they avowed that he had started the quarrel that lead to his death, which suggests that he did have a reputation for violent quarrels.

Marlowe matriculated in January 1581, and received his BA in 1584, despite being absent for seven weeks when university regulations only allowed scholars four weeks absence. From 1585 he is more absent than usual, and has more money to spend at the buttery which suggest he is now working for the government, meaning the Privy Council, Francis Walsingham and Lord Burghley. But Marlowe had had extra money from the very beginning of his career at Cambridge making the suggestion that Parker scholars were Parker spies more than tenable.

That Parker Scholarships involved spying is supported by the close relationship John Parker had with Archbishop Whitgift. John Parker had been surveyor for Archbishop Parker and keeper of the archbishop's palace at Canterbury. It seems he continued in this role after his father's death, working for Archbishop Grindal during his suspension, after the quarrel with the Queen over preaching,[16] and then Archbishop Whitgift. From Whitgift he leased property in Canterbury in 1586 and also in Kent,

---

15   Honan, P. ibid pp.108-109. Marlowe's brother-in-law, John Moore, 'remembered that Christopher (Marlowe) had read it (the will) "plainly and distinctly".
16   John Strype (1710), *Life and Acts of Edmund Grindal, Archbishop of Canterbury*.

at Boughton [17](Kent was where Marlowe's inquest was held in 1593). Thus, John Parker seems on good terms with Whitgift, and he is resident in Canterbury. He is also an MP and a wealthy man, paying £2000 for the manor of Nunney Castle, Somerset, in 1576. Whitgift was as interested in Catholics as in Separatist, what more natural than that Archbishop Parker's son should continue his father's work of keeping an eye on scholars at Cambridge as part of his charitable work of providing a university education for poor but clever young men?

Returning to Marlowe's career, the anomalies start as soon as he arrives in Cambridge. Why did he go up to Cambridge in December 1580, when Pashley would still hold his scholarship till the following March? Why was he able to spend three times his weekly Parker scholar's allowance in the second week of his residence?

He was accommodated in the newly furbished Parker scholar lodgings, which had formerly been a storeroom. He shared with two students from Norfolk, who in March following received 13/- to Marlowe's 12/-, showing they had been in college for a week longer than him. [18] Were they also matriculating in March? And the Bursar had added Marlowe's name in the accounts as a scholar and then crossed him out and replaced it with Pashley's. Kuriyama says that Corpus Christi was paying for Marlowe until he could matriculate, and expected that the moneys would be

---

17   *Parker Correspdence.* (Parker Soc.), pp. x-xi, 379-81; Strype, *Parker*, passim; *HMC 7th Rep.* 630, 642; Strype, *Whitgift*, i. 46; *CSP Dom.* 1598-1601, p. 527; C3/284/39; PCC 39 Pyckering; Add. 48018, f. 294v; *DNB* (Parker, Matthew); Lansdowne. 97, f. 177; R. Masters, *Corpus Christi*, ed. Lamb, 337. Ref Volumes: 1558-1603
18   Bakeless, J. *Christopher Marlowe*, 1938, p.72.

repaid, or rather be covered by later absences, as most scholars did not claim their whole allowance; as she says 'the college came to his aid'. [19] But why did the college support Marlowe? Is it that, since the Parker scholarship lasted for only six years and it took slightly longer than this to gain an M.A. the college countenanced early arrivals? Marlowe is put onto the list of pensioners for the year ending 24 March 1581 (1580 OS). Pensioners were scholars who had private means to pay their fees and board. How is Marlowe on this list and also able to spend 3/6 [20] in a week in the previous December unless he is being paid in some other capacity than scholar? The college is not likely to have paid him more than his scholarship fund, as they wanted the money back at some point.

Certainly his father cannot have been funding Marlowe – and was more likely, if funding was needed at this point, to suggest waiting till his son could matriculate and receive his stipend, the meanwhile probably helping in the family business. So if not Marlowe senior, then who is giving money to Marlowe over and above what the college might be loaning him against his later scholarship? It looks suspiciously as if it can only be John Parker, making sure one of his spies is properly settled in place for the beginning of the 1581 Lent term.

***

We have little enough documentation on Marlowe, but Shakespeare is even less well documented. Most

---

19   Kuriyama, *Christopher Marlowe A Renaissance Life*, p.43 '
20   Boas, ibid, p.10.

intriguingly his education seems to have been truncated and yet his plays are full of classical references and knowledge of high society. Can such a man actually have written the plays ascribed to him? Or was the author another man with the requisite education and contacts? And in both families there is the mention of membership of the old religion – Catholicism, and in Marlowe's case of homosexuality, not a word or concept known to the Elizabethans, but nonetheless a crime under the law since the time of Henry VIII, though prosecutions for it are rare to non-existent. Compared with Marlowe's life, Shakespeare's is one long gap until 1592 when he is apparently mentioned in Greene's Groat's Worth of Wit. Where was Will whilst Kit adorned Corpus Christi and the London stage?

Many explanations have been given of Shakespeare's lost years, meaning those years between 1585 and 1592/3, when Henry VI Part II and Venus and Adonis appeared. But we know almost nothing of Shakespeare's life between 1564, when he was baptised in Stratford, and 1592/3 when he appears in London. There are a few scattered dates in the 1580s. There is nothing else until the publication of Greene's Groat's Worth of Wit, which speaks of a 'crow in borrowed feathers' a 'shakescene' at the end of 1592. About Christopher Marlowe we can be pretty sure where he was in general between 1579 and 1587 – Canterbury, at the King's School, and at Corpus Christi, Cambridge.

Between Shakespeare's baptism and his marriage in 1582 there is a clearly a gap. We can guess that Shakespeare, as the son of a prominent man and a member of the corporation, went to the grammar school in Stratford, since this was a privilege extended to the sons of the city council members; otherwise we know nothing of his childhood. However, when John Shakespeare was accused of evading tax and taking part in illegal wool trading [21] that privilege came to an end, and Shakespeare's education came to a full stop. But there is no record of him being apprenticed in Stratford, nor anywhere nearby. So what happened to William, surely a boy wanting an education, despite his later writing of schoolboys going unwillingly to school, for an education was a ticket to the prospect of advancement in Elizabethan England?

We know that William Shakespeare was born within two months of Marlowe into a similar household. Shakespeare was baptised on 26th April 1564, so Old Style in a different year to Marlowe, and also came of people of the middling sort. His father was a glover (sometimes he is confused with Marlowe's father and called a shoemaker) and became an officer of the council, and an ale toper – in modern terms in charge of the enforcement weights and measure laws. However, unlike John Marlowe who, though caught in petty corruption in the matter of forty shillings of the council's money, mostly prospered in Canterbury, John Shakespeare fell from grace. He had originally been much better off than John Marlowe, the possessor of land and houses from his wife Mary Arden's family. However, an unwise, but certainly profitable, venture into illegal wool trading brought him low and he was dismissed from the council and lost his wife's lands in order to pay their debts. William was probably removed from the grammar school, since free attendance was a privilege of council members' sons, and with John's debts payment would be out of the question. William's education was truncated and the chance of going to university ruined – and also his father was

---

21   Greenblatt, *Will in the World*, p.63.

revealed as dishonest, convicted of a serious crime in Elizabethan times, for the wool trade provided much tax and evading it was a criminal offence. John Shakespeare was probably lucky that he only lost land and money. But this marks out William Shakespeare as the son of a man who was not averse to shady dealing. William himself was not above lying about his family when it came to getting his somewhat disgraced father a coat of arms.

Much controversy and various suggestions of Shakespeare's whereabouts have been posited for the so called 'lost years' between 1585 and 1592. The favourite and often considered most likely is that Shakespeare became a strolling player and that this led to his being linked with Lord Strange's Men, with whom he is later associated. This neatly fills one gap and may also account for his absence from the record before 1585 as well, 1578, when fourteen, being a reasonable guess for when a boy might join a strolling players' troupe since there would be female parts to play for a beardless boy, as women did not take part in acting on the commercial stage in England. Other suggestions are that he was a tutor, a musician or player in a Catholic household in Lancashire, or some country place, as suggested by John Aubrey. This suggestion is remarkably persistent, even though Aubrey cannot be considered a reliable source. [22]

The suggestion that he became a strolling player, though unprovable, is attractive, for acting troupes appeared in Stratford and it is likely that Shakespeare saw plays

---

[22] Dick, O.L. (ed) Aubrey's Brief Lives and Honan, A. ibid p.54. Aubrey says he had the information from William, son of Christopher Beeston, a colleague of Shakespeare's in the Lord Chamberlain's company.

performed. For an adventurous youth, perhaps one liable to get into trouble locally (there is always the legend of being caught poaching on Sir Thomas Lucy's land, although it has about as much provenance as King Alfred burning the cakes![23]), the life of actors going from place to place must have seemed appealing. And this could be a possible explanation for Shakespeare's disappearance from Stratford. Perhaps for a youth disappointed in ambition because of the need to leave the grammar school, a band of players, maybe attached to some gentleman's household or patronage, might well have seemed a way out from the narrow life of Stratford. His mother's property had been sold, the Shakespeares were no longer prosperous. One less mouth to feed would probably appear as a blessing. And so young Shakespeare could be off, adventure and a possibly brilliant, or at least reasonably prosperous, future ahead if he managed to reach London and join some nobleman's troupe. Except that players were vagrants and vagabonds, so that if Shakepeare

---

23   Ibid p. 45. But one might say the story encompasses a truth in the same way that Alfred burning the cakes does (that he was preoccupied with the important matter of fighting the Danes, whatever else he was doing) which tells us something about the nature of the young William Shakespeare, that he was a daring young man, although the incident described may not actually be true, and the Lucys have always denied it was true. The story seems to originate in notes made by Richard Dawes c.1688, and in the first biography of Shakespeare, written by Nicholas Roe in 1709. That Shakespeare wrote about hunting does not mean he actually hunted, either. There were books available on 'the chase' for him to read. (Source: Shakespeare Institute Library, Mason Croft, Church Street Stratford-upon-Avon Warwickshire, https://silibrary1.wordpress.com/2015/12/21/sing-lousy-lucy-shakespeare-and-the-roes-of-charlecote/).

left with a troupe it would probably have been in the teeth of family opposition.

A more recent theory is that Shakespeare spent his lost years, that is from 1585 to 1592, at sea.[24] Evidence for this is generally taken from the apparently highly accurate descriptions of sailors, ships and sailing in his plays [25]. But Shakespeare was working in London, the greatest port in England, and an international trading port. His opportunities to meet sailors and examine and discuss ships were manifold and as likely to have happened as his being at sea, or indeed being a co-author with Christopher Marlowe, acquaintance with whom by Shakespeare is nowhere found though frequently assumed. It is clear, too, that even if Shakespeare travelled he had not gone much futher than France or the Netherlands. In *A Winter's Tale* Shakespeare has people shipwrecked in Bohemia. 'Shakespeare in a play brought in a number of men saying they had suffered shipwreck in Bohemia, where is no sea near, by some hundred miles." said Ben Jonson, who prided himself on his knowledge of the world. [26], of this error. This hardly argues wide travelling or knowledge of the sea.

---

24   Holden, A., William Shakespeare, p 43, followed by Duff Cooper's theory that Shakespeare was a soldier in the Netherlands, based on Philip Sydney's mention of 'Will, my lord of Leicester's jesting player'.

25   . Act I, sc i of The Tempest contains accurate nautical language: 'Heigh, my hearts! cheerly, cheerly, my hearts!/yare, yare! Take in the topsail. Tend to the/master's whistle. Blow, till thou burst thy wind,/if room enough!' But this is no more than might be picked up in the port of London. It is not particularly technical.

26   From *Halleck's New English Literature* by Reuben Post Halleck. New York: American Book Company, 1913. and http://www.shakespeare-online.com/biography/benjonson.html

Thus far neither the suggestion that he was a strolling player nor the idea that he was a seaman are certain, and besides, we know he was in Stratford in November of 1582, when he married Anne Hathaway who was three months pregnant, so he was presumably in Stratford the previous August too. So where was Shakespeare if he was not permanently in Stratford, given there is no record of his apprenticeship or employment there or in a nearby town?

To sum up, Shakespeare shows knowledge of various spheres of life, but it is unlikely that he took part in all of them, and seafaring is not a good grounding for a future playwright. Becoming a strolling player has its charms, and would be a good background for someone who eventually became a playwright, except that playwrights, as Greene pointed out, tended to have some extended education, not just the background of the stage, and Shakespeare does show knowledge of classical legend, history, and (possibly) courtly life – which requires the ability to study and to learn, abilities which are acquired through extended education. Even if, as was the case, the books were available to read, it needs a mind trained to gain information from them in order to obtain knowledge. It seems Shakespeare had that ability to study, taught by education. So if he had been educated beyond fourteen, where was that education got?

Since the early twentieth century the suggestion that Shakespeare was in Lancashire, as suggested by Aubrey, has been debated and at different times his presence there has been in ascendancy but also several times struck down. It has been mooted that Shakespeare was in the household of Alexander Hoghton of Lea Hall and Hoghton Towers. This supposition is based on two facts, the first that John Cottam, teacher at Stratford grammar school from 1579 to 1581, returned to his home in Tarnacre in Lancashire after the arrest of his brother Thomas Cottam, a Catholic priest who was executed with Edmund Campion in 1582. It is supposed that John Cottam knew of the secret Catholicism [27] of the Shakespeare family.

    The possibility that the Shakespeares were recusants is founded on John Shakespeare's excuses for not attending church because of his debts (a frequent excuse of recusants) and on a document found in the rafters of their house in Henley Street. This document was a profession of Catholic faith and was eventually published in Edward Malone's biography of Shakespeare in 1790. The actual document is now lost. According to Holden it is a translation of Saint Carlo Borromeo, Cardinal Archbishop of Milan's last testament, written in 1570. The testament was translated into English and printed at the request of Jesuit missionaries, led by Edmund Campion, when they visited Milan in 1580. Edmund Campion then returned to England and visited Lapworth, probably on his way to Lancashire, where he was entertained by Mary Shakespeare's kinsman[28] by marriage Sir William Catesby (father of the leader of the Gunpowder Plot, Sir Robert Catesby). It may be that a copy of the

---

27   Holden, A., ibid pp 23-26.
28   Kinship, whether by blood or marriage, was very important to the Elizabethans. Witness the connection between the Vaughan and Devereux families. Vaughan' stepmother , Lettice, was sister-in-law to Dorothy Devereux, Countess of Northumberland, and this gave William Vaughan connections at court which enabled him to learn some of the facts concerning the death of Christopher Marlowe at Deptford. (Honan, P. ibid, p.365).

testament was given to John Shakespeare when invited to meet Campion, or that John Cottam passed it to him before he himself left for Lancashire. Given this information about the Shakespeares, Cottam might well arrange for the employment of the eldest of John Shakespeare's sons in a Catholic household.

The second fact is that Alexander Hoghton's will names as an annuitant William Shakeshaft and gives him an annuity of £2 per annum, a middling amount where the lowest is 13s.4d and the highest £3.6s.8d.

Alexander Hoghton of Lea Hall, near Preston made this will dated 3 April 1581, not long before he died, and set up a controversy that lasts till this day. The annuity left to Will Shakeshafte, names him as one of Hoghton's household 'now dwelling with me', and a person who he also recommends to Sir Thomas Hesketh[29], a fellow recusant (he was arrested in 1581 as 'a disaffected papist') and kinsman of Alexander Hoghton's second wife, Elizabeth. [30] So far, not controversial but preceding this recommendation is the bequeathing of 'instruments belonging to musics (sic), and all manner of play clothes' so that one can infer Alexander Hoghton kept a troupe of players or at least some actors and musicians in his household and that William Shakeshafte was one such. [31] Hoghton's will was not published until

---

29   The father of Richard Hesketh, who was part of a plot now known as the Hesketh Plot, which intended to put Lord Strange on the English throne. https://great-harwood.org.uk/about/people/Families/hesketh.htm
30   Holden, A., ibid pp 53 and 60.
31   Greenblatt, S., ibid p.104.

1860 and attracted no attention until the twentieth century. This is not particularly surprising since the arguments about the authorship of Shakepeare and Marlowe's plays did not arise until later in the nineteenth century, mainly as a result of the 'romantic' view of authors [32] starving in garrets, writing only when inspired and exhibiting 'Bohemian' behaviour, which Shakespeare did not fit, but Marlowe did (or seemed to – he did not really meet the starving in a garret persona, and probably did not wait for inspiration to write a play).

Edmund Chambers [33] first made the connection and wondered if Shakeshafte was an actor, and later raised the possibility that Sir Thomas Hesketh, on a visit to Lord Derby was the means of introducing Shakespeare to Lord Strange's Men – with whom Shakespeare was later definitely connected. Chambers was basing this leap on the surmise of Oliver Baker in 1937 [34] that Shakeshafte might have been Shakespeare and joined Sir Thomas Hesketh's players and thereby been introduced to the players in Lord Derby's employment. Lord Strange was Lord Derby's eldest son, which is how the connection is made. This surmise is based on an enigmatic record of one of Hesketh's visits to Lord Derby, in 1587, when he might have brought players with him.

---

32 A view Anthony Trollope fell foul of when he explained his writing schedule, which showed admirable application but no romantic inspiration or Bohemian tendencies.

33 Chambers, E.K., The Elizabethan Stage, Oxford, Clarendon Press (1923).

34 Baker, O., In Shakespeare's Warwickshire and the Unknown Years, Simpkin Marshall Ltd, (1937)

Douglas Hamer, however, in 1970, suggested that the identification of William Shakeshafte (or Shakestaff, according to Greenblatt) with William Shakespeare was dubious on two fronts. [35] First, Shakeshafte is a very common name in Lancashire, and particularly around Preston, where the Hoghton estates were, and second that Shakespeare was too young to be Will Shakeshafte, based on the provisions of the will.

Hamer investigated the frequency of the name Shakeshafte in Lancashire and Warwickshire. What he found was that Shakeshafte is a common Lancashire name. [36] Hamer looked at the Rolls of the Guilds of Merchants and found between 1542 and 1602 several Shakeshafte households in Preston and its environs. In 1582 he found seven Shakeshafte households within the borough of Preston, with fifteen males listed. There were also several families of Shakeshaftes who did not claim the rights of freemen, and are not, therefore, included in the Preston rolls. Lea Hall, the residence of Alexander Hoghton [37], lies in the centre of the area covered by the Rolls of the Guilds of Merchants and the areas where non-freemen Shakeshaftes are resident. Not only this, but the Preston rolls include four Shakeshaftes with the Christian name William among

---

35   Hamer, D., 'Was William Shakespeare William Shakestaffe?' Review of English Studies, (1970).

36   Bearman, R., 'Was William Shakespeare William Shakestaffe?' Revisited, Shakespeare Quarterly, (2002.

37   Hoghton Towers is also associated with Alexander Hoghton and William Shakeshafte. Lea Hall seems to have been used as the family's main residence until Hoghton Towers was built in 1565 (source: Old Lea Hall, a hint of Preston's Past, ashtonribble.com, Ashton-on-Ribble's community web, 2016).

fifteen males of that surname [38]. On the other hand Shakeshafte is not a common name in Warwickshire at the time.

Secondly, the annuity paid to William Shakeshafte is said to be too large for a young man such as William Shakespeare would have been in 1581. It is £2 per annum, a large amount, considering the range of annuities listed in Hoghton's will, for a seventeen year old who could only recently have joined the household. Not only is £2 a large amount for such a young man, but if Shakeshafte was the last remaining annuitant he would become eligible for £16.13s. 4d. Such an annuity suggests a retainer with long service, and Hamer surmises that the recipients may be age related to the money left them. If one arranges the annuities by amount then the recipient of the largest amount, £3.6s.8d, would be the oldest and the two people receiving £1 each per annum are the youngest, making Thomas Sharp who received the largest amount the oldest and William Ormshaw and Roger Dickinson the youngest, as they received the least. Thus, £2 is in the middle, which suggest a recipient of middle age.

Although it has been disputed that the annuities of Hoghton's will are arranged by age, because two of the men mentioned in the will are older than Thomas Costen (who was twenty-nine in 1581 when he was listed to receive £1 per annum) the objections are not conclusive. Henry Bond and Thomas Barton may be mentioned only as guarantors; they are both much older than Costen and they do not receive annuities at all. Does their naming in Hoghton's will annul the supposition that Douglas Hamer made, that

---

38   See Appendix IV for list.

Shakeshafte looks to be the wrong age to be William Shakespeare and is much more likely to be a middle-aged Lancashireman? Even if the annuities are not age-related, there still remains a third problem with identifying Shakeshafte with William Shakespeare, which is that Shakespeare, as well as being only recently employed, was not from Lancashire and was unlikely to remain there. The payment of a life-long annuity to such a person would have been an onerous and difficult task for Hoghton's executors and it seems unlikely it would have been arranged. Why would Alexander Hoghton, who gives only £1 to Costen, employed in the dangerous job of messenger when Thomas Hoghton was in exile in Liege because of his recusancy, give a boy of seventeen who had been recently employed, a life-long annuity which was also going to be augmented whenever a fellow annuitant died?

It seems most unlikely, even with the possible connection to Lord Strange's Men through Thomas Hesketh's visit to Lord Derby, possibly with players, in 1587, which seems a little late for purposes here, since Alexander Hoghton had died several years before!

In 1581 William Shakespeare was seventeen, which led Hamer to consider him too young to be Shakeshafte. It is quite legitimate to ask why Alexander Hoghton would leave such a young man so considerable a sum. There may, of course, be a reason, but the evidence may not only be highly circumstantial but rather tortured, yet nonetheless the will is intriguing.

In summary, Hamer's two arguments of disparity in age and frequency of Shakeshafte as a Lancashire surname but not a Warwickshire one, do, on the face of it, appear finally to destroy the suggestion that the William

Shakeshafte of Alexander Hoghton's will is William Shakespeare, the son of a Stratford-on-Avon glover.

But do they?

There is some evidence [39] that the names Shakestaff and Shakeschafte were both used by William Shakespeare's grandfather, Richard. Spellings in the sixteenth century varied, for example Marlowe is variously called Marlow, Marley, Morley, Marlyn, Marlen and Marlin[40] in the buttery records at Cambridge and Cotham was a variant of Cottam.[41] Honigmann [42] suggests that Shakeshafte could be simply a name that Shakespeare used whilst in Lancashire, or was used by others for him. So William Shakeshafte becomes a possibility now, either as a variant adopted by a young man going to Lancashire or as a misspelling by Alexander Hoghton's scribe [43] for William Shakespeare.

Perhaps there is also no real reason to suppose the amounts of annuity in Hoghton's will relate to age in any way. Not everyone mentioned in Alexander Hoghton's will is a beneficiary. Of twenty-nine people listed only eleven receive an annuity. The amounts left may reward loyalty or seniority rather than age, so youth may be no barrier to the identification of Shakespeare with Shakeshafte.

That Shakespeare was the intended annuitant is not impossible, especially considering the link between Stratford-on-Avon and Catholic Lancashire found in John Cottam, and in Shakespeare's father.

---

39 Holden, ibid, p.54.
40 Greenblatt, ibid, p.104.
41 Holden, ibid.
42 Honigmann, E.A., *Shakespeare: 'the lost years'*, MUP, 1985.
43 Who would probably be more familiar with the name Shakeshafte.

John Cottam may have taught William Shakespeare until John Shakespeare's disgrace meant his son was turned out of the grammar school. It is possible that John Cottam, seeing a likely scholar in William, and being aware of the Catholic leanings of the Shakespeare family, suggested that he go to Lancashire[44], specifically to Alexander Hoghton's household and from there go to Rheims to train as a Catholic priest. This would get William the education he needed and a future beyond the bounds of Stratford. Whether this plan was approved by William himself is doubtful, after all he got a young woman pregnant in the summer of 1582, putting paid to any career as a priest, since he married her. But such an opportunity for advancement could not be turned down by the now less than prosperous Shakespeare family. William need not become a priest, but he might get patronage, sponsorship and an education from the arrangement; at the very least he was, again, one less mouth to feed in Stratford.

This may seem an unlikely turn of events. But connection between Lancashire and Stratford-on-Avon, through its grammar school was of long standing. John Cottam had been his predecessor's choice for the post at Stratford, and that predecessor, Thomas Jenkins, was the only non-Lancastrian to hold the schoolmaster's job at Stratford between 1569 and 1624. Jenkins was preceded by another Lancashire man, Simon Hunt, who went to Douai and became a Jesuit. Hunt links Stratford to Douai and to Lancashire recusants, specifically the Hoghton family,

---

44   This journey may be the origin of the poaching story, as an explanation for William disappearing suddenly. He would have needed a passport, too, which might have been issued for a servant travelling to join a new household.

because Douai was the recipient of donations from Thomas Hoghton, Alexander Hoghton's brother, a recusant so unrepentant that he lived and died abroad. Douai was the original foundation of the English school, which Cardinal Allen removed to Rheims when Douai became too uncomfortable for them (and one of the school's related descendant is now in Lancashire, at Stonyhurst a school first founded in St. Omer [45]). In William Shakespeare's time the school was in Rheims (the removal had taken place in 1578 [46]). Thus there is a strong connection in 1580 between the schoolmasters at Stratford, the Hoghton family in Lancashire and the English school at Rheims, where Catholic priests were trained in order to return to England to support Roman Catholics here and work for the conversion of England and its invasion by Spain in order to put either Mary, Queen of Scots, or Philip II of Spain on the throne instead of Elizabeth. Being a Catholic priest, or going to Rheims to train was tantamount to treason. This fact explains the one remaining problem with the will – that Shakeshafte was living in Alexander Hoghton's household in 1581. Alexander Hoghton is highly unlikely to have said: *William Shakeshafte, who is in Rheims* in his will. Suggesting Shakeshafte's absence in any way would have implicated Hoghton, his family and associates, and Shakeshafte's family in treason. So Shakeshafte must be 'dwelling' with Hoghton. It is the only safe choice, especially in the heightened atmosphere of the 1580s, when the succession was in question, Mary Stuart was suspected of plotting her cousin Elizabeth's downfall and a Spanish

---

45   Where a First Folio has recently been found – Daily Telegraph, Rory Mulholland in Paris, 25 Nov 2014
46   Holden, ibid, p.54.

invasion was feared, and in Lancashire Edmund Campion was at large pursuing the Catholic Church's agenda for re-converting England. However, even this problem of Shakeshafte 'now dwelling with me' is more easily resolvable. The will may not have been written in August 1581, but much earlier for it details the provisions for disposal of Hoghton's lands made between Alexander Hoghton and his brother, Thomas. These provisions were set in a deed 'berringe (the) datte the twentythe daye of Julye in the yeare of our lord God one thowsande fyve hundreth and fourescore' [47]. Fourscore is eighty, so the date the deed was set up was 20 July 1580, when William Shakeshafte, aka William Shakespeare, would have been 'dwelling' with Alexander Hoghton. Though wills tended to be made at the point when a person thought they were going to die, a recusant in England in the 1580s faced that possibility every day. Why should not the will (or at least its first draft) have been begun in 1580, and not when Hoghton felt the actual pangs of death upon him? Certainly, if he employed a lawyer to write a deed, the writing of the will would seem to be a logical addition, so that deed and will would tally (Elizabethans were great litigants, after all). By the time Alexander Hoghton actually had the will completed both Thomas Hesketh and Thomas Hoghton might well have already suggested that William Shakeshafte was ripe for Rheims and that the sooner he went hence the better, especially as Edmund Campion was there in Lancashire encouraging Catholics to continue in their rebellion against

---

47   Bearman, R., ibid Appendix: Excerpts from the will of Alexander Houghton, 3 August 1581 adapted from Records of Early English Drama: Lancashire, ed. David George (University of Toronto, 1991).

Elizabeth and their hopes in a Catholic succession. The earlier date seems just as likely as the later, and explains the term 'now dwelling with me', allowing for William Shakeshafte/Shakespeare to be already gone in 1581, probably aware of the provisions of Hoghton's will. Again, Hoghton would be unlikely to change the wording of the will, supposing the anomaly occurred to him, even if it was recopied in August 1581 (and the copyist would surely not presume to do so).

But William Shakespeare did not go to Rheims as his subsequent marriage to Anne Hathaway shows. So if, as it seems, he is William Shakeshafte, where is he and what is he doing, and why does a seventeen year old, surely newly arrived and not certainly then resident in Hoghton's household, get such a large annuity if he has not gone to Rheims?

Two reasons spring to mind. One is that Hoghton had a relationship with William Shakespeare so close that he wished to secure his future with financial assistance and also patronage, since he recommends Shakeshafte both to his brother Thomas and to Sir Thomas Hesketh.

But what close relationship could exist? It is possible that there is some hint of homosexuality in addition to the suggestion that Shakespeare, the son of a possible recusant, was meant to be a priest, off to Rheims to train, with money to help him. Shakespeare's sexuality has often been in question, and the acting profession itself held many temptations, particularly with young boys playing women's parts - but such a relationship with Hoghton is currently unprovable. But what if Shakespeare had left Lancashire in 1581? It is then possible that Hoghton **thought** Shakespeare was in Rheims and gave him money to support himself there. The amount is not far different from that given to

Christopher Marlowe as his Parker Scholarship, though Shakespeare's is for life, not just six years.

Thus, in 1580, aged sixteen, it is possible that William Shakespeare set out to go to Rheims, but perhaps with a different intention from that assumed by Hoghton (and his friends) who probably provided both the money necessary for the journey and the cover, most likely, given the interest in acting, a troupe of travelling players.

Chapter Five

Mind the Gap
You See What You Expect To See

In December of 1580, having got a place at the King's School at the eleventh hour, Christopher Marlowe set off for Corpus Christi, Cambridge, the holder of a Parker scholarship and with a promising, if perhaps not entirely welcome, career before him.

It has already been noted that Archbishop Parker was an evangelical, a man in the forefront of the protestant reforms. It seems unlikely, then, that any boy chosen as a Parker scholar would have Catholic sympathies or be accused of intending to go to Rheims. And yet, and yet…both of these accusations were thrown at Christopher Marlowe. How can that be? In the edgy world of the 1580's, when men jumped at shadows lest they be informers, and minded their words even among their intimates for fear of the stake or the rope, there is one solution that springs to mind. Marlowe is known to history as a spy and it is usually suggested that he was recruited, perhaps by Walsingham, in 1583 after he had taken his B.A. But by then there are already rumours of Catholic sympathies at Cambridge, and Marlowe has already shown a propensity to be absent from college for long stretches of time, and to have extra money, particularly at the beginning of his residence. When he arrives on 10 December 1580 he is already free with money even though his scholarship does not fall due until the following term. His father was in no position to give his son an allowance so from whence the money? And why, that being the case, did Marlowe go up to Cambridge many weeks before his scholarship fell vacant? Perhaps he was eager to attend and start his new life as a proto-gentleman, or perhaps he had a more sinister reason for going up early to do with the nature of being a Parker scholar – a reason which would mark Christopher Marlowe out not as a Catholic sympathiser at all, but as a protestant firebrand. For he was, as earlier surmised, there to spy on his fellow scholars, as Corpus Christi, like many Cambridge colleges, had become the home of many recusants who were hopeful of going to Rheims to join the priesthood

But perhaps he did not go up to Cambridge at all.

When Marlowe apparently goes to Cambridge William Shakespeare has usually been supposed either living at his family home, a burden on his father's stretched budget, or having joined a group of strolling players on tour towards London – but if he was with Lord Strange's men it is odd that he does not arrive in London until 1592. However, it is suggested in Chapter Four that he was at Hoghton Hall in Lancashire, in the household of Alexander Hoghton, using the name of William Shakeshafte, intended to go to Rheims and train as a Catholic priest – although not necessarily happy to be in that position. Precisely what his role was in Lancashire may never be known, but he, as William Shakeshafte, was left an annuity of £2 per annum in Alexander Hoghton's will dated August 1581.

This gap between Marlowe arriving in Cambridge in December 1580 and not matriculating, that is formally joining the university as a scholar and receiving his scholarship, until March 1581 is significant. Why is he there? Some authorities have suggested that the record crossing out Marley (sic) and replacing it with Pashley (Marlowe's predecessor) is an error and that Marlowe was fully a scholar receiving his payments in the Michaelmas term. But the evidence does not support this. Marlowe is only listed after March 1581. It is not a matter of guesswork. Paying scholarships was an important financial undertaking and the paymasters were not likely to be mistaken as to whom they were paying, (the more especially as there were financial problems and irregularities at the college [67]). If Marlowe is replaced by Pashley for the Michaelmas term then he was not getting his scholarship money, and although it is backdated, he is still not in receipt of it until March. Why did he arrive so early and with more than sufficient money for his keep, so that he can be described as a pensioner by Peter Roberts [68], before he was paid his scholarship? What is he doing and how is he funded?

The answer lies in the accusation that Christopher Marlowe was intending to go to Rheims in 1585, and in the apparently abiding dislike of him emanating from Richard Baines. There is some relationship between Baines and

---

67   Roberts, P. Christopher Marlowe at Corpus, 1580-87, in Pelican - The Magazine of Corpus Christi College, Cambridge Easter Review, p32.
68   Ibid. p28.

Marlowe – in *The Reckoning* Nicholl suggests they met as co-spies after 1585, when Baines, having been released from his imprisonment in Rheims after being betrayed by a colleague as an English government spy, returned to England.

The rumour set up in 1587, that Marlowe was going to Rheims, had a basis in truth. But the truth was that Marlowe had been to Rheims, not that he was going. The basis for this is supported by his nemesis, Richard Baines, who seems to have pursued Marlowe for several years, with the intention of harming him. Why this was will appear in later chapters. For the moment it is sufficient that there are two possibilities concerning how Marlowe found himself in Rheims, and who was actually at Cambridge – as Christopher Morley, so called in the Privy Council's letter.

Possibility One

It may be that what Marlowe was doing in December 1580 was travelling to Rheims, because two young men, both wanting an education, are loose and unaccounted for in the run up to Marlowe's entry to Cambridge, and both those young men end in the same career with what clearly appears to be an extended education, which one of them has no evidence of having – and that there is a connection between them, which cannot be pinpointed or identified and yet seems clear from their work. True, Marlowe is in Canterbury, but where was William Shakespeare, a boy who has lost his chance at an education because of his father's financial irregularities and who is probably destined to be trained as a Catholic priest as this is his only remaining opportunity for gaining learning, that necessity for an Elizabethan on the make? It can surmised that Shakespeare was with a troupe of strolling players making their way from

Lancashire to Kent, where lies Dover a port from whence it is possible, with the right connections, to take ship and travel to Rheims. He would be carrying with him funds for his journey and his sustenance. There was probably already a place on board a suitable ship, and though Rheims might not be aware of Shakespeare's imminent arrival (under an assumed name) they would recognise his provenance because of the Hoghton family's close links to the college, as benefactors and unrepentant English recusants. We can also surmise that he had somewhere to visit in London before he set off for Rheims.

***

Lancashire was a centre of recusant activity and Shakespeare, in a troupe of players, was moving out of it towards the south east. He must have set off with a settled purpose, but not the one Alexander Hoghton was paying for and therefore had an interim point of call in London on his journey to Rheims. Francis Walsingham [69] was known to look out for likely youths to recruit into his spy network. A somewhat reluctantly intended Catholic priest would be a good choice, if that disaffected young man was also one of intelligence, as William Shakespeare was, and eager to make his way. But I believe that Walsingham's plan only reached fruition when Shakespeare met Marlowe, a committed Protestant already recruited to spy on Catholics as a Parker Scholar. Shakespeare was probably recruited in Lancashire with the intention he should go to London before going to Rheims, and meet Walsingham or one of his subordinates. We do not quite know what Marlowe was doing in the

---

69   Cooper, J., *The Queen's Agent, Francis Walsingham at the Court of Elizabeth I. Faber and Faber. 2011*

summer of 1580, but he was already recruited and it would not be impossible that he too was called to London, it is anyway on a possible route to Cambridge in the sixteenth century. There in London a remarkable thing happened. Walsingham saw that he had a double agent – two boys remarkably alike, one a young Catholic looking for a lucrative career outside the church, the other fired up by Protestant zeal, and probably pecuniary interest as well, to spy on Catholics. Christopher Marlowe and William Shakespeare met. To all intents, and Walsingham's purposes, interchangeable twins.

The reason that this is a possibility is that Marlowe and Shakespeare do seem to have collaborated. Shakespeare seems to be in London by 1592, writing plays, and yet there is no recorded meeting of Shakespeare with Marlowe. When Marlowe dies many people write about his death, and depending on their view of him, did so either to praise him or condemn him. But not William Shakespeare. He says nothing about Marlowe's death, not just in 1593 but not ever. Except for an oblique reference in *As You Like It* Shakespeare never mentions the man whose plays and work seem to be linked so closely to his own, and with whom he seems to have worked on *Henry VI*. In London Marlowe knows Nashe; he was at university with him and maybe worked on *Dido* with him. Marlowe knows Greene - and Greene does not like Marlowe and says so. Chapman finishes Marlowe's *Hero and Leander*. Gabriel Harvey knows Marlowe, and is quite condemnatory of him - they were at Cambridge at the same time and Marlowe spoke against Harvey on occasion, saying he belonged to the 'Age of Iron', which was insulting, suggesting that Harvey's intellect was of the lowest age of history, the best being the

Age of Gold and the worst being the Iron Age [70]. (Each successive age marked a deterioration in civilization. Marlowe would have known of these ages from Virgil.) Everyone knows Marlowe - except Shakespeare. And no-one knows Shakespeare at all until 1592 at best. It is as if the death of Christopher Marlowe is Shakespeare's cue to come on stage and into the light. But if not in London, where was William Shakespeare? He was not in Stratford, there is no record of his activities there after the conception of his twins in 1584. True, he could be with a troupe of players. But then why does he make no mention of Marlowe later, or any mutual acquaintance remark that Shakespeare and Marlowe met, or lived near them. Kyd says he lived with Marlowe around 1591. No-one says they lived with Shakespeare, and though the paper trail for Shakespeare as an author of his plays and poetry, as well as a shareholder in the Globe, a resident of London and a man of substance in Stratford, is a clear trail, it does not start until after Marlowe has made his exit. And yet there is evidence that Marlowe and Shakespeare collaborated. So what is the solution to the non-existence of Shakespeare whilst he was collaborating with Marlowe? It begins to look as if Shakespeare and Marlowe were the same person - which might certainly account for suggestions that Marlowe was in more than one place at once, for example, being tutor to Arbella Stuart and being in London, and explain why parts of plays by Shakespeare look remarkably as if they are by Marlowe. If they were the same person then at Marlowe's death in 1593

---

[70] The current age is that of Iron. Previous ages are those of Gold, Silver and Bronze - each declining from the previous age in intellectual ability and in culture. To say this of Harvey is a potent insult.

Shakespeare would have to emerge, because his alter ego had gone; he could not continue as Marlowe because Marlowe was supposed to be dead. And on cue, he emerges, which looks very non-coincidental, and could well be linked not to their playwriting careers, but to the darker career of secret agent, which culminated, so we are told, in a dinner at Deptford.

But we think we know what Marlowe and Shakespeare looked like – certainly Shakespeare, for we have his funeral monument and the portrait in the First Folio. But actually we do not really know. We have the Corpus Christi portrait that has been believed to be Christopher Marlowe. The picture was found in Corpus Christi college, actually in the building where Marlowe had lodged as a Parker scholar. It had been used as shelves at some point and, when discovered during renovation work in 1952, had been used to support a gas fire. It was rescued from the skip [71] but it was not immediately recognised as Marlowe, or even a sixteenth century portrait. Examination at the time led to the identification using circumstantial evidence. It is an attribution, not an absolute identification, based on clothing, date and the motto written on it. The portrait shows a young man in expensive finery and is painted in 'the twenty-first year of his age'. It also has the motif of an upturned torch and the motto 'that which nourishes me consumes me', (in Latin: Quod me nutrit me destruit}. A similar phrase (perhaps taken from a translation of an Italian or Latin play) turns up in Shakespeare's *Pericles*, II, ii, 33-4. It was not an uncommon motto and one quite attractive to youth, which in the Elizabethan era as now, tends to self–

---

71   Honan, P., ibid pp.112-115.

dramatization and exaggeration. We do not actually know who the sitter is but its confident outlook and rich dress has chimed in with our modern construction of Christopher Marlowe, and it is the right age for him in 1585, because it is done in his twenty-first year, when he was twenty.

In 1585, Christopher Marlowe was twenty-one: in his twenty-second year because he was born in February 1563 Old Style. The year still began in March (on the 25), not January. William Shakespeare was in his twenty-first year up until late April 1585, when he turned twenty-one, and was born in 1564 whether Old or New Style. Marlowe turned twenty-one in the February of what was officially still 1584.

If the portrait is of either of these young men, it is of William Shakespeare, and he would have ample reason to say that which nourished him consumed him, for he was living a lie and Christopher Marlowe, that student rumoured to be going to Rheims, was already there.

But we do know what Shakespeare looked like – we have his bust at Stratford-on-Avon, and at least one copy of a portrait from the folios. They show a balding man, clean-shaven or with a goatee beard, and a little heavy. They are done late in life. But Shakespeare was a flourishing man, why are there no other portraits? Edward Alleyn is pictured and also his wife, for example, and we know something of the looks of Raleigh's friend George Gascoigne [72], enough for some to suggest he was a sorrowful and broken man. People of the middling sort, living within the community of playwrights and actors, did have portraits, often for publicity

---

72   Lyons, M., *The Favourite,* p. 82. The portrait is in Gascoigne's *The Steele Glas.*

or to go into the frontispiece of their published work, why not Shakespeare? And indeed, why not Marlowe? The reason that springs to mind is that there was already that portrait at Corpus Christi, perhaps hanging in the Parker scholar lodgings, and it showed a truth that by 1592, when Marlowe was apparently well-known in theatrical circles, and Shakespeare supposedly just entering them, was dangerous for both of them. They were very alike – so alike they could swap places, like the two Dromios and Antipholuses or Viola/Cesario and Sebastian or, more significantly, like Simon Magus and his double. Indeed, Marlovians often point out that the First folio portrait of Shakespeare is like an older version of the Corpus Christi portrait. [74]

The confusions caused by twins was a subject twice used by Shakespeare, first in *The Comedy of Errors*, and later in *Twelfth Night*. T*he Comedy of Errors* is based on a play by Plautus[75] (an odd choice of inspiration for a man with small Latin and less Greek), and concerns two sets of twins, with the same names, who are both in the town of Ephesus, but unknown to each other. The complications, accusations and general mix ups are the subject of the play. *Twelfth Night's* probable sources include *Gl' Ingannati* ("The

---

73   Edward Alleyn had himself portrayed as *Dr Faustus,* and his first wife had a portrait done upon her marriage.
74   Wiilliams, *Shakespeare, thy name is Marlowe,* p.53, for example.
75   Plays by Plautus were part of the Cambridge curriculum. Duncan Salkeld. Shakespeare among the Courtesans: Prostitution, Literature, and Drama, 1500-1650 Anglo-Italian Renaissance Studies. Farnham: Ashgate, 2012.

Deceived, Cheated, Dupes"), and Gonzaga's *Gl' Inganni*[76] (again, odd choices for someone without a university education) – *Gl' Inganni* includes a heroine called Cesare, who dresses as a young man. The plot of the play as presented by Shakespeare is based around the ideas of misrule and disruption usual during the celebration of Epiphany or Twelfth Night itself, when topsy turviness ruled, servants took the place of masters and general mayhem was allowed for one night only. It concerns a brother and sister so alike they are mistaken for each other (it is not stated that they are twins, but many believe that they are). Viola believes her brother Sebastian has drowned, and he believes she has drowned. In order to survive in Illyria, Viola dresses as a boy (cross dressing was popular in the Elizabethan theatre, especially as female parts were played by young boys) and falls in love with her employer, Duke Orsino. But his beloved, Countess Olivia, thinking Viola is a boy, falls in love with her. Complications arise when Sebastian arrives, knowing nothing of his sister's activities, and finds himself in difficulties as he is taken for 'Cesario', Viola's alter ego. The plot unwinds so that Olivia marries Sebastian, Orsino marries Viola, and normality is restored. The genesis of Shakespeare's interest in twins is

---

76   Boas, G., *Sources of the Plot, in* The Touchstone *Twelfth Night,* p.91. Boas notes that Rich's *History of Apolonia and Silla,* (published 1581) may be the source of both stories. Girls masquerading as boys, and the triangular love plot, including a cross-dressed girl, were very popular. Boas was probably following *The Works of Shakespeare: Twelfth Night or What You Will*. Ed. Morton Luce. London: Methuen and Co., 1906.

usually attributed to being the father of twins [77] himself, but his twins were fraternal, a boy and a girl (like Viola and Sebastian). Fraternal twins are no more alike than any brother and sister might be, but Shakespeare suggests in both plays identical twins, even in the case of Viola and Sebastian. And he is quite aware that if you expect to see one person you will see them, even when presented with someone not quite like.

What is less well recognised is that Christopher Marlowe based one of his plays, *Doctor Faustus*, on a character associated with a twin or a double: Simon Magus. [78] According to Simon Magus' legend he created a double who could take his place on various occasions, by changing the face of one of his followers or servants. This worked so well that the man, Faustus, was taken for Simon whenever Simon Magus needed this to happen. Doctor Faustus is a man who sells his soul in order to have earthly wealth and his story is closely linked to that of Simon Magus, indeed he calls himself Simon Magus's double, referring to the look-a-like story [79] so it looks as if Marlowe too has an understanding of the effect of twins and the truth that 'you see what you expect'.

And so, Shakespeare knew in *Twelfth Night* that you see what you expect to see. When Olivia meets Sebastian

---

77 In the play, interestingly since many believe its main characters derive from Shakespeare's children Hamnet (who died) and Judith, it is stated that Sebastian and Viola's father is dead. I had thought this suggested Marlowe was the father of Hamnet and Judith, but this seems unlikely because of the chance that Anne Hathaway would realise he was not her husband.

78 Riggs, p 233. Faustus identifies himself with Simon Magus, including, in Marlowe's play, conjuring up Helen of Troy.

79 ibid p 233-4.

she 'sees' Cesario, for who else would she expect to see? Everyone mistakes Sebastian for Cesario in the same way – they see what they expect. My younger brother is so like me – particularly in our twenties and thirties – that from the point of view of looks we could easily have played Viola and Sebastian as twins even though we are of different heights and I am dark and my brother fair – in photographs now it is difficult sometimes to distinguish between our faces, especially photographs done when hair styles (long and curly) for women and young men were similar. In another instance, even more remarkable, for my mother-in-law's ninetieth birthday my husband and stepson arranged a lunch at a local public house [80] for my mother-in-law, my stepson's partner, their four children, and me. My husband sat on my right, opposite his mother and his son's partner, and the teenage and early twenties sons and daughter were ranged around. Just after we had sat down my husband got up and went to the bar with my stepson. The rest of us continued talking and then my husband came back and sat next to me and joined the conversation with me, his mother, his grandchildren and his son's partner, looking at us and speaking to us for several minutes. I looked up to see where my stepson was and saw him talking to my husband at the bar; they seemed to be amused. I looked in surprise at the man on my right, wearing my husband's black broad-brimmed hat and his red jacket and realised it was my brother-in-law, who dresses quite differently from my husband. We had all been duped by seeing what we expected, dressed in the appropriate clothes, because we

---

80   April 2010, Leicester. The public house was the Uncle Tom Cobley on Freeman's Common.

were not expecting to see my brother-in-law, who lives two hundred miles north of us. We saw what we expected, James Clarke, not Brendon Clarke, wearing the clothes James Clarke wears, in a place we knew Brendon Clarke could not be – except that he was – and this despite my brother-in-law having long, iron grey hair and beard still in profusion and my husband having what he resolutely terms 'ash blond' hair and beard (long, but not in such profusion as his brother's) and the brothers not looking particularly alike. They are, in fact, regularly confused by people who do not know one of them well! Thus, it is not surprising that with a strong resemblance to each other, Marlowe and Shakespeare could change places and be accepted, because no-one except possibly Francis Walsingham knew there were two Marlowes, not one. Change of dress and hairstyle, and the assumption that there was only one man was enough.

This interchangeability of two young men who were very alike is what was realised when they met in 1580, possibly in London, possibly under the aegis of Elizabeth's master spy, Francis Walsingham – or at least a near subordinate of his. The portrait does not show the young Marlowe, in the twenty-first year of his age but Shakespeare, and already he knew that the work he was engaged in could destroy him. Indeed, when he met Richard Baines, probably later in 1585, it very nearly did. For Baines recognised Christopher Marlowe, and must have been very confused, so confused that he dare not accuse Marlowe directly of having been to Rheims, where he had met him, but had to be circumspect. Perhaps he was not sure. It was some time since he had seen his former colleague, and he had gone through testing times. So, rather than accusing directly, he set about the rumour that Christopher Marlowe was about to go to Rheims and nearly cost Shakespeare his degree, and put him in danger of arrest and possible death.

But we are getting too far ahead here. What evidence is there for Marlowe or Shakespeare having anything to do with Francis Walsingham and how was the swap managed? It is most unlikely, even in the sixteenth century when a sixteen or seventeen year old was mature enough to set out alone for Cambridge (sixteen was the normal age to start at university and some scholars entered as young as twelve), that two young men decided to swap places in order to become a spying duo. I think it more likely they were swapped intentionally by someone else. It may have been clear to Walsingham's recruiter that Shakespeare was a good Catholic – after all he had been chosen to go to Rheims – though possibly a reluctant priest, but one who could easily be brought over to the side of those opposed to Elizabeth I and Protestant England, in which case he would become extremely dangerous because of his attachment to Walsingham's spy network. Marlowe on the other hand had been picked as a potential spy at Canterbury; he would be highly unlikely to turn to the Catholic cause because he would see the Catholic priesthood and the access it gave him to recusants as an opportunity both to spy and to make his way in the world under Walsingham's patronage. Shakespeare possibly also lacked enough good Latin for the Rheims course (for we have no way of knowing how much schooling he had, although his references to schools and schoolboys suggests he found it unpleasant [81]) but could, if

---

81 Jaques 'whining' schoolboy in *As You Like It* and also (perhaps significantly?) Jack Cade in *Henry VI Part II*, a text now attributed to Marlowe (2016). Holden, ibid, p.42.

he arrived at Cambridge early, before he actually started a course, and attended lectures officially, become proficient enough to get through the university course, perhaps not as well as Marlowe would have done, but adequately enough. Marlowe would have been able to act because the King's School included in its curriculum, like most Elizabethan grammar schools, reading and performing plays, usually in Latin or Greek. He would have, in the short time he was at the school (and perhaps at the petty grammar school he had presumably attended beforehand), participated in these readings and performances. Thus he would have fitted into a band of strolling players well enough if that was necessary to get him to Dover. It is thus possible that Walsingham decided to swap them, the good Catholic boy for Cambridge, where he could be used as a spy on fellow students, the hopeful Protestant spy for Rheims.

The swap must have taken place in London, Marlowe took Shakespeare's place in the acting troupe, perhaps making a straight swap, or more probably joining them on their way to Dover simply as someone needing to travel in a group, and boarding the ship that Shakespeare had passage arranged on. In the meanwhile Shakespeare continued on the road that Marlowe had apparently started out on from Canterbury, perhaps with another acting troupe, but certainly with a group of other travellers leaving London, and with his keep provided by Walsingham.

As to acquaintance with Francis Walsingham, there is the play *The Massacre at Paris*, ascribed to Marlowe, full of detail of that event, which Walsingham and his household witnessed while in Paris as ambassador in 1572, and to which Shakespeare or Marlowe would have had access, if he were working for Francis Walsingham. Where but

Walsingham's household he could have had this information, covering both the massacre and the politics behind it, is uncertain, but in Walsingham's household was a man who wrote an account of the massacre which was not published until the seventeenth century and who could give a first hand account – as could Walsingham. [82]

Robert Beale, Secretary to the Privy Council, and married to Francis Walsingham's sister-in-law, Edith St. Barbe, also wrote an account of the Paris massacre, as an eye witness, *A Discourse after the great murder in Paris and other Places in France (*or *A Discourse by way of a letter to the Lord Burghley)*, but it does not seem to have been published; his papers were retained by his son-in-law, Sir Henry Yelverton[83]. Beale was Walsingham's secretary while he was in Paris, and carried letters to and from London, including reports to Burghley. He deputised for Walsingham on several occasions as secretary of state, and seems to have continued to be associated with him until Walsingham's death, Walsingham naming him as deputy governor of the Mines Royal in 1581. Other sources for the *Massacre* might have included François Hotman's *De Furoribus Gallicus (A Plain Report of the Furious Outrages in Fraunce)*, published in 1573, [84] which Shakespeare, as Marlowe, could have had access to, along with Hotman's life of Admiral Coligny. But Hotman was in Bourges during the St

---

82   Cooper, J. The Queen's Agent, pp 42-43.
83   Yelverton's library at Easton-Maudit was sold in 1784, and the British Museum had the manuscripts it contained.
84   The Queens Agent, ibid p.79.

Batholomew Massacre (from which he fled) and was not an eye-witness, therefore, to the events in Paris as Beale was.

If Beale's account of the St Bartholomew Massacre was used for the play then the writer was likely to have been in contact with Walsingham and his household. It may be that meeting Beale was the inspiration for the play, rather than that the playwright sought information on it. But it may be that Sassetti's [85] manuscript was also available in Walsingham's household, because Sassetti worked as an agent of the English spy system set up by Sir Francis Walsingham, and had done so at various times from about 1570, continuing to do so until the 1580s, [86] and he was also resident in London, where he met Giaocomo Castelvetro, [87]

---

85   Sassetti's account of the St. Bartholomew Massacre was not published till after 1611, after it had been discovered in Venice. *Archives Internationales D'histoire des Idees / International Archives of the History of Ideas, The Massacre of St. Bartholomew,*Volume 75 of the series pp 99-154.

86   'Sassetti lavorò pur non continuativamente come agente del sistema spionistico inglese messo in piedi da sir Francis Walsingham', (Trans: Sasseti had worked, though not continuously, as an agent for the English spy system set up by Sir Francis Walsingham). Sources: - Dizionario Biografico degli Italiani - di Igor Melani - Volume 90 (2017): J. Tedeschi, *Tommaso. Sassetti's account of the St. Bartholomew's day massacre*, in *The massacre of St. Bartholomew. Reappraisals and documents*, ed. A. Soman, The Hague 1974, pp. 99-111; Id., *Introduzione*, in T. Sassetti, *Il massacro di San Bartolomeo*, ed. J. Tedeschi, Roma 1995, pp. 7-30; J. Cooper, *The Queen's Agent, Sir Francis Walsingham and the rise of espionage in Elizabethan England*, New York-London 2012, *passim*.

87   Sassetti's report on the massacre was in MS form when found in 1611 in the house of James VI's tutor, then in Venice, Giacomo

who later had a copy of Sassetti's manuscript. Therefore it might be that Marlowe had read Tommaso Sassetti's account at Francis Walsingham's as well. If Marlowe had access ot Beale's account, and also Sassetti's he must have been both a welcome and a frequent visitor. This suggests that Walsingham's double-spy was an important agent, as witness also Burghley's championing of him to the Cambridge authorities, and not a minor part-time worker in the secret service as has been supposed. If that is so, the events at Deptford are even more intriguing; Burghley went out of his way to protect Marlowe at Cambridge, why put him in danger at Deptford?

But if Marlowe took Shakespeare's place at Rheims with Hoghton funding, and Shakespeare took up Marlowe's role as Parker Scholar and spy, at Cambridge, and was used whilst there as an agent by Burghley and Walsingham on several occasions, quite likely going to the continent on various missions, then many of the mysteries of Marlowe's life are explained.Marlowe.

Castelvetro. The MS was found by Dudley Carleton, English ambassador to Venice, when Castelvetro was arrested. Carleton searched Castelvetro's lodgings for incriminating papers before the Inquisition did so. Tedeschi J. (1974) *Tommaso Sassetti's Account of the St. Bartholomew's Day Massacre*, in: Soman A. (eds) *The Massacre of St. Bartholomew. Archives Internationales D'histoire des Idees / International Archives of the History of Ideas,* vol 75. Springer, Dordrecht . Castelvetro met Sassetti when both were in London ('che proprio a Londra lo conobbe' – they just knew each other), Dizionario Biografico degli Italiani - Volume 90 (2017). Their acquaintance in London was likely when Castelvetro acquired the MS.

Chapter Six

Going to Rheims

As he left London and was going towards Dover what sort of the place was it that Marlowe was heading towards? The English school at Rheims and Douai was led by Doctor, later Cardinal, William Allen and provided a route for displaced Catholic Englishmen to get the education now denied them in England because of their religion. In some ways it was a displaced Oxford University, offering the same curriculum and taking in similar scholars. The school was funded by Phillip II with two hundred ducats a year but this was not enough to sustain it and the school was reliant upon donations such as those from the Hoghtons. For English recusants entry was by vocation to be a seminary priest and many men, young and not so young set out on the journey that for many ended on an English scaffold. Doctor Allen was quite clear that what he was producing at Douai and later Rheims was a fifth column not only sent to give the comfort of the mass to English Catholics but also to promote rebellion against the English state, especially after Elizabeth I had been excommunicated in 1570. When one realises that Catholic priests were the spearhead of a projected and hoped for invasion of England one begins to understand why Burghley and Walsingham were so relentless and merciless in their search for the priests and their hidden congregation. They feared rebellion funded by Spain in order to set a Catholic monarch on the English throne and the return of Catholicism – which by the 1580s most of the population had rejected. Spain was in the throes of the Inquisition's search for heretics. That a Catholic monarch would bring the Inquisition into England was a real possibility. In such fear any means was considered allowable in order to prevent what would be a civil war such as were taking place in France (though those was in essence less a religious war than a breakdown of the state into warring factions). The English renaissance was threatened by outside powers determined to destroy the emerging society and it took all of Walsingham and Burghley's energies and Elizabeth's wit to circumvent that intention.

Sixteen seems young to be setting out abroad to become a Catholic priest, and by implication a traitor and a criminal in one's own country. But Marlowe and Shakespeare were not alone in setting out on such a difficult and dangerous journey.

It is quite difficult to work out who went to Rheims from England to join the English mission. False names were frequently used and it is not always clear who the men were. Additionally, although there are forty English martyrs listed, and many more who were beatified, the true names of those priests who died on the scaffold as recusants and traitors are not always known. Thus tracing a particular person is frequently quite difficult. Sometimes all that exists is a name and some dates. The list of scholars at Rheims and Douai is also incomplete.[1]

Notable among graduates of Douai-Rheims was Edmund Campion who was executed in 1582. He was a graduate of Oxford and came to Lancaster to promote both reconversion of the English and the replacement of Queen Elizabeth with a Catholic monarch. Looking at dates of arrival and of ordination it took five to seven years to complete the course at Rheims. Some men arrive and are ordained within a year; for example, John Amias (or Amyas, but also known as William Anne), a widowed cloth merchant, entered Rheims in 1580 and was ordained in 1581, but this was not the usual pattern. In general, young men entered the college aged nineteen or twenty, having studied at Oxford or Cambridge beforehand (plenty of work for Parker scholars spying within the university), and were ordained several years later, then proceeding to England where their life expectancy if caught was sometimes short – although some priests were imprisoned for many years, making the prisons themselves good recruiting ground for converts. Typical of such entry are Christopher Bales (1564-1591) who went to Rheims in 1583 aged nineteen, and George Haydock who was ordained in 1581 aged twenty-five. Less typical, but indicating that Shakespeare could have been entered at Rheims in 1580, is Robert Southwell, the poet, who entered Douai in 1576, aged fifteen, and Edmund Genneys (1567-1591) who was converted to Catholicism aged sixteen and went immediately to Rheims – he took the name Ironmonger, which suggests he was the son of a tradesman like Marlowe and Shakespeare. He was

---

1   List of Catholic Martyrs - Wikepedia, 2012.

ordained in 1590, aged twenty-three. His fellow martyr, Polydor Plasden (1563-1591) was ordained in 1586, aged twenty-three, so being about sixteen when he started his studies at Rheims. So their age was no barrier to Marlowe or Shakespeare entering the English college.² Finding a route out of the country was more of a problem as travel licenses were required to move about the country at this time and passports needed to leave it, but this difficulty would have been circumvented in Shakespeare's case by being sponsored by the Hoghton family who would know how to arrange a passage to the seminary. Undoubtedly there was a safe ship for Shakespeare to take across the Channel and funds provided for his board and lodging on the way. The troupe of players would be a good cover (and presumably would have travel licenses provided by a patron) but because of the swap Shakespeare probably arranged to leave them in London to allow Marlowe to join a ship. Once in Rheims, presented as Hoghton's protégé and using an assumed name, Marlowe could settle in to training as a seminary priest; he certainly had the Latin and was a good scholar we must presume. And all the time he is corresponding with England, planning to spy on those who intended to undo Elizabeth I's settlement.

As funding of the scholars was dependent upon donations from sympathisers the regime was simple. Each scholar had a gown and a three cornered hat; dinner, the main meal of the day, was a simple broth made with root vegetables. Following on the possible hardships of reaching Rheims the enclosed world must have seemed frugal indeed.

---

2   Sixteen remained the lowest age of entry into a seminary into the twentieth century.

We have a description [3] of a fairly typical journey by a young man called John Chapman who went to Rheims in 1579. He went from Dover to Calais in the company of English and French merchants and paid two shillings for his passage. Once arrived in France he travelled the one hundred and fifty miles to Rheims on foot, using Latin in order to communicate and staying at what he describes as common inns. On arrival he was admitted without ceremony by the Vice President, Doctor Baily, and handed over twenty shillings. Marlowe probably took the same route, and would have been provided with money to hand over by Walsingham, for England's spymasters where determined to undermine the work of Allen's seminary.

Richard Baines also made this journey, almost certainly also with the knowledge and help of Burghley or Walsingham, for he too was determined to use Catholic connections to spy upon Catholic plotters in England. Arriving in 1578, the year before Chapman, he would have been a senior contemporary to Marlowe. Baines' intention at Rheims was to undermine the vocations of the seminarians by questioning particularly the frugality but also by scoffing at the leaders of the school. He chose the younger seminarians as he thought that they were more open to the infiltration of anti-authoritarian ideas within the community. One of those younger colleagues would have been Marlowe, several years junior to Baines who had already gained his MA from Caius College in 1576. Since Caius was home to such men as John Ballard, who was instrumental in the Babington Plot, and Rheims-defectors

---

3   Nicholls, ibid, p.147.

such as Sayer and Fingelow, [4] it is possible that, like Parker Scholars at Corpus Christi, Baines was already acting as an informer before he himself set out for Rheims. While there he sent information, in the form of notes, back to England about his fellow scholars.

One of those fellow scholars, a younger colleague in whom he confided his intention to use his ordination to spy on Catholics, betrayed him to Doctor Allen, whom Baines wanted to kill. How such a confidence came about is inexplicable except in one situation: it sounds like pillow talk, which suggests that Baines and his betrayer had an intimate relationship. However it came about, such confiding in a colleague, close and sympathetic as he might seem, would suggest that Baines would have become something of a broken reed from the point of view of the English spy system – but, in fact, that is not the case, he continued to work for the English secret service for many years.

There is no record of who it was betrayed Baines, as in the event Baines did not reveal his betrayer, and Doctor Allen did not name him either. Given the prevalence of assumed names among graduates of Rheims, the name might mean nothing to us in any event. But I believe the informant was Christopher Marlowe for two reasons. First, for what Baines wrote in his confession about the person who had betrayed him, and second, for his actions against Marlowe, when there is no evidence that he knew Marlowe well.

---

4   "Fingley, John, alias Finglow, John (FNGY573J)" A Cambridge Alumni Database. University of Cambridge.

First, Baines writes in his confession: 'And that good Priest my deare louing fellow, whom I would haue had partaker of my wicked and damnable reuoult I cry him mercy euen vpon my knees, and thanke him (though to the carnal wordly [sic] man it might be compted an iniury that he discouered al my counsel vnto his superiors and myne) for els I had been without doute damned for euer more.'[5]

This statement suggests that the relationship with his colleague was close. So close that whoever his betrayer was, enmity might well last for years – Baines was tortured because of this betrayal, and to be betrayed by one that is called 'my dear loving fellow' (words which suggest both anguish and anger) will leave a bitter taste for a long while – and might even result in Baines' wishing to cause the man's death. And second, Baines shows in his actions in 1592, at Flushing and 1593 with his Note to the Privy Council, an insatiable dislike of Christopher Marlowe, and a wish that he might die.

In conclusion, from Baines' activities at Rheims it is fairly clear that there must have been a system of drop boxes such as those listed by Robert Poley in 1590, so that communication back to England was possible. This affects the relationship between Shakespeare at Cambridge and Marlowe in Rheims – and it may be that it was possible for Marlowe to travel back to England as well as send messages. Such travel might well be necessary for seminarians in order to maintain their 'cover' in England, for the priests ordained at Rheims travelled undercover in England to do their work, which would hardly be possible if it was well-known that

---

5   Marlowe Studies translation. The full text is in Appendix V.

they had been absent abroad without a break for several years, suggesting that they were unrepentant recusants. Such information as Baines (or Marlowe, or later Gilbert Gifford) could provide on the residents at the English school would thus be vital as it would allow a tie-up with otherwise quite innocent seeming travelling Englishmen.

While Marlowe was presumably ingratiating himself in Rheims by betraying Baines, and getting ordained, Shakespeare was taking advantage of the education on offer at Cambridge. He probably had told his family that he was joining a troupe of strolling players – and this cover would have done both for Rheims and Cambridge – but he clearly was able to communicate with them. Again, the system of drop boxes would have provided a communication route, and would not have seemed strange to his family. Many men travelling about the country would have needed places for messages to be left for them and Shakespeare would have had use of the spy-networks drop boxes in England.

That Marlowe and Shakespeare swapped places in 1580 and Marlowe took Shakespeare's place at Rheims is my first possibility. The following chapter outlines the second.

Chapter Seven

A Holder of Horses [1]

In Chapter Five it was said that there were two possible ways for Christopher Marlowe to be in Rheims and detailed in Chapter Six how he actually got there and some of his possible activities. However, there is a second possibility, still suggesting that Marlowe had been recruited as a spy in Canterbury, a town noted for its Catholic sympathies, and suffering loss of income and position since the destruction of its prime tourist attraction, the shrine of its martyr, St Thomas Becket, and a place where government agents might well find suitable candidates for Walsingham's spy network. It was also suggested that the Parker Scholars themselves

---

1 Arriving in London, Shakespeare 'driven to the last Necessity, went to the Playhouse door and pick'd up a little Money by holding the horses of those who had no Servants.' (*Conversations ... with the people of Stratford-upon-Avon (1715)* Betterton). Shakespeare Institute Library: 'Sing Lousy Lucy': Shakespeare and the roes of Charlecote, Posted on December 21, 2015 by sililibrarian.

were set to spy on fellow students at Cambridge, a former stronghold of the new Protestantism but by the 1580s nurturing Catholicism. Shakespeare, hailing from Lancashire, was intended for Rheims, but had been recruited to the spy network and then Walsingham swapped two young men he saw as 'twins' in order for a more favourable outcome for each as a spy.

But there is a second possibility, which involves Walsingham less in Shakespeare's life.

Possibility Two

The second possibility revolves around our lack of knowledge of Shakespeare's whereabouts from 1564 until 1592, excepting his marriage and the conception of his three children between the summer of 1582 and February 1585. Shakespeare has been supposed a travelling player from 1585. Prior to 1582 he was either with a travelling troupe or, as has been suggested by several studies, living at Hoghton until December 1580[2].

The second possibility for Shakespeare taking Marlowe's place at Cambridge involves supposing that he was at Hoghton until after August 1581, when Hoghton's will was signed (though, as suggested earlier, this is not necessarily when it was written), supported somewhat by Hoghton saying that 'one Shakeshafte' was 'dwelling with him'. Given that dwelling may not mean actually living with someone, for it might mean being part of a household but not living-in, or being on that household's business elsewhere, in another, related, house, it is not necessary that Shakespeare actually be at Hoghton, but there is a possibility he was still there until 1581. If this is so, then Shakespeare

---

2   Chapter Four above.

left Lancashire with money in his pocket and the intention of going to Rheims, as supposed by Alexander Hoghton. But he did not go, he returned to Stratford and met Anne Hathaway (and possibly Anne Whateley of Temple Grafton) and was in the position of having to marry her in November 1582.[3]

There are stories about Shakespeare that defy investigation. One of them is that he fled Stratford-on-Avon because he had been poaching in the Lucy's park (a capital offence) another is that he held horses for a living outside theatres in London. The Lucy family has always denied any truth in the poaching story [4] but the horse holding story has not been refuted. Like the tale of Shakespeare being a tutor it has some ring of truth. A young man who had joined a troupe of players might well be holding horses outside the theatre for patrons to earn extra money, especially if he had reached that slightly uncomfortable stage in life where he was too old to play women's parts but not quite old enough for substantial male roles – so that the part of a spear carrier (though this is so close to Shakespeare's name one wonders whether it is wishful thinking), passing servant or messenger were his likely opportunities for appearance on stage. He

---

3 There is some doubt that Anne Whateley existed and that her name in the register at Worcester is a clerk's error. But perhaps it records Shakepeare's wish which was thwarted by Anne Hathaway's family, who forced him to do the decent thing and marry her.

4 There is no legal documentation for the deer poaching story, and the Lucys had no deer park till after 1618. However they had rights of warren, so there would have been hares, rabbits etc to take. Ibid.

might also do it as an extra job when the theatres were closed.

  Possibility two for the role swap between Marlowe and Shakespeare involves quite heavily some understanding of how student life works. If Marlowe (and not Shakespeare) did go up to Cambridge in December 1580, possibly after a meeting with Walsingham or one of his aids in London then he also, at some point, went to Rheims. This may have been his remit from Walsingham – or, as is more likely, it may have been his own decision because he saw more traction in becoming an embedded Catholic spy, with its possibilities for acting as a double agent and thus being more lucrative, though more dangerous. He must have been there before the betrayal of Richard Baines and his imprisonment in May 1582, but not all the time for he had to appear at Cambridge also. Which is where the mechanics of student life come in. Marlowe's place in the Buttery lists was occasionally taken by other scholars, including the Protestant martyr, Greenwood, and Pashley's scholarship lasted until March 1581. So Marlowe did not have to be in attendance at Cambridge all the time as long as he could get someone else to sign him in – a thing that students do for each other to this day. He could follow a similar procedure at Rheims – although he probably was not enrolled as a candidate for the priesthood at this point, but as an ordinary scholar studying the general course. What reasons he gave fellow students for his absences we do not know but they will most likely be along the lines of illness in the family, family occasions, girlfriends (or boyfriends), pressing work (and Cambridge students were allowed leave of absence to work with other scholars [5]) and the even more pressing need to visit and carouse with friends – for these are the reasons given by absenting students now. But by the end of 1582, having done such swaps for over two years Marlowe's position at both Cambridge and Rheims would have been getting difficult. Some people would be asking questions and there might have been pressure at Rheims to study for the priesthood, for Marlowe would have seemed an ideal candidate, able and a good actor perhaps, and apparently, the holder of strong Catholic sympathies against Elizabeth I. And he had discovered the traitor, Baines, in their midst. The constant travelling would have been arduous and expensive, and though Marlowe had his Cambridge scholarship and possibly money from Walsingham he might have been seeking a way out.

Marlowe is absent for a week of the Michaelmas term and would most likely be travelling via London to Canterbury for Christmas. He possibly also needed to report to Walsingham on his activities, if he had already been recruited as a spy. Shakespeare had married in late November, possibly against his will and wishes. There is no record of him being in Stratford after the marriage, so it is quite possible he did the decent thing and then left, joining a troupe of players on their way to London to begin an acting career while he thought about his missed opportunity of getting an education in Rheims. He would be getting his annuity from Hoghton, and it would keep him in London, but he also had a wife to support and a coming child. He would need all the money he could scrape together and

---

5   Roberts, P. Christopher Marlowe at Corpus, 1580-87, in Pelican - The Magazine of Corpus Christi College, Cambridge - Easter Review.

holding horses earns money – not much, but perhaps the difference between eating and not eating or paying for lodgings rather than having to sleep somewhere in the theatre or in a doorway. So he is holding horses when he is not required on stage or backstage. It is coming towards Christmas, he does not want to go back to Stratford and Christopher Marlowe walks into his life, perhaps by accident (or maybe by Walsingham's design, for it may well be that Shakespeare **had** been recruited as a spy in Lancashire and has just been noticed in London). Whether accidental, with Shakespeare not yet having entered Walsingham's orbit (or perhaps having rebuffed tentative overtures and been dropped), or designed by Walsingham, they meet. If it is an accident, Marlowe, more astute perhaps than Shakespeare, at once notices the resemblance. Shakespeare, perhaps mourning his education and wondering how he is going to progress in his new profession as an actor (legend has it he was not a good one, but as he appears in several cast lists this seems unfounded), is open to suggestion. A swap, so that Shakespeare takes Marlowe's place in Cambridge, is suggested. Shakespeare has his annuity and Marlowe has his scholarship and spy money. It is possible. All that is necessary is to make the swap smooth. From Marlowe's point of view Shakespeare taking his place in Cambridge is the easiest option. Marlowe will by now have a working knowledge of French which Shakespeare will not have – and although Shakespeare has the entrée to Rheims through his Hoghton connection he may appear to Marlowe as less likely to stay the course or to become a danger to Marlowe by becoming a Catholic agent for Allen and Rome – so he may not feed Marlowe the information he needs. It would also be logistically easier to make a swap in England. Shakespeare might very easily be introduced to both Marlowe's family and his fellow students and his lecturers at Cambridge in the space provided by Christmas.

Shakespeare would go home to Canterbury with Marlowe, perhaps dyeing his hair and changing his appearance by growing or shaving his beard. Extra padding (available in an acting troupe) would make him appear stouter. He would be introduced as a fellow student from Cambridge. After Christmas the journey to Cambridge would be done together, perhaps just before the beginning of the Lent term. Shakespeare, still looking stouter and with or without facial hair, would be introduced to Marlowe's contacts as his 'country cousin'. Shakespeare as an intelligent young man would imbibe the knowledge necessary to get on at Cambridge, then they would swap and Shakespeare would become Marlowe at Cambridge while Marlowe himself set off for Rheims, perhaps able to use Hoghton's name now as his patron (Hoghton had died in 1581 and it would be possible for Marlowe to suggest that he had only just learned of his legacy) and begin training as a seminary priest in 1583. Shakespeare would continue at Cambridge and carry out Marlowe's mission as both a Parker Spy and Walsingham's agent at Corpus Christi.

But where is the evidence of such a swap? It is in the Buttery books and Audits of Corpus Christi, and in Shakespeare and Marlowe's plays

Chapter Eight

Parker Scholar

Marlowe signed the buttery book at Corpus Christi, Cambridge on 10 December 1580. He used the name 'Marlin' and spent one penny. He continued to spend throughout December and into January and February, sometimes as much as fifteen pennies a week (1/3d) [1] but 'Marlin' does not become registered at the college until March, when the previous Parker Scholar, Pashley, completes his degree and departs. And who was Marlin? It is assumed that this is Christopher Marlowe, entering Cambridge on his scholarship, since Marlin was one of the ways that he spelled Marlowe. And can it be anyone else? Two young men are looking for an education and a future in 1580, from similar backgrounds and with similar beginnings in education. Also similar are the rumours of continuing Catholicism in their families.

---

1   Honan, P., ibid pp.82-88.

Under the terms of the first set of possibilities, detailed in Chapter Five, when Marlowe arrived in London he met William Shakespeare, on his way to Rheims to train as a Catholic priest in order to spy, and it was abundantly clear to Walsingham, who had them interviewed, that he had a small miracle before him, two boys so similar that they could swap places. It was probably also clear that Shakespeare was not likely to finish the course at Rheims, or might become a dangerous Catholic agent, because he was not committed either to it or to spying on Catholics, but that Marlowe was committed and had better Latin for the job. So they were swapped. 'Marlowe' thus arrived early, which he would not have otherwise done, so that he could take advantage of attending lectures and improving his Latin before he took up his scholarship. It also gave him time to embed himself among the possible Catholics he had been engaged, as a Parker scholar, to investigate.

If this is the situation, he has the money to do this from Walsingham, and he is not Marlowe, but William Shakespeare, so desperate for an education denied by his father's bankruptcy that going to Rheims to train as a priest was a draw to a young man who later shows how unsuited he was to this role.

But William Shakespeare was in Stratford in 1582, probably August, getting Anne Hathaway with child, and Christopher Marlowe was in Canterbury in 1585 [2] signing a will. How can Shakespeare be both in Cambridge and Stratford-on-Avon, how can Marlowe be in Cambridge, Rheims and Canterbury? The answer lies in Robert Poley's drop boxes and the Cambridge Buttery Books, which tell a

---

2   Honan ibid p.p. 105-6.

tale of absence and at least once of someone taking Marlowe's place at Cambridge.

So how can Shakespeare both be at Cambridge and having an affair with Anne Hathaway in August 1582 – this date is based on the birth date of Susannah Shakespeare on 26 May 1583, roughly forty weeks later – and get married in a hurry on November 28 1582? The Buttery records show how, in the absences from Cambridge, many of those absences simply the allowed time off for scholars.

Someone calling themselves Marlowe arrives in Cambridge on 10 December and begins eating at the Buttery, spending quite substantial amounts of money on occasion. He is enrolled as a Parker scholar in March 1581 and then receives the scholarship money. If he is in Cambridge he will have been able to attend lectures and although he would not be able to use the books in the Parker collection he would most likely be able to borrow books from other students, possibly even Pashley, the resident Parker scholar whom he was to replace. He almost certainly lodged in the building where Parker scholars were housed. Being at Cambridge before he formally became a Parker scholar would allow for some brushing up on his knowledge – Shakespeare' attendance at the Stratford-on-Avon grammar school under John Cotham meant he would have had enough Latin to cope with the catching up necessary for someone who had not had Marlowe's longer education. That he never quite caught up is attested by the examination results allotted to Marlowe – quite poor considering that he must have had a powerful intellect and been a good scholar in order to have been given a Parker scholarship after such a short time spent at the King's School. Later, of course, Shakespeare allowed people to believe, as Jonson said, that he had 'small Latin and less Greek' – a necessary lie to cover his association with Marlowe.

Previously, little attention has been given to the absences from Cambridge prior to 1585, when Marlowe begins to be absent for longer periods which do not necessarily match up with what would be considered normal absence times such as late summer. The theory that he was not recruited as a spy until 1585 is questionable because of the persistent rumours of Catholic contacts, which suggests a much earlier dalliance with spying though the agency of the Parker scholarships. But there are earlier absences which support my theory that Marlowe and Shakespeare, possibly under the aegis of Walsingham, swapped places.

The tables that follow cover the years 1580 to 1587. They are arranged to show Marlowe's absences across those years. They are followed by tables showing the events we know of in Shakespeare's life between 1582 and 1587.

Tables 1a and 1b below show Marlowe's Audit [3] and Buttery [4] entries from December 1580 until 1587. The Buttery records are incomplete for 1585-86. [5]

---

3   Honan P., ibid pp.82-88.
4   Boas, F. S., Christopher Marlowe: A Biographical and Critical Study, pp.12-14.
5   Bakeless, J., *The Tragicall History of Christopher Marlowe,* Vol 2 p.301. 'Discovered by the college authorities and place in the strong room of the Estates Bursury, 1935. Marlowe entries discovered by the writer (John Bakeless) ,1936. The records give a week-by-week account of the poet's purchases and thus a clue to his comings and goings from 1580 to 1586. It thus covers the year 1585-86 missing from the Audits.'

Table 1a – Terms 1 and 2

Year	Term 1	Buttery weeks	Term 2	Buttery weeks
	Michaelmas		**Lent**	
	Sept/Oct-Xmas		**Jan-Mar**	
1580-81	- ?		12/-	
1581-82	13/-		13/-	
1582-83	12/-		13/-	
1583-84	12/-		13/-	
1584-85	3/-	2,3,4,7,10,11,12 entries	7/-	9 weeks entries
	Sept/Oct-Xmas		**Jan-Mar**	
1585-86	Unknown, assumed present	2 weeks out	Unknown, assumed present	3 weeks out
1586-87	9/-		5/6	

Table 1b – Terms 3 and 4

Year	Term 3	Buttery weeks	Term 4	Buttery weeks
	Easter		**Summer**	
1584-85	4/-	No entries 5-12th	5/-	No entries 4-12th
1580-81	13/-		12/-	
1581-82	13/-		7/-	
1582-83	6/-	No entries 4-9th but in college on 22nd April [6]	14/-	
1583-84	13/-		11/6	2.5 out
	Easter (3)		**Summer (4)**	
1584-85	4/-	No entries 5-12th	5/-	No entries 4-12th
1585-86	Absences	1 entry before last 2 weeks of term	Unknown assumed present	All 14 weeks
1586-87				

From the tables it can be seen that Marlowe's first entry in the Buttery records is 10th December 1580. He continues spending at the Buttery until he is formally listed

---

6   Boas, ibid. p.9 – Marlowe was in college when his sister, Joan, was married on 22 April 1582. (Boas source: John Bakeless, Christopher Marlowe, p.26 (1938)).

as a Parker Scholar in March. He attends well during 1581, with only two weeks missing in the Trinity term – when he received only twelve shillings, against a usual fourteen shillings. In 1582 there is a change. He takes seven weeks off for the summer, covering August. This makes it possible for Marlowe – aka William Shakespeare – to return to Stratford, meet Anne Hathaway and get her pregnant (pregnancy lasts between thirty-eight and forty-two weeks). He would not have known she was pregnant when he returned to Cambridge but would have received news of this through the drop-box system he would certainly have arranged with his family. He is absent for a week in the Michaelmas term, which gives him time to marry Anne – although it is possible his absence does not actually coincide with the marriage date, 27 November, but that Marlowe returned from Rheims (perhaps to visit Canterbury in order to hush suspicions of his presence in Rheims) and took Shakespeare's place. More likely is it that the entries are uncertain. In 1583 there is an absence of six weeks in the Easter term (Easter was 10th April) which would allow Shakespeare to be in Stratford for the birth of Susannah. There are no more absences until the Trinity term of 1584 when he is allotted only eleven shillings and sixpence, meaning an absence of between two and three weeks – long enough to visit his wife in Stratford and father twins, especially as Easter fell on 1 April in that year. Hamnet and Judith were born the following February. Of course, twins can be born early so the conception date could be later but for the moment the dates fit, and Shakespeare was absent again for three weeks in the Lent term, allowing time to see the new arrivals.

Table 2 shows the dates for Easter from 1580 to 1587, from which it can be seen that some of Marlowe's absences coincide with it:

Table 2 – The date of Easter 1580-87

Year	Easter
1580	3 April
1581	26 March
1582	15 April
1583	10 April
1584	1 April
1585	21 April
1586	6 April
1587	29 March

Looking at Table In 1585 Christopher Marlowe signs Katherine Benchkin's will on 19 August. [7]. Bakeless, in *The Tragicall History of Christopher Marlowe*, referring to absences in November 1585 says: 'This corresponds to Marlowe's absence from Corpus in the sixth and seventh weeks after Michaelmas, 1585, or the latter part of November.' Relating 'this' time in November to the matter of the Benchkin will [8], adding that John Malowe making a

---

7   Her son, John Benchkin, came up to Corpus Christi 30 June 1585 (Honan, ibid, p. 107).

8   'Marlowe's absence for two weeks in the Michaelmas term of 1585 is explained by documents discovered in 1939 by Frank. W. Tyler, Esq. In the autumn of that year Mistress Catherine Benchkyn, of Canterbury, made her will, and young Christopher Marlowe, then visiting his family in Canterbury, witnessed it'. Bakeless ibid p Vol 1 p. 74. (1942

depositon of it on 5th October 1586 'sets the time as about a year before'[9]. Catherine Benchkin's will was signed in August 1585, so these absences do not relate to the will at all. However, Shakespeare may well have had reason to be in Stratford at the end of 1585, as the father of a young family.

The pattern of presence and absence is easier to follow with the terms and absences listed from the Lent term rather than Michaelmas, so that events follow the calendar year rather than the academic. The date of Easter has been inserted to show how the pattern fits with this. Tables 3a and 3b below are adjusted to show the year from January to March.

Table 3a – Lent and Easter terms

Year	Lent (2) Jan-March	Easter (3) April-June	Date of Easter
1580	-	-	3rd April
1581	12/-	13/-	26th March
1582	13/-	13/-	15th April
1583	13/-	6/- (6 weeks missing)	10th April
Year	Lent (2) Jan-March	Easter (3) April-June	Date of Easter
1584	13/-	13/-	1st April

---

and 1970 eds).

9   Bakeless, ibid. John Marlowe appears to have made his deposition on the will rather late.

Year	Lent (2) Jan-March	Easter (3) April-June	Date of Easter
1585	7/- (9 wks buttery)	4/- (no buttery 5-12)	21st April
1586	(3 wks missing)	Absent (1 entry before last 2 weeks)	6th April
1587	5/6		29th March

Table 3b – Summer and Michaelmas terms

Year	Easter	Summer/Trinity (4) July-Sept/Oct	Michaelmas (1) Sept/Oct-Xmas
1580	3 April	-	Buttery entry 10th Dec
1581	26t March	12/- (2 weeks missing)	13/-
1582	15 April	7/- (7 weeks missing)	12/- (1 week missing)
1583	10t April	14/-	12/-
1584	1 April	11/6 (2.5 weeks missing)	3/- (2,3,4,7,10,11,12)
1585	21 April	5/- (no buttery 4-12) (Benchkin will signed)	2 weeks missing – 6th and 7th weeks after Michael-mas or the latter part of Nov-ember.[10]
1586	6t April	(14 entries)	9/- (entries first 4 wks)
1587	29t March		

The information we know of for William Shakespeare fits Marlowe's Cambridge pattern:

---

10   Bakeless, J. ibid. Vol 1, p 75 (1945 edition)

Table 4a – Shakespeare:1580-83

1580	1581	1582	1583
Easter 3 April	Easter 26 March	Easter 15 April	Easter 10 April
		Susannah conceived approximately August	Susannah baptised 26 May
		Marries Anne Hathaway 27/28/11 [11]	

Table 4b – Shakespeare: 1584-87

1584	1585	1586	1587
Easter 1 April	Easter 21 April	Easter 6 April	Easter 29 March
Twins conceived approximately April/May [12]	Twins born 2 February		

Thus it is perfectly possible to reconcile Shakespeare's marriage and the conception of his children with him being at Cambridge, remembering that there is no

---

11   The marriage license was granted on 27 November for 'Wm Shaxpere et Anneam Whateley de Temple Grafton'. The marriage took place on 28 November between 'William Shagspere on the one party and Anne Hathwey of Stratford in the diocese of Worcester, maiden'. Source: shakespeare-online.com/biography/shakespearemarriage. 28 Nov 1585 was a Sunday.

12   But maybe as late as June as twins can be born early.

employment record for him in Stratford during these years. In arguing this it is necessary to be aware that had Shakespeare been a strolling player at this time he could have equally well been in Stratford at the right times – although the arrangement of his marriage might have been fraught as a troupe of players would rather less reliably be picking up messages from stations on their tour. At Cambridge it is quite possible for Shakespeare to receive regular communications from his family, as well as from his contact from Walsingham's spy network, through drop boxes which might be fairly permanent, and which would anyway have a means of passing a message to another drop box if necessary. Walsingham's secret service was quite sophisticated and there was always a need to be able to pass on information secretly.

Thus far the swap arranged by Walsingham works. Marlowe is in Rheims and Shakespeare is in Cambridge getting the education he needs to become a playwright.

If this second hypothesis is the probable one, and that Marlowe and Shakespeare did not swap places until the end of 1582 the time-table still fits. Marlowe flits between Rheims and Cambridge, paid for by Walsingham, possibly signed in at Cambridge by his friends. As suggested by Peter Roberts[13] the Buttery and Audit records of Corpus Christi are in disarray during Marlowe's time at Cambridge. There is no certainty of any dates and Marlowe, whether it is the real Christopher Marlowe or William Shakespeare, could be absent for any length of time without the records showing this. Marlowe is absent in 1587 for thirty-five weeks of the year – which is ***one*** reason the college does not

---

13 Christopher Marlowe at Corpus, 1580-87 in Pelican, Easter 2014 p.26.

want to give him his M.A. – and we cannot be sure of his presence there at any time. Whenever the swap took place the absences in the Buttery Books and the gaps in the scholarship payments allow Shakespeare ample time to go back to Stratford to father his twins if he joined Corpus Christi in December 1582 or January 1583. The drop box system being used by Marlowe would still accommodate Shakespeare and the role of strolling player would cover his absence from Stratford, whilst his £2 a year from Hoghton would amply cover his expenses – or rather Marlowe's at Rheims.

A later swap is just as likely as the earlier one (though it leaves the Cambridge portrait still being Marlowe, this is not significant) and that Walsingham therefore did not know of it. Shakespeare would take on the role of Parker scholar-spy and also the work paid for by Walsingham. He and Marlowe could communicate by means of the drop boxes and the secret services courier system utilizing them without anyone except themselves knowing that there were two Marlowes.

In 1587 when the Privy Council write their letter telling Corpus Christi to give 'Christopher Morley' his M.A. they are writing of Shakespeare, although they do not know this. As to the letter itself, it need bear no relation to what Marlowe was actually doing, it is simply a cover letter to stop Corpus Christi making a fuss about the Privy Council's spy being absent from Cambridge.

Marlowe, at Rheims, could, in 1582, now accept a place to train for the priesthood and would be in good odour with Dr. Allen having revealed Baines, still in prison at this point, as a spy within their midst. That he too was a spy would not be apparent.

Both Shakespeare and Marlowe would have been able to proceeds in their respective educations. Shakespeare, in the persona of Marlowe at Cambridge, was undoubtedly working for Walsingham's spy network and was probably working undercover on the continent when absent from Cambridge, particularly in 1587, the year of Mary Stuart's execution.

On graduation, both proceed to London. Marlowe as an ordained seminary priest, probably dressed in the clothes of a gallant, a popular guise among his fellow priests. In London Shakespeare-as-Marlowe would have visited Walsingham to give a report of what he had been doing and to plan his next assignments. He must also have made plans with Marlowe himself. Neither of them, perhaps, were aware of the ticking bomb represented by Richard Baines, still intent on revenge for his sufferings at the hands of Dr. Allen, his ploy to tar Marlowe with the Rheims brush having failed thanks to the Privy Council. It looks suspiciously as though Baines was not aware that Marlowe was Walsingham's spy and so did not expect any intervention on Marlowe's behalf. By 1587 Baines was either in the pay of Walsingham or Burghley, or about to join another network – perhaps that of the rising Earl of Essex.

Having settled with Walsingham's spy network it appears that Shakespeare as Marlowe started a career writing plays. Marlowe almost certainly set off to infiltrate Catholic households, using drop boxes to pass information back to Shakespeare.

Chapter Nine

'The Play's the Thing'

After receiving his M.A. the young man known as Christopher Marlowe went to London to join the literary circles around the city and the court, thus breaking the condition of his scholarship, that he should be ordained. His intended career was that of writer, both of poetry – Marlowe had made a translation of Ovid whilst at Cambridge[1] – and plays. He had probably already written *Dido, Queen of Carthage.* His translation of Ovid was scurrilous enough to be burnt by Archbishop Whitgift in 1598, so we can imagine it was popular among the reading public who were not of extreme Protestant leanings. We do not know when *Dido*

---

1 Riggs, The World of Christopher Marlowe, suggests that Marlowe translated Ovid after its publication by Thomas Vautrolker in Marlowe's third year at Cambridge (1582/3). Riggs suggests it 'shows traces of an apprentice piece' (Riggs, p. 99) suggesting it was translated by a student. Shakespeare had less education than Marlowe, so the translator is more likely to be him.

was performed, although it is possible it was presented by the boys of St Paul's – which were well known for their theatrical activities – or perhaps at Cambridge, where students often put on plays for festival days. But Marlowe had an immediate success in London with *Tamburlaine the Great* – a play of sweeping action and romance, telling the story of a shepherd who becomes a great emperor. It is based on contemporary knowledge of Timur Lang, and shows acquaintance with the history and geography of the Middle East as known to Elizabethans. It was so successful that Marlowe wrote a sequel, known to us as *Tamburlaine Part II* – an equally popular play. Whilst writing Marlowe was entering the society of the University Wits, those playwrights and poets who had studied at Oxford and Cambridge and who held themselves a cut above contemporaries who had not had a university education – people like William Shakespeare or Thomas Kyd. It was a society in which everyone knew each other, and Marlowe presumably became well-known among playwrights working for the companies of actors and the new theatres. Or rather, William Shakespeare, under the name of Marlowe, became well-known, if my theory is correct.

Exactly when the young Marlowe/Shakespeare arrived in London is unknown. He most probably travelled from Cambridge by the route he had taken when he had first gone up to Corpus Christi, and arrived in the early summer of 1587. He would have found a city of perhaps 200,000 people, spread over both banks of the Thames; a city of contrasts, with the houses of well-off merchants and the aristocracy cheek by jowl with lock-up shops and street stalls; a city full of the wealthy and the abjectly poor, with beggars on the streets and no safety, particularly at night. [2] He probably found lodgings in Norton Folgate, or the close by Shoreditch, then as now rather rakish areas, peopled with actors, writers and prostitutes. There were also two theatres there, the Theatre (constructed in 1576 by James Burbage), supposed to be the first theatre constructed in England, [3] and the Curtain, both built outside the jurisdiction of the London magistrates, as Norton Folgate was a liberty within the metropolitan area. The theatres themselves, modelled on the inn yards where actors usually performed, were rather temporary structures which could be dismantled at need (Shakespeare and Burbage did dismantle the Theatre and relocated it across the river in Southwark, after Giles Allen, the owner of the land the Theatre was built on, claimed he

---

[2] A century later Samuel Pepys records having to escort two ladies home at night, leaving his wife to make her own way in their carriage with a friend. Women needed male protection as it was not safe to be abroad at night in London in the 1660s. Fanny Burney, in the 1770s, could not make the short journey from the theatre to her home on foot after she became separated from her friends.

[3] http://www.william-shakespeare.info/william-shakespeare-globe-theatre.htm. But there is some evidence that the unnamed theatre built in Newington Butts predates the Theatre by a few months, being opened by Jerome Savage on land and tenements leased from Richard Hicks on 25th March 1576, which seems to have been a theatre (Ingram (1992) pp 153–157, p. 164, p. 166, and Wickham *et al* (2000) p 320) Hicks calls Savage a low fellow who got his living by play acting. Henslowe may be refering to Newington Butts in his diary, when he writes 'ne'. He uses this term against *The Massacre at Paris*, being performed in 1594. If 'ne' stands for 'new' instead, then it is an odd addition as *The Massacre* was performed by Lord Strange's men in January 1593 and so was not 'new

owned the building as well as the land when the lease ran out in 1598 [4]). Inside they had a wide space, the pit, and galleries around three sides with the stage sticking out into the pit, (called an apron stage) with a curtain at the back (which could be opened to reveal a scene) and one or two galleries above (which would make the balcony for *Romeo and Juliet*, or the window out of which Katerina looks in *The Taming of the Shrew*). On stage there were seats for specially privileged spectators. Behind the stage there were dressing rooms and prop rooms.

With a new and growing appetite for plays among the general population[5], these theatres needed playwrights to feed them. If Marlowe already had contacts in London he probably used them to get access to actors. It is possible that he knew Greene[6] and other university graduates. He would have come to know the printers around St Paul's, who were in the market to publish popular plays. The acting companies presented whatever the public wanted, and performances might end with a bear baiting, with jugglers or acrobats.[7] But there was also a demand for a variety of

---

4   Though the story of the removal of the building is a little convoluted, some versions saying the Theatre was moved (and Richard Burbage had a legal right to the materials) others saying it was another theatre, in Blackfriars, which was illegally dismantled because the government would not allow the site to be used for performing plays (on petition of local, wealthy, residents). Source: william-shakespeare-globe-theatre.htm. and Britannica.com/topic/Globe-Theatre.

5   Honan, P., Christopher Marlowe, Poet and Spy, p.162.

6   Who apparently wrote quite disparagingly of him in his Groat's Worth of Wit, 1592, see below.

7   Honan, P, ibid, p. 161-2

plays, and a troupe, under the repertory system,[8] might perform several plays in a week. Those plays might be comedies, histories, or moral allegories and the playwrights of London were providing them to a growing market. Into this came Marlowe, perhaps with *Tamburlaine* already nearly finished. The play was performed by the Lord Admiral's men, the part of Tamburlaine being taken by Edward Alleyn, perhaps one of the greatest, certainly a popular, actor of his time. So famous was he in the part of Tamburlaine that his (attributed) portrait in the role appears in Richard Knolles' *The General History of the Turks*, published in 1597.

Success breeds success and Marlowe followed up *Tamburlaine* and the equally popular *Part II*, with *The Jew of Malta*, *Edward II* and *The Massacre at Paris*. None of these plays was published in book form in his lifetime, however. He also wrote several poems, including *The Passionate Shepherd*[9] and the unfinished *Hero and Leander*.[10]

Meanwhile, the Marlowe who had been at Rheims was returning home, not necessarily for the first time because he may have had leave of absence to visit his family in 1585 [11] when he witnessed a will in Canterbury and read it 'plainly and distinctly', - although this may have been Shakespeare, who would have been introduced to Marlowe's family and after the absence of some years could have, for a short time, passed as the son of the house. (That

---

8　　ibid
9　　Shakespeare published this as his own poem in 1599, possibly by mistake.
10　　Hero and Leander was completed by Chapman.
11　　ibid, p.109.

Marlowe travelled back to Cambridge with John Benchkin, supports the idea that it was Shakespeare, since Benchkin might have noticed a swap.) But now Marlowe returned as a fully-fledged seminary priest apparently dedicated to overthrowing the rule of Queen Elizabeth, but actually a young man about to be employed as a spy on her Catholic subjects.

The two probably met in London, before Marlowe, the priest set off to carry out the work he had trained himself for, the infiltration of Catholic households.[12] He might have been travelling about the country, disguised as a gallant, just like John Penry, who is described as wearing a 'sky blue cloak', more than likely playing the part of a dissolute young fellow, so that his expectant Catholic hosts may have been entirely surprised – and disarmed – by his appearance (he would have introduced himself by password). He needed them to trust him and they would expect a seminary priest to be a man dissembling his true vocation. Fulfilling expectations would enable Marlowe to carry out his mission. His findings he sent, via drop boxes or maybe through the agency of travelling actors, to Shakespeare in London. Shakespeare meanwhile was cultivating friendships in literary circles, where he would have met several other spies, for example Thomas Watson (who had been at Douai in the 1570s), with whom he was involved in an affray which resulted in a death.

One of the people he probably made a close relationship with is Thomas Nashe, who may have

---

12 If the exchange took place in 1582 then Walsingham will have known nothing of Shakespeare's existence. He might have been surprised by the amount of intelligence he received from Marlowe.

collaborated with him on *Dido*. (Nashe was one of the University Wits, having attended St. John's college as a sizar[13] and graduated in 1586 and so may have been acquainted with Marlowe at Cambridge.) Murphy[14] suggests that not only was Marlowe collaborating with Nashe but that plays ascribed to Shakespeare are Marlowe's, and that the anonymous *Edward III*, also attributed to Shakespeare, on the evidence of vocabulary, is Marlowe's. But the contention here is the opposite, that the plays attributed to Marlowe were written by William Shakespeare, under the name of Marlowe, they having swapped places, so that it is Shakespeare who knows, and collaborates with Nashe.

The evidence from the Buttery entries shows that Shakespeare taking Marlowe's place at Cambridge is possible. What evidence is there for the opposite assertion, that the man who seems to have collaborated with Nashe and went to Cambridge was the man who wrote the plays ascribed to William Shakespeare, and was Christopher Marlowe from Canterbury?

The evidence is said to be mainly in the texts of Shakespeare's plays and poetry and that evidence not only suggests that the same person wrote the plays, or most of

---

13   At Cambridge a sizar is a student who receives some form of assistance, for example meals, lower fees or lodging during his (or now her) period of study, sometimes in return for doing a defined job. There were three types of students at Cambridge in Marlowe's time: pensioners who paid their own fees, scholars - like Marlowe - who had a scholarship, and sizars, like Nashe.

14   Murphy, D., (2013) *The Marlowe-Shakespeare Continuum*, Scholars Publishing.

them, attributed to Christopher Marlowe and William Shakespeare, as suggested by many Marlovians, but that the writer had attended Cambridge University and also went into exile. This same evidence supports the theory that Shakespeare was the author of Marlowe's work, and not the other way around. To show how this might be needs an examination of the various arguments for Marlowe's authorship.

For example, Donna Murphy[15] suggests there is evidence that the writer of *Tamburlaine* shares rare vocabulary with Nashe. Murphy concentrates on terms such as 'burly-boned', which appears in *Henry VI, Part II*, a play always attributed to Shakespeare. – for example: Cade [16], (to his sword): 'Steel, if thou turn the edge or cut not out the **burly-boned** clown in **chines of beefe**.' (IV.ix.56-7), comparing this to similar words in Nashe's *Almond for a Parrot*,[17] *Piers Penniless* and *The Unfortunate Traveller* – and 'forty foot', which appears in *The Jew of Malta*: '**Within forty foot of** the **gallows**,' (IV.ii.16-20), as well as in *The Unfortunate Traveller* and *Have at You to Saffron Walden* (Nashe's 'confutation of the sinful Doctor'[18] Gabriel Harvey, who had his living in Saffron Walden). Thus, on this

---

15   *Review of Donna Murphy's The Marlowe Shakespeare Continuum*, Peter Farey's Marlowe Page.
16   It is now thought (2017) that the scenes in Henry VI involving Jack Cade (and also Joan of Arc) were written by Marlowe. By this time, 1592, Shakespeare was attempting to move away from his Marlovian style, although it persisted for some years, and that the passages in Henry VI are unintentional lapses. Other sources: Bakeless, 1938 and Riggs, 2004.
17   1590. One of at least two anti-Martin Marprelate tracts commissioned by ecclesiastical authorities and written by Nashe.
18   Oxford Shakespeare.

argument, the writer of *Tamburlaine* and the writer of *Henry VI* are the same writer because they share a vocabulary with Nashe, who had gone to Cambridge - and Murphy is of the opinion that the writer is Marlowe, who was at Cambridge at the same time as Nashe. Actually it only suggests that whoever wrote *Tamburlaine* and *Henry VI*, knew Nashe.

In further support of the theory that the hand in Shakespeare's plays is Marlowe's, it has been suggested that the vocabulary used in several of Shakespeare's plays shows familiarity with Cambridge usage, something which would not be known to a writer who had not been at Cambridge. The terms are 'act', 'to commence' and 'to proceed', which both, apparently, refer to the procedures for obtaining a degree. The term 'act' referred to the sillogistical[19] dispute a degree candidate had to take part in. If he was successful he was said to 'commence'[20] to his degree. Both these terms are used in Shakespeare's work. For example:

When he to madding Dido would unfold

His father's *acts, commenced* in burning Troy!
(*2 Henry VI* , 5.2.117–8)
and:

---

19   To argue, using syllogisms. For example: Only someone who had been to Cambridge would know specialist Cambridge terms. Henry VI contains specialist Cambridge terms. Therefore the writer of Henry VI must be Marlowe who went to Cambridge, not Shakespeare, who did not. Or the infamous: Immortals live to be 100. Bertrand Russell died at 99. Therefore Bertrand Russell is not an immortal (anonymous philosophy lecturer, Keele, 2/2/1970).

20   This term is still used for graduands attending a congregation, where they commence to a degree - become 'graduates'.

Hadst thou, like us from our first swath *proceeded*
The sweet *degrees* that this brief world affords . . .
Thy nature did *commence* in sufferance, time
Hath made thee hard in't.
(*Timon of Athens*, Act 4, Scene 3 (my bold).) [21]

However, these words bear other meanings and are hardly unique to Cambridge University, even in the sixteenth century. It is also clear that the meanings intended in the plays is not the meaning used at Cambridge: '(H)is father's acts, commenced in burning Troy' quite obviously means 'the things he did' 'began' in burning Troy (i.e. when Troy burnt) – and have nothing to do with maintaining a disputation or entering into the state of having a degree. The words do, however, have the look of puns on the Cambridge meanings. Because that is so, it makes it possible the writer of *Henry VI part II* and *Timon of Athens* might have attended Cambridge, but alone the use of the words is not conclusive of this or that the writer is Marlowe. In any case may not this Cambridge usage be from Nashe as well, since Shakespeare and he are collaborating? The evidence supporting Marlowe being Shakespeare equally supports Shakespeare being Marlowe. A Shakespeare who had taken Marlowe's place at Cambridge would know Nashe and also share his vocabulary. Not even the use of 'keep' to mean dwelling, as found in:
... all the skyey influences
That dost this habitation where thou *keep*'st
Hourly afflict.
(*Measure for Measure*, 3.1.8–11)

---

21   Farey, P. *Shakespeare and Cambridge,* The Marlowe-Shakespeare Continuum blog.

for example, which usage is also found in *Hamlet*, *Henry IV Part I*, *The Merchant of Venice* and also *The Massacre at Paris*,[22] does not confirm that the writer attended Cambridge, where the use of 'keep' to mean 'dwell' supposedly originated, and therefore shows that Marlowe was the author of Shakespeare's plays. There is no evidence that Shakespeare did not go to Cambridge, and the Buttery Books suggest that his attendance, as Marlowe, is possible, and explain how it was that Marlowe: could be 'going to Rheims'.

Similarly, the term 'jades of Asia' is used in *Henry IV Part II*, Act 2, sc.iv, lines 160-164, echoing, perhaps, the kings of Trebizon and Soria being harnessed to a cart, in *Tamburlaine Part II*, Act 2, sc.ii, lines 36-38. Also, in *King Lear*, Cordelia is compared to 'barbarous Scythians', abother allusion to *Tamburlaine II*[23] These echoes argue collaboration, and also a writer who is repeating himself unconsciously – something that all writers do. If it can be used to indicate one author for both canons, the author is Shakespeare.

Pursuing the linking of Marlowe and Shakespeare's vocabulary, Williams, in *Shakespeare, thy name is Marlowe*,[24] makes a similar assertion to Donna Murphy's, but based on frequency of word use, saying that the profile for Shakespeare exactly matches that of Marlowe. Williams

---

22   *The Massacre* text is probably a composite 'actors' copy' with additions made from other plays, put together at Philip Henslowe's behest, and thus the use of *'keep'* more likely confirms Shakespeare's authorship, than Marlowe's, since much of the text echoes him.

23   *Lear*, 1,i,113-120, and *Tamberlaine Part II*, 2,iv,19. Honan, ibid, p193.

24   Williams, *Shakespeare, thy name is Marlowe*, p. 15.

takes notice of the work of Mendenhall (1901), who, having been asked to investigate the likelihood that Francis Bacon wrote the works attributed to Shakespeare, devised a method of analysing word use in order to get a profile of the writer – a fingerprint, if you like. Mendenhall practised his method on various authors, including Dickens, Julius Caesar and Cervantes, as well as his targets, but could not show that Bacon was the author of Shakespeare. However, he found that Marlowe and Shakespeare's use of words matched.[25] Williams (and Mendenhall) immediately saw this as evidence that Marlowe was Shakespeare. But evidence that Marlowe had a vocabulary profile identical to Shakespeare's does not prove in any way that he wrote the plays attributed to Shakespeare. It could as easily prove the opposite or that they heavily collaborated, despite there being no evidence they ever met. Absence of evidence of course, is not evidence of absence.

It is hardly now disputed that Shakespeare collaborated with other playwrights, for example Fletcher in *The Two Noble Kinsmen* – a re-working of the *Knight's Tale* from Chaucer's *Canterbury Tales* – and *Thomas More*,[26] a

---

25 This idea is reiterated in P. Farey's *A Deception in Deptford'*, which includes examples of Shakepeare and Marlowe's similar usage.

26 Hand D is supposed to be Shakespeare – matching some of his five extant signatures. There is some stylistic evidence that he wrote, or re-wrote, A and C. C shows signs of dictation in the line: 'that I[']ll appear. before no king Christened but my good Lord Chancellor . . .'. There is also a contraction of time and historical events in scenes 6 and 7, said to be typical of Shakespeare's style. Shakespear in Compositon, **Evidence for Oxford's Authorship of "The Book of Sir Thomas More"**, Fran Gidley, The Oxfordian, Volume VI, 2003. Though this analysis comes from an Oxfordian source none of the above points made in the article go anywhere near

play written originally by Anthony Munday and Henry Chettle, but revised by various other playwrights, including Shakespeare (Hand H). However, by far the most pervasive hand supposed to be found in the plays of Shakespeare is that of Christopher Marlowe. If Shakespeare was in London, under the name of Marlowe, from 1587, then it is not Marlowe's hand in Shakespeare that we find, but that Shakespeare is the main author of plays ascribed to Christopher Marlowe, with some input from Marlowe himself, who had already perhaps written the play *Timon*[27] before he left Canterbury. Marlowe possibly also suggested some of the subjects of the later plays, and much of the background colour.[28]

The Marlovian position is that Marlowe went into exile in 1593 and from somewhere abroad was sending plays back to London, to be performed under the name of an actor/manager called William Shakespeare. There are several reasons for this surmise, as detailed above: repetition of lines, of vocabulary and similarity of style in places. However, they do not conclusively point to the Marlovian theory and the difficulty with the theory is lack of knowledge of where Marlowe went after May 1593, and how he supported himself. The contention here suggested is that the similarities do support one main author, but that the author in question is Shakespeare, not Marlowe.

---

proving Shakespeare's work was done by the Earl of Oxford, who anyway died in 1603.

27   A play, written about 1580, based around Drake's circumnavigation.

28   It might even be possible to track Marlowe's travels after 1593 through the locations of Shakespeare's plays.

And Shakespeare does have an affinity for foreign locations, particularly Italy and Greece, for his plays. It may be that, after 1593, he and Marlowe continued to correspond and that Marlowe's real contribution to the works of Shakespeare is plot ideas and location detail. After all, Shakespeare describes places in some detail, for example, from Othello, where Iago tries to make Othello jealous:

It is impossible you should see this,

Were they as prime as Goats, as hot as Monkeys,
As salt as Wolves in pride and Fools as gross

As ignorance made drunk.' (3.3.405-408)

This is, apparently, a description of a fresco in Bassano del Grappa in Italy. It has been suggested by Roger Prior, that this means Shakespeare went to Italy.[29] However, though such a suggestion is plausible given that we know so little of Shakespeare's activities before 1592, such information could as easily be gleaned by having a correspondent who had visited Italy, especially if, as I suspect, both correspondents were still acting as agents for the Privy Council and therefore had access to secret service drop boxes.[30] Such activity could well explain the suggestions that Shakespeare was (still) a Catholic, since he would, perforce, be associating with continuing recusants. It is possible that 'I'll drown my book' in *The Tempest* does not only refer to Shakespeare's writing no more plays, but

---

29 Roger Prior. "Shakespeare's Visit to Italy," *The Journal of Anglo-Italian Studies*, Vol. 9 (2008). The University of Malta.

30 Just as drop boxes were used at Cambridge and by Richard Baines at Rheims.

also that he has ceased to collect information for the government. That information, sent from abroad, might also encompass Italian names for characters[31] – although London itself was cosmopolitan enough to provide such names, and Shakespeare would have been able to read literature set in Italy as part of his research. In opposition to this idea being the main source of Shakespeare's knowledge, M. Duff suggests[32] that the Dark Lady of Shakespeare's sonnets is Emilia Bassano[33], (the mistress of Sir Henry Carey, the Lord Chamberlain, and the son of Mary Boleyn[34]) whose family came from Italy and who matches some descriptions of women in both the plays ascribed to Marlowe and those of Shakespeare. If the Dark Lady sonnets were written between 1591 and 1595[35], as may be suggested by the vocabulary, then it is unlikely that Emilia Bassano had met

---

31   The names and locations may have been used to cover the real message contained in a letter, if Marlowe and Shakespeare were still working for the secret service.

32   See Duff, M., Marlowe and the Dark Lady, 2011, in P. Farey's marlowe-shakespeare.blogspot.co.uk, which suggests that Emilia Bassano was the Dark Lady of Shakespeare's sonnets, and that references to her and to Italy indicate that the author of Shakespeare's work was Marlowe.

33 Emilia Bassano has also been suggested as a candidate for the authorship of Shakespeare's plays.

34   Some think Carey was Elizabeth I's half-brother as Mary Boleyn was Henry VIII's mistress, but it is more likely that his elder sister, Catherine, was Henry's child.

35   Hieatt, A. Kent, Hieatt, Charles W., & Anne Lake Prescott. 1991. "When Did Shakespeare Write 'Sonnets 1609?'" *Studies in Philology*, Vol. 88, No. 1 (Winter, 1991), pp. 69-109. The authors show that there are early rare words but no late rare words in the Dark Lady Sonnets 127-152, hence their claim for early composition, 1591-95. Duff's footnote.

Shakespeare, who is unknown in 1592, and whose connection with the London theatre does not really begin until 1594. But, Duff surmises, she might have met Marlowe, then a rising star on the London theatre scene, and he might have been her lover (there is no actual proof that Marlowe was homosexual, only Baines' accusation in his Note). She further offers as proof of Marlowe's Shakespearian authorship the use of names from the Bassano family in several of Shakespeare's plays (e.g. *The Winter's Tale, Othello* and *The Comedy of Errors*[36] – this last is one of Shakespeare's 'twin' plays) as well as in *Dr Faustus*, where the description of Alexander the Great's 'paramour' matches a description of Emilia Bassano. That Bassano del Grappa may be near the Bassano family properties in Italy (about forty miles from Venice) also makes the suggestion that Marlowe knew Emilia Bassano possible, especially as Bassano herself apparently owned property in Norton Folgate.[37]

But *if* Emilia Bassano met the author of *Dr Faustus* before 1593, then, according to my theory, she met William Shakespeare, and the Marlowe who went to rural Italy and saw the Bassano fresco, was not the man who had written the Dark Lady sonnets, but his double. Which leaves

---

36 Duff does not list Bassanio in *The Merchant of Venice* as a connection, along with Antonio, but it looks like a play on a version of Emilia's name: Bassoni.

37 The Bassano theory is not convincing. There are other 'dark ladies' available, more accessible to Shakespeare. Since both Marlowe and Shakespeare probably lived in Norton Folgate it is possible they knew Bassano as a landlady, since she owned a tenement there. It may even have been a brothel, as discussed below in Chapter Eleven on Thomas Watson and the Hogg Lane affray.

Shakespeare as the author of the sonnets and Marlowe as the progenitor of backgrounds and plots.[38]

But it is part of this contention here that neither Emilia Bassoni nor any other candidate so far put forward for the part is Shakespeare's Dark Lady. The identification of her also sheds light on Shakespeare's life and the theatre world of London in the sixteenth century. Examining the lines particularly of Sonnet 130 tells an altogether different story of possible identification, only tentatively explored by literary historians. Duncan Salkeld suggests that far from being a lady of the court, or an influential man's mistress, the Dark Lady was a prostitute called Black Luce or Lucy Negro, and that she ran a brothel in Clerkenwell, holding the tenancy from Philip Henslowe, who mentions her colleague (and his bailiff) Gilbert East in his diary.[39]

Sonnet 130 is supposedly a parody of an Elizabethan love sonnet, but that may not be the case. It is just as likely to be an accurate description of Shakespeare's beloved, who was black.[40] The first lines of Sonnet 130 describe a woman with dark eyes, lips less red than pale pink coral (which suggests a pale brown), brownish breasts and wiry hair:
My mistress' eyes are nothing like the sun;

---

[38] But Shakespeare does not show as much knowledge of foreign locations as anti-Stratfordians imagine: for example he sets plays in Venice without mention of the canals.

[39] Mail Online: *Was Bard's lady a woman of ill repute?* 'Dark Lady' of Shakespeare's sonnets 'may have been London prostitute called Lucy Negro, 27 August 2012 '

[40] Duncan Salkeld. *Shakespeare among the Courtesans: Prostitution, Literature, and Drama,* 1500-1650 Anglo-Italian Renaissance Studies. Farnham: Ashgate, 2012.

Coral is far more red than her lips' red;
If snow be white, why then her breasts are dun;
If hairs be wires, black wires grow on her head.
(Sonnet 130, lines 1-4)

It is the hair like wires that is the most emphatic and clear description. In such a way might one describe the hair of a woman from sub-Saharan Africa. Added to dark eyes, described in Sonnet 127 as
'raven black', and brown skin this suggests a woman who is not white. It is no satire on beauty but a description of a beautiful black woman. And Sonnet 127 goes on to mourn that her beauty is not recognised:

In the old age black was not counted fair.

Or if it were, it bore not beauty's name;
and
But now is black beauty's successive heir/
And beauty slandered with a bastard shame,
(Sonnet 127 lines,1 - 4)

Lucy seems to be known to Henslowe and thus is likely also to be known to Shakespeare, who was moving in theatrical circles, but probably also the circles of vice and gambling, in Shoreditch and Norton Folgate. There is also clear confirmation from the connection that Henslowe (and his son-in-law, Edward Alleyn) was involved in prostitution as well as the theatre. Her identification as the Dark Lady of the sonnets looks convincing. But the sonnets are not written by Marlowe.

It is suggested, in pursuance of Marlowe's writing from abroad, that some of the sonnets attributed to Shakespeare speak of the sorrow of exile. In *The Story the Sonnets Tell,* A.D. Wraight suggests that there are three persons associated with Shakespeare's sonnets: William Hatcliffe; Henry Wriothesley, Earl of Southampton; and Thomas Walsingham. She suggests the sonnets may be divided into three: numbers 1 to 17 which address a young man who should be thinking of marriage, and commissioned by Lord Burghley who wanted to promote a marriage between Henry Wriothesley and his kinswoman, Elizabeth de Vere. Since Lord Burghley was Chancellor of Cambridge University, Wraight suggests he knew Marlowe and commissioned the sonnets from him[41]. The second subset is to Thomas Walsingham, and a third, smaller subset to William Hatcliffe, a student at Grays Inn. Without sonnets 1 to 17 and those addressed to William Hatcliffe, says Wraight, those to Walsingham tell a story of exile, with Marlowe taking ship from Deptford on 30th May 1593, the ultimate goal probably Italy.[42]

The first that needs saying at this point is that authors do not write directly from their experience to the page; it is distilled, and some experience is vicarious, not the author's own experience but the product of his meditation on someone else's experience and his own knowledge of human nature. It is also necessary to remember that Renaissance thought patterns and beliefs were different from those of later centuries or our own. For example, it is almost

---

41   Burghley was elected as Chancellor of Cambridge University in 1559, and was Chancellor when Marlowe was at Corpus Christi. There is no reason to suppose he met Marlowe.

42   Wraight identifies a significant Italian bent in Shakespeare's plays after 1593, for example in Twelfth Night. But Wraight moves on, in *Shakespeare, New Evidence*, to suggests that Marlowe is M. le Doux, but P. Farey and G. Caveney show this person to be Catherinus Dulcis, alias Catherine le Dou(l)x.

impossible for us to imagine the sheer terror of Romeo on learning he is to be banished from Verona[43], for our world is much wider than his, we are less dependent upon family ties and families are more scattered. For Romeo, his whole world, all his friends and acquaintances and his entire family, was in Verona. He was being asked to leave the very womb that nourished him and go on a journey of too well imagined dangers (footpads, brigands and so forth) to a destination completely alien to him and also probably dangerous. In *The Taming of the Shrew*[44], for example, a traveller is cozened into pretending to be a suitor's father because he is told the wholly believable tale that travellers from Mantua, whence he comes, are liable to be murdered in Padua because of a dispute between the rulers of those cities. His fear is real, and so is Romeo's, but it is beyond our easy comprehension that such a short distance, in what we consider to be the same country, could wreak such havoc on a person, because we are not living in the fragmentation of states and allegiances that was sixteenth century Italy. Thus, when a writer speaks of his pain at being in exile, his actual experience of exile may be that of being in London and not Stratford, where his family and attachments are, not that he has flown the country of his birth. The mental distance of Stratford from London is slight for us, and so we imagine a much further exile, but for an Elizabethan the mental distance was much more like our feelings on being

---

43   I am indebted for this example of the Renaissance idea of exile to David Didau's blog, The Learning Spy, on teaching context in English literature.

44   Interestingly, in the same play Lucutio is disguised as coming from Rheims.

moved from the UK to Russia: total dislocation for some time, and to some extent constant.

So when Shakespeare writes sonnets about being in exile, it does not mean he is 'abroad'[45] but that he is away from the familiar sights of his home in Stratford, quite far enough to make him feel uncomfortable and unsettled in his new place, where he knew hardly anyone and had to scramble for patronage and income among a throng of strangers. And it may be that for Shakespeare, born in the Midlands, being a stranger was always the case for him in London - he was never a Londoner, only resident there for the time being.

Much is also made, by Wraight, of Sonnet 74, which speaks of arrest and bail, both words associated with imprisonment and release on surety, just as had happened to Marlowe before the events on 30 May 1593, and again associating the sonnet with the hand of an exiled Marlowe, not an at home Shakespeare.

Wraight particularly chooses the lines:

But be contented: when that fell arrest
Without all bail shall carry me away (Sonnet 74, Lines 1-2)

However, it would appear that both 'fell arrest' and 'without all bail' do not refer to being arrested (and Marlowe

---

45   Two hundred years later Jane Austen, in Mansfield Park, sent Maria Rushworth into exile 'abroad' with her aunt, Mrs Norris – there is no suggestion she went to a foreign country, only out of her known circle and into the social exile meted out to a woman divorced for adultery. To some extent 'going abroad', at least by the 1700s, referred to going out of the domestic sphere and into the world: 'abroad' also has the general meaning of 'being about' in the world.

was not arrested in 1593, but asked to answer questions from the Privy Council. He was on bail, but for an affray with constables) but to death, from which there is no escape and no return - and from which we are all 'given bail' until the day we must stand in death's court. The terms 'arrest' and 'bail' are again used metaphorically (as with the remarks about Dido in Henry *VI part II*), not literally by someone who has first hand experience of these events. The sonnet is about how a person is remembered after they are dead, not about being arrested and taken away.

Of more interest is the line 'The coward conquest of a wretch's knife', which might suggest a reference to Marlowe's death, especially alongside 'a reckoninge in a little room' found in *As You Like It*.[46] But the wretch in question does not have to be a murderer. What 'wretch' might carry a knife with which to cut away life? Surely a barber surgeon who is cutting away a limb or a diseased part - and such a knife wielder was very likely the cause of death in the patient, on bail, at that point, from death. Perhaps the writer thinks of being dissected too, by an anatomist, but more likely is it that the phrase may be a metaphor of death itself - a knife which cuts the thread - or for the Fate Atropos, who cuts the thread of each life in its time.

---

46   Williams, in *Shakespeare, thy name is Marlowe,* attempts to prove that Marlowe wrote *As You Like It* from the line 'for all your writers do consent that ipse is he: now, you are not ipse, for I am he.' (Act V, sc.i), which is spoken to William, Audrey's lover. Williams says there is not context for these words and therefore they mean that the author is saying he is not William (Shakespeare), but someone else. However, a reading of the scene shows that Touchstone is trying to substitute himself for William as Audrey's prospective husband. Thus: 'WILLIAM: Which he, sir? TOUCHSTONE: He, sir, that must marry this woman'. (ipse is a rhetorical term meaning an assertion without proof).

But the line is, on examining those lines above it, not a reference either to Marlowe's death or Death personified:

My spirit is thine, the better part of me.
So then thou hast lost the dregs of life,
The prey of worms, my body being dead,
The coward conquest of a wretch's knife, (Sonnet 74, lines 8-11)

It is part of a list, and as with the lines above 'the dregs of life' and 'The prey of worms', given as an example of how the body, which is capable of 'being dead', is inferior to the spirit. The body is 'the dregs of life', something which will decay as 'the prey of worms', something which can be killed by any 'wretch's knife'. The spirit, 'the better part' of any person, is not the bitter leas in the cup, not capable of decay, not able to be killed by anything or anyone. It is immortal. The body is not, but is described as 'base'. So instead of being a reference to Marlowe's supposed death,[47] it is a part of a metaphor for the mutability of the body as opposed to the immutability of spirit. The worth of the body is only in what it contains: the spirit:
And that is this *(my spirit)*, and this *(my spirit)* with thee remains.[48] (Sonnet 74, Line 14)

Thus the evidence of the sonnets does not support the author being Christopher Marlowe, and therefore cannot

---

47   And why would Shakespeare make a reference to something he knew did not happen, if, as I am suggesting, he and Marlowe were working together as one, and Marlowe had not died in Deptford?

48   The whole of Sonnet 74 is quoted in Appendix V. Lines discussed are underlined.

support him as being the main author of Shakespeare's work. Remembering that writers work from distilled experience, then the sonnets are Shakespeare's distilled experience from his own life and his knowledge of other people's lives, both in his own world and from the world of literature which he inhabited. There is some evidence to suggest that the authors of both Marlowe and Shakespeare's plays could be by the same man, or two men collaborating closely, some of which can be interpreted as showing Marlowe to be the author of Shakespeare's plays, but a substantial amount might suggest quite the opposite, that Shakespeare was Marlowe.

But taken with other evidence, for example that Christopher Marlowe was co-author of *Henry VI*, it is suggestive that the same person, or persons, wrote both sets of plays. William Shakespeare, the same age as Christopher Marlowe, does not become known as a playwright until after Marlowe's death, which strongly suggests a connection between the two writers. While Marlowe lived he and Shakespeare appear to have worked together, once he was dead then Shakespeare properly emerges in his own right. That Shakespeare began to emerge before Marlowe died suggests that the two were separating anyway.

To sum up at this point, there is no provable reference to Shakespeare being a known playwright before Marlowe's disappearance. The plays of Marlowe and Shakespeare share many stylistic devices, as well as type of plot (history plays, magicians, twins) and vocabulary. They also share an interest in exotic locations. As time goes forward, Shakespeare's style diverges, but this is perhaps because he needs to distance himself from any connection with Marlowe, as to be discovered as having been Marlowe would open him to great danger, probably imprisonment and perhaps death. But it is difficult for a writer to change their style completely, odd words and phrases keep re-appearing, as do topics. Considering the amount of time spent on writing one play (Shakespeare averaged two a year before the turn of the century, and one a year as he got older and more involved in other financial dealings) it is not surprising that echoes of Marlowe continue in Shakespeare's work, nor that Shakespeare continued his interest in classical literature (albeit intimating, as Jonson says, that he had 'small Latin, and less Greek'[49]) as a source of plots. Finally, the first mention of Shakespeare is in late 1592, when his poem *Venus and Adonis* is published. Before this date there is no real evidence of his existence in London, except the reference to 'Shakescene' in Greene's *Groat's Worth of Wit*, which suggests a writer of some standing, who has been working in London for a while and will be easily recognised by the allusions used to identify him. It has been assumed Shakescene is Shakespeare, but are there any other contenders who can be identified as the Upstart Crow?

---

49   Aubrey's Brief Lives

Chapter Ten

Some Groat's Worth of Wit

In his *Groats Worth of Wit*, Greene writes (after a long passage on the untrustworthyness of actors): 'Is it not strange that I, to whome they all haue beene beholding: is it not like that you, to whome they all haue beene beholding, shall (were yee in that case that I am now) bee both at once of them forsaken? Yes, trust them not: for there is an vpstart Crow, beautified with our feathers, that with his Tygers hart wrapt in a Players hyde, supposes he is as well able to bombast out a blanke verse as the best of you: and being an absolute Iohannes factotum, is in his owne conceit the onely Shake-scene in a countrey. O that I might intreat your rare wits to be imploied in more profitable courses: & let those Apes[1] imitate your past excellence, and neuer more acquaint

---

1   'Apes imitate your past excellence' - this seems very like actors, and persons who buy plays from playwrights, not a playwright. But Jonson's *The Poet Ape'* also brings to mind someone who is not a playwright who is writing below standard plays and poor poetry - and

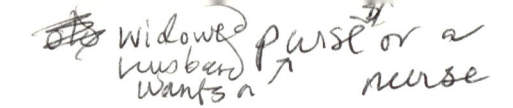

them with your admired inuentions. I knowe the best husband of you all will neuer proue an Vsurer, and the kindest of them all will neuer proue a kind nurse: yet whilest you may, seeke you better Maisters; for it is pittie men of such rare wits, should be subject to the pleasure of such rude groomes.'[2]

Above are the main lines in Greene's *Groats Worth of Wit*, supposedly referring to Shakespeare. The argument that Shakespeare is referred to here is not convincing. Born's argument in *Why Greene was angry with Shakespeare*[3] as to why the above paragraph refers to William Shakespeare, cites many literary scholars who support the view that Greene is attacking Shakespeare. Born further contends that there is a reason why Greene was angry with William Shakespeare and this was because Shakespeare had improved Greene's last work, *A Knack to Know a Knave*[4], particularly by changing the part of Ethenwald, to improve the subplot of the wooing of Alfrida. Lord Strange's men performed *A Knack to Know a Knave* in 1592, along with a play Henslowe lists as *Harey Vi*, which

---

Edward Alleyn has some plays recorded in Henslowe's diary, listed as 'his'. Henslowe uses this pronoun to indicate a playwright in other entries.

2   Greene in Harrison, ed., Groats-werth of Witte, pp 45-46.

3   *Why Greene was angry with Shakespeare,* Born, Hanspeter, in Medieval and Renaissance Drama in England, 2012.

4   This play is not in Greene's canon, and is currently considered anonymous. Born suggests the construction and style are typical of Greene, and that this is the play Greene refers to as that Nashe 'lately writ' with him. Born supports this view by citing Paul E. Bennett, 1952, coming to the same conclusion. If it is not Greene's play then Born's argument falls.

was performed in March. Born and others have taken this to suggest that Shakespeare was at this time working for Lord Strange's Men, but there is no evidence that this is the case. It was not necessary that a playwright be part of a troupe of actors in order for them to purchase his plays. Players might contract with a playwright for several plays, as indeed Greene intimates in *Groats Worth*, but this is not actually necessary. Given that, it is a moot point that Shakespeare, rather than some other playwright, tampered with *A Knack*. The changes might have been made in rehearsal, or the play may have been sent out to be improved. All playwrights in Elizabethan London were in the habit of plagiarizing and re-writing other writers' plays. There was no such thing as copyright and plagiarism did not exist as a contentious issue. Greene himself plagiarized other authors. Why should he suddenly take against one particular writer who may have altered his play? And Greene is not attacking playwrights in *Groats Worth*, he is attacking actors. Apart from all this *Henry VI Part III* is thought to be a composite work on which Shakespeare collaborated with other writers, notably Christopher Marlowe, whom there is evidence to suggest was in any case Shakespeare's doppelganger.

Greene has been read as containing attacks on both Marlowe (Marlin) and Shakespeare in *A Groat's Worth of Wit*, edited by Henry Chettle[5] and published by Thomas

---

5   Henry Chettle c.1564-c1606, dramatist and pamphleteer. Greene's Groats-werth of Witte was entered in the stationer's register in 1592, 'at the peril of Henry Chettle'. (*Chisholm, Hugh, ed. (1911).'Chettle, Henry' ,Encyclopeida Britannica **6** (11th ed.). Cambridge University Press. p.113.*). The title page refers to *Piers Penniless* not taking on the work, which may be an oblique reference to the possibility that Nashe was also

Nashe after Greene's death in September 1592. But Greene is actually warning playwrights, and Marlowe in particular (but also Nashe whom he urges to give up literary quarrels, and Peele), to save their souls and live better lives, as well as to keep themselves out of the clutches of players. And then Greene writes of one 'Shakescene' who he calls an 'upstart crow' and 'johannes factotum' (jack of all trades) flaunting 'borrowed feathers'. It has generally been accepted that this refers to Shakespeare as it also uses some lines from Henry VI Part III. The apposite lines are: 'Yes, trust them not: for there is an upstart Crow, beautified with our feathers, that with his 'Tiger's heart wrapped in a Player's hide', supposes he is as well able to bombast out a blank verse as the best of you: and being an absolute *Johannes Factotum*, is in his own conceit the only Shakescene in a country.'[6] The words 'tiger's heart' are from *Henry VI Part III*, when York says 'O, tiger's heart wrapped in a woman's hide!' on seeing Margaret of Anjou with his dead child's blood on her handkerchief. Thus the lines would appear to be aimed at William Shakespeare, whose *Henry VI Part III*, probably written in 1591, was likely performed in 1592, before June 23 when the theatres were closed.[7] But the words follow Greene's (or his editor, Henry Chettle's) warning to his contemporaries not to trust actors, those 'puppets' who 'speak from our mouths' – that is, translate the playwright's words into action and intonation on stage. Also, the quotation from Henry VI replaces

---

suspected of writing *Groats-Worth of Witte*.
6   Quoted from Greenblatt, S., p213.
7   Though the evidence for performance is Greene quoting form it, yet he must have seen the play sometime in 1592, else he could not quote it - there was no published copy.

'woman's hide' with 'Player's hide' – which suggest Greene is talking about an actor, not a playwright. There is no clear evidence that Shakespeare was acting in 1592, except Greene's comment, if we accept he *was* talking of Shakespeare. But if Greene is not attacking Shakespeare, then who is he attacking? The end of the *Groat's Worth of Wit* contains a retelling of Aesop's fable, *The Grasshopper and the Ant*, wherein the heedless grasshopper plays all summer whilst the industrious ant collects food for the coming winter. In the extremis of the grasshopper the ant refuses help. When winter bites the grasshopper begs the ant to give him food, but the ant refuses. The ant says:

Pack hence (quoth he) thou idle lazie worme
My house doth harbour no vnthriftie mates:
Thou scornedst to toile, & now thou feelst the storme,
And starust for bode while I am fed with cates.
Vse no intreats, I will relentlesse rest,
For toyling labour hates an idle guest.[8]

This is a clear rejection of a wastrel. Greene, in *Groats Worth of Wit*, is saying that he has been a wastrel, and that now he is in need no-one will help him. Particularly the untrustworthy players, and especially the one he calls 'Shakescene' and 'upstart Crow'. Greene is by August 1592 in great need, sick and poor. To whom did he go for help in his extremis? That information may well be the clue that explains who 'Shakescene' is.

---

8   Greene in Harrison, ed., Groats-werth of Witte, pp 48-49.

Neville Barker[9] puts forward a quite plausible argument that the intended recipient of this particular piece of vituperative spite *is* an actor. His first contention is also mine, that Greene is speaking to fellow playwrights (Marlowe among them) and warning them against actors who but mouth the lines they write, yet get all the credit for a play. Reading what Greene writes it seems clear that he *is* talking about actors. Borrowed 'feathers' distinctly suggests someone using the plumage belonging to another, and this is what actors do – they borrow the words of others. Thus, it looks as if an actor is the target of Greene's ire, rather than a playwright. Greene also calls actors 'puppets' - 'Puppets (I meane) that spake from our mouths'. And he is urging *playwrights* to stop writing plays.

Next, Greene never names Shakespeare. Shakescene might look like a play on his name, but other playwrights are named much more clearly: merlin[10] for Marlowe is a clear play on the way that gentleman spelled his name at Cambridge, where 'Marlin' appears in the Buttery Books, and may also refer to *Dr Faustus*, where the main character is a magician, but Shakescene suggests one who makes the scenery shudder, and looks pretty much like calling an actor a 'barnstormer', a pejorative term for someone who might 'bombast out a blank verse'. Who might that be?

There is some evidence that Greene had been borrowing money, as his income from his writing (and he seems to be the first playwright to make a living from his

---

9   Barker, N. *Shake-scene and that Upstart Crow,* The Marlowe Society Journal, 36, Spring 2011. Rubinstein, in *Who Wrote Shakespeare's Plays,* makes the same point: why would Greene target Shakespeare, an unknown playwright?
10   A merlin is also a bird of prey, perhaps hinting at a a contrasting picture of Marlowe from his friends calling him 'kind Kit Marlowe'.

work) had fallen off as other writers grew in popularity he was suffering hard times. He had borrowed from the actor Edward Alleyn and had not repaid him and thus Alleyn (who was apparently notably generous to fellow actors and playwrights) then refused all further help to the struggling, and now dying, playwright. Greene was not a man who took such behaviour in a good spirit and probably blamed Alleyn for his predicament. When *Henry VI part III* was performed in 1592 by Lord Strange's Men, the leading actor of that company was Edward Alleyn, and he played the Duke of York, the speaker of the line 'tiger's heart'. If Greene meant to pick out Alleyn for his comments then quoting a line for which he was probably famous would make clear his intention, and it is arguably more likely that he would pick out the well-known Alleyn, whose nickname was 'Shakescene' because he literally shook the scenery on stage, rather than the unknown Shakespeare, even if he was an actor. Additionally, according to Henslowe's records, Alleyn did write some plays (possibly including *Tambercam*,[11] a clear plagiarisation on *Tamberlaine*, by its title), as suggested in the story that Greene puts forward in *Groat's Worth of Wit*, when he first meets his patron[12]– so if a playwright is intended as well as an actor, that playwright could quite easily be Alleyn, especially if he was using the plays he performed in as source material for his own work. Other evidence that Alleyn is intended, not

---

11   Marlowe seems to have quarrelled with Alleyn over this plagiarism, which may have had implications for Marlowe's writing career, since it was actors who commissioned plays for companies.

12   The fable of the Upstart Crow involves a crow dressing up in the feathers of other, more spectacular birds. The symbolism suggests plagiarism – rife in sixteenth century England.

Shakespeare, is that in the *Roberto* story, the actor says that he is rich enough to build a windmill. Edward Alleyn is recorded as having built a windmill but there is no evidence that Shakespeare did so. This would appear to point much more to Alleyn as Greene's target, than the unknown Shakespeare.[13] In conclusion of this point, after *Groat's Worth of Wit* was published Henry Chettle copiously apologized to a person who felt themselves to be attacked: 'About three months since died M. Robert Greene, leaving many papers in sundry booksellers' hands, among other his Groatsworth of Wit, in which a letter written to divers play-makers[14] is offensively by one or two of them taken, and because on the dead they cannot be avenged, they willfully forge in their conceits a living author [...] With neither of them that take offence was I acquainted, and with one of them I care not if I never be. The other, whom at that time I did not so much spare as since I wish I had, for that, as I have moderated the heat of living writers and might have used my own discretion (especially in such a case, the author being dead), that I did not I am as sorry as if the original fault had been my fault, because myself have seen his demeanor no less civil than he excellent in the quality he professes. Besides, divers of worship have reported his uprightness of dealing, which argues his honesty, and his facetious grace in writing that approves his art.'[15]

---

13   The use of quotations from what is now known as Shakespeare's plays *Henry VI Part I and Part III* merely shows that the work had been written and performed, which we know from Henslowe's Diary. Greene tells us nothing about the author of that play.
14   Both writers and actors are 'play-makers'.
15   Preface from Henry Chettle's *Kind Heart's Dream* (the subject is a dream in which five ghosts or spirits rail against contemporary abuses, and

Usurer

It was Chettle[16] who had edited the book, taking out comments that he thought most likely to cause trouble, but he missed the 'upstart Crow' passage and does not seem to have worried about the Roberto and Roseus story, which is suggestive of Alleyn as the target. Shakespeare would have had little influence in 1592, but Edward Alleyn, and his stepfather-in-law Henslowe had great power to offer work to writers, and to cross them could mean financial ruin for a playwright. Such a grovelling apology seems unapt to a very new playwright, but very apt if being offered to Alleyn and Henslowe. The term 'play-makers' is used, but Alleyn fits this description as being a writer as well as an actor just as much as Shakespeare, and Alleyn was much better known, and had been in dispute with Marlowe over plagiarism, which would be common knowledge in theatrical circles.

But there is more to Greene's situation than a spat with Edward Alleyn over a loan. As was said above Greene had borrowed money from Edward Alleyn, and not paid it back. This caused Alleyn to ignore Greene's pleas for help when his plays were no longer fashionable and he was struggling to make money out of pamphleteering and was also unwell. Alleyn, we have already noticed, is recorded as being generous to his friends, lending them money when they were suffering bad times. I am going to turn this idea of Alleyn helping his friends on its head, with support from Robert Greene, Thomas Watson and Christopher Marlowe. John Allen, Edward Alleyn's brother was an innkeeper, as their

---

desire Kind Heart to publish what they say).

16   He may have written some or most of it, according to some modern scholars, and appended the dead Greene's name.

father had been. He also leant £14 (a huge sum) to William Bradley, who did not pay the money back at the term and therefore suffered a default clause meaning he had to pay back £40. John Allen is clearly a money lender, otherwise it is odd that there would be such a penalty clause in the agreement with William Bradley.[17]. Bradley was killed by Thomas Watson, aided by someone identified as Christopher Marlowe (noted as a yeoman, not a gentleman in the inquest record) in Hogg Lane in September 1589. Bradley had previously asked for Watson, Hugh Swift and John Allen to be bound over to keep the peace, because, he, Bradley was in fear of his life from them. This was not mentioned at the inquest - which made it much more likely that Thomas Watson would be allowed a plea of self-defence. Chapter Eleven goes more into the details of the fight in Hogg Lane, and its ramifications for Shakespeare and Marlowe. Here the focus is on Edward Alleyn's loan to Greene, and Greene's death from a surfeit of pickled herring and Rhenish wine.[18]

Greene owed Alleyn money. Bradley owed Alleyn's brother money. Both died in rather odd circumstances. It strongly suggests that Alleyn, the actor of Marlowe's plays, was a money lender (this is borne out by Greene's comments) among his other ventures, of bear and badger baiting and cock fighting. All these activities involve betting; taken together with Alleyn's support of Marlowe's plays, Marlowe's support of John Allen's cause in Hogg Lane, and that John Allen owned several inns where plays could be performed along with bear and badger baiting and

---

17   In The Merchant of Venice, Shakespeare seems to know all about money lending and terms of trade. Shylock demands a pound of flesh from Antonio as bond for a loan - which is to be paid if Antonio defaults.
18   According to Gabriel Harvey.

cock fighting - with all the accompanying betting, and also probably prostitution, as theatres inhabited red light districts - strongly suggest that we are looking at an organization that we can name as an integrated business venture. The fact that Bradley's loan results in a fatal fight suggests that the business venture supported its aims and continued prosperity by use of a gang, and possibly a protection racket. Greene is on the other side of this business and its gang. He seems to have had his own gang, and has for a partner a woman who is rumoured to be a madam and whose brother is a known cut-purse, Cutting Ball, who was later hanged at Tyburn. It is also possible that Bradley was Greene's strong man. Greene says in his *Groat's Worth of Wit*, that he never pays back loans, an odd thing for a playwright on the London circuit to say, unless he is in the position of being able to back up this habit with force. It looks as if Greene was in the position of being able to do that, because the people surrounding him appear to be of the sort who could support his position with violence. In other words, like Henslowe and the Allens, he is a ganglord, though not such a powerful one as Alleyn.

So we have to see that it is highly possible that Alleyn is dropping Greene's work, and encouraging others to do so, in favour of Watson and Marlowe/Shakespeare, because Greene is becoming intransigent, and setting up his own racket and not keeping his deals with Alleyn. It may be that Greene's comments about 'borrowed feathers', 'upstart crows' and 'Shakescene', which he almost certainly voiced before he put them in his book, may have persuaded both Malowe and Shakespeare that Greene knew of their deception and was about to unmask them. Since Marlowe was spying as a Catholic priest and Shakespeare was masquerading as Marlowe to Burghley, it would have been highly inconvenient for them to be revealed as two people, especially so if Walsingham was also unaware of the ploy. So Marlowe, or probably Shakespeare, had a vested interest in backing John Allen in Hogg Lane and Edward Alleyn - who more likely saw the comments about borrowed feathers, and particular the name Shakescene, as aimed at himself - over Greene's work. That Greene died essentially of food poisoning is also rather suspect. The effects of food poisoning are very similar to being simply poisoned.

Put simply, we are looking at gang warfare between a gang lord, Edward Alleyn or perhaps his stepfather-in-law (and this marriage rather looks like the amalgamation of two businesses into one) and a rival gang leader, Robert Greene, who is branching out onto Alleyn's turf. If this is so, then Alleyn's rule of Norton Folgate and Shoreditch almost certainly puts into the shade the activities of the Richardsons and Krays in the twentieth century. Such a situation makes clear how impecunious 'gentlemen' playwrights are eking out their livings: they are spying for the government, or some other lord, and helping to police a redlight area and protection racket as well as carrying out their own private scams. Greene himself points out that 'coney-catching', the tricking of innocent citizens or tradesmen for money, is not the worst thing that can be done. As a gang leader he is quite well aware of the lengths to which the dubious fraternity of playhouse owners will go to make sure their profits are not infringed on by rivals. It also explains the events in Hogg Lane and Marlowe's reputation as a brawler, Watson's as a confidence trickster and Greene's association with a known cut-purse.

That Alleyn and Henslowe[19] are powerful ganglords then explains Chettle and Nashe's desire to distance themselves from the 'upstart Crow' attack in *Groats Worth of Wit*. They are not just in danger of losing their livelihoods, which is bad enough, but possibly their lives as well. That they also apologise to Marlowe suggests that the playwright is part of Alleyn and Henslowe's operation and perhaps even an enforcer - the curious fight in Hogg Lane throws light on this possibility.[20] They would not be at all bothered about the reaction of a scarcely known playwright such as Shakespeare.

Returning to an examination of the *Groat's Worth of Wit*, if, as suggested, Greene is not writing of Shakespeare [21] then it is now possible to say that there is no real mention of Shakespeare in London until the publication of *Henry VI parts I and II* (and *Venus and Adonis*). The two plays seem to have been in the ownership of the short-lived Pembroke's Men, who published versions of *Henry VI Parts I and II* and also *The Taming of a Shrew*, in 1594[22]. Curiously Pembroke's Men flourished only between the summer of

---

19   In Chapter 9 Henslowe is noted as renting out a tenament which is used as a brothel.
20   See below Chapter Eleven – Thomas Watson, Gangs - and Romeo and Juliet.
21   The view that Greene is referring to Alleyn as the upstart crow is put forward by Ros Barber in the University of London's Who Wrote Shakespeare course: Video 4.3 The Upstart Crow as Edward Alleyn, based on Greene's speaking of puppets, in reference to actors, and naming only Marlowe, Nashe and Peele as playwrights . If Shakespeare were meant, surely Greene would mention him.
22   Riggs, The World of Christopher Marlowe, p281.

1592,²³ when they were extremely popular apparently rivalling Lord Strange's Men, some of whose players had moved to the new band, and the end of 1593, as though they had been formed just to perform the Henry plays.²⁴ *Venus and Adonis* was published in 1592 – after Marlowe has ceased to be a player on the London stage (*The Massacre at Paris*²⁵ was performed in January 1593 – the last performed of the plays attributed to Marlowe in his lifetime). After that Marlowe is with Thomas Walsingham writing *Hero and*

---

23   There are said to be equivical mentions of Pembroke's Men as early as 1575 according to Pembroke's Men's Wikipedia entry, but I can find no clear evidence of this.

24   Perhaps this is the case, and Pembroke's Men had been formed to produce these history plays, giving the Elizabethan populace a view of the problems that occurred when a succession was disputed. Burghley in particular was working for the Scottish solution - that James VI should succeed his cousin as King of England as well as Scotland. The other heirs, such as Stanley, could be seen as both divisive (Stanley was favoured by Catholics) and dangerous, especially as many heirs were female (Stanley had no sons) and perhaps Burghley and his fellow Privy Council members felt that another queen would be a queen too many - return to normal service, under a male sovereign, might be their preference. So putting on plays about the Wars of the Roses could be seen as propaganda in favour of an obvious and male successor in James of Scotland.

25   As noted in Chapter Nine, *The Massacre at Paris* contains many lines very similar to other plays attributed to Shakespeare and Marlowe (see Appendix 1). But the version which has survived appears to be an actors' copy, so the similar lines are most likely caused by actors remembering speeches from other plays, not necessarily consciously, and putting them into the *Massacre*. Thus, these repetitions are indicative of very little except the incompleteness of the surviving version of the play.

Leander and meeting Frizer, Poley and Skeres in Deptford, and then nothing.

If all this is the case then it confrims that there is no evidence for Shakespeare's existence in London before Marlowe's death. If Shakespeare had been Marlowe then by 1592 the swap was wearing thin, and Shakespeare was wanting to put forward his own identity, tentatively at first, and after Marlowe's disappearance, fully, with some attempt to distance himself from his doppelganger, not always successfully. He remains loyal to some of the ideas and concerns that he had as Marlowe, for example using Medea's speech from Ovid's *Metamorphosis* (published by Arthur Golding in 1575) as the model for Prospero's speech in *The Tempest*, beginning 'Ye elves of hills, brooks, standing lakes and groves,' and ending, interestingly: 'I'll drown my book' (V.i), when he finally retires from acting and writing in London.

Taken all together, a picture begins to emerge of theatre land being also gang land, and Shakespeare/Marlowe appears to be very completely involved in it, as well as in the world of secret agents and spies. (Certainly Shakespeare shows good knowledge of how gangs work in *Romeo and Juliet*.[26]) From either of these activities trouble is likely to come, and Shakespeare/Marlowe is very likely to be involved.

---

26   Clearly better knowledge than that of the workings of a Renaissance royal court.

Chapter Eleven

Of Thomas Watson, Gangs - and *Romeo and Juliet*

In 1592 Thomas Watson was involved in a scam. The last of many that he devised. Although recognised in his time as one of the most popular playwrights and poets, he spent a great deal of his energy trying to swindle people. In this he was not particularly unusual among well educated but impecunious young men in Elizabethan England.

    Thomas Watson was born in 1556, so was nearly ten years older than Shakespeare and Marlowe. He was in his time more popular and better known than either of them, along with the scrivener's son, Thomas Kyd. None of his plays in English survive, but his Latin verse does, as do his madrigals. He was described, by his employer, Cornwallis, as one of the best writers of tragedy, but also one who could make up tricks, japes and incidents in his plays, much as he did in life.[1] There is some evidence also that he was the first

---

1   Dictionary of National Biography, 1885-1900, Volume 60, Sidney Lee, *Thomas Watson (1557?-1592)*

to write blank verse[2], and may have influenced Marlowe and Shakespeare.[3] In 1585 he published his *Compendium memoriae localis*, on memory, which owes a lot to the work of Bruno's *De Umbris Idearum* (The Shadow of Ideas), which used a mnemonic wheel, and the memorization system based on loci attributed to Simonides of Keos. That Watson is interested in the work of Bruno suggests he himself is interested in, and happy to make use of, astrology, mysticism and magical ideas, as is suggested below by his connection with the woman Anne Burnell. He is a shadowy figure in the London of the 1580s, and what little is known of him suggests a wandering life.

Thomas Watson was brought up by his uncle after his parents died in 1559. He went to Winchester and to Oxford before 1570,[4] but also studied at Douai, and travelled abroad for about seven years, when he learned French and Italian. He was, inevitably one feels, an employee of Francis Walsingham, and travelled with him and his cousin Thomas Walsingham in 1581, whilst Francis Walsingham was negotiating a marriage between the Duke of Anjou and Elizabeth I. When Walsingham died in 1590, Watson wrote an elegy in which he mentions becoming friends with Thomas Walsingham on the banks of the Seine. He was certainly friends with Christopher Marlowe [5], to such an extent that he may be considered to have saved Marlow's life in the fight with William Bradley in 1589. He also knew the

---

2   DNB ibid.
3   Hess, W. Ron, *The Dark Side of Shakespeare*, Writers Club Press 2002, p88.
4   *The Oxford Companion to English Literature* 7th ed., ed. Dinah Birch, Oxford: OUP, 2009, p1050.
5   Or more probably Shakespeare. Watson may be the source of some of Shakespeare's ship knowledge.

playwright Lyly and the poet (and spy) Royden, who later went to Scotland. Indeed, Thomas Watson was himself part of Walsingham's intelligence network (he carried letters from Paris in 1580). He may also be counted among the University Wits, which included Gabriel Harvey (a continuous detractor of Marlowe), William Nashe and Robert Greene. He also knew John Allen, the brother of the actor Edward Alleyn. Watson also seems to have been on the fringes of Elizabethan literary society, his Eclogue on Francis Walsingham's death shows long association with the family and clear gratitude for their help.[6]

So Watson's career was somewhat varied. We know he attended Oxford before 1570 and then goes abroad, possibly to Padua - but we do not know if he attended the university there. He is at Douai in 1576. Dr Allen took non-Catholics to study 'humanities, philosophy and juris prudence'[7] and kept them at his own expense. Watson may have been at Douai for several months before going to Paris on 15th October and then returning to the college in May. This amount of travelling about by Watson suggests that Marlowe would have been able to do the same several years later, and that continuous attendance at the school was not expected. Watson left for England in August of 1576. In England he became, according to Nicholls, loosely attached to a group calle the Areopagus[8] which seems to have been

---

[6] (Chatterly, 2003) Chatterly, A, Marlowe Society Newsletter no. 23, 2003.

[7] Honan, P, Christopher Marlowe, Poet and Spy, p. 136. This is probably the route Marlowe first took at Rheims.

[8] Nicholls, p. 210. The Areopagus (literally Ares' (or possibly the Erinyes') large rock) was the court of ancient Athens. Both Ares and Oedipus were tried there, according to legend.

a gathering of literati including Spencer, Philip Sydney (married to Francis Walsingham's daughter), Edward Dyer and Gabriel Harvey, though Thomas Walsingham may have been on the fringes as well, as Nashe reports him telling 'spurious tales and doggerel poems about follies'[9] of Gabriel Harvey.

By 1581 Watson is living in St. Helen's, Bishopgate, listed as not attending church. This suggests that Watson was a secret Catholic, which is also borne out by the marriage of Poley, another Catholic, in 1582 to Anne Watson, who may be Thomas Watson's sister or cousin. Watson at this time seems to have been living on his wits rather than his verse and becomes a fringe player in the case of Anne Burnell, who claimed to be the daughter of Philip II of Spain, citing as evidence the testimony of a Nottinghamshire witch who told her she had marks of royalty on her body. During Anne Burnell's interogation 'one Watson, a wise man in St Helen's, that could tell strange things' emerges. On being sent for, Watson admitted knowing Anne Burnell but avoids saying anything about their dealings, merely reporting that a witch had told the woman she was 'better born than she was taken for'. The entire tale has all the marks of a scam by a young man bent on making money out of gullible women. It seems that being a confidence trickster to was part of Watson's stock in trade, as well as beautiful Latin verse and popular plays. This is borne out by the trick played on the Cornwallis family, where Thomas Watson's brother-in-law, Thomas Swift, was employed as a lutenist. Swift was in love with the fourteen year old Frances Cornwallis, Watson was tutor

---

9   Nicholls, ibid.

to her brother, William (and may have been spying on the family as well, as being a tutor was often a cover for a government spy [10] and Sir Thomas Cornwallis had been investigated for recusancy). Watson, whose scheme it was, persuaded Frances to sign a bond of promise to repay a loan, but in actuality what she signed was a promise to marry Thomas Swift. Frances is then persuaded to write a compromising letter in order to get back the bond, and her brother encourages this. Eventually the deceit is discovered by their father. Oddly, both Thomas Watson and his other brother-in-law, Hugh Swift, an attorney who drew up the bond, were dead before the matter could come to a resolution - it had been referred to the court of Star Chamber - one buried on 26th September 1592, the other on 6th October (according to Nashe). Only Thomas Swift survived, though he was apparently punished.

The reality behind all these machinations is that there were few places for young men of education, and in order to survive they had to be quick on their feet, earning money where they could. So poets were spies; playwrights could spin a tale off stage as well as on. The Elizabethan world was a harsh one in which to make ones way and patronage was needed; thus Watson's Eclogue to Francis Walsingham; he was indeed grateful to the family and he wished to continue to be so. Walsingham's widowed daughter, Frances Sydney, married the Earl of Essex, a powerful source of patronage; she was also sister-in-law to Mary Sydney, Countess of Pembroke, a poet in her own right who gave

---

10   It is possible that 'one Morley' was spying on Arbella Stuart and her grandmother, Elizabeth Cavendish, probably at the instigation of Burghley, whilst being employed as at tutor . See below p193, and Appendix 1.

patronage of other poets.[11] Watson, like any other sixteenth century playwright, would be looking for patronage wherever he could. But patronage was not only available from aristocrats such as Essex, but also from actors themselves, as Greene had found to his cost. And actors were enmeshed in the world of the theatre with its sleazy background and dubious hangers on. And, as suggested in Chapter Ten, it looks very much as though the ganglord in Norton Folgate is either Edward Alleyn, or his stepfather-in-law, Henslowe, who are not only involved in producing plays but in gambling and bear and cock fighting, probably along with Alleyn's brother John Allen. Alleyn inherited the brothels run by his father-in-law too. Henslowe and Alleyn[12] both lend money, and Henslowe records in his diary the names of playwrights he made loans on surety to, including Marlowe, Greene, Henry Chettle, George Chapman, Thomas Dekker, John Webster, Ben Jonson, Anthony Munday, Henry Porter, John Day, John Marston and Michael Drayton. Shakespeare and Burbage do not

---

11 In the light of Watson's need to raise money where he could it is interesting that Marlowe does not figure as a confidence artist at any point. This argues that he did not need to. Given that six plays would have netted him around £48 it suggests he had a second source of income which was steady and at least a competence. Watson was working for the government but he continues in his shady practices, suggesting he is not earning as much as Marlowe does from his work as a secret agent. This suggests that, contrary to received opinion' Marlowe was a highly rated agent for someone - probably Walsingham and Burghley - and was, like Robert Poley, quite well paid.

12 Chapter 10 above examines Alleyn as a moneylender. Greene, in his *Groat's Worth of Wit*, implies that Alleyn is a moneylender for profit in the passage where he writes the semi-auto-biographical story of Roberto and Roseus. Roseus, the actor who promises Roberto his patronage, is generally considered to represent Edward Alleyn, with Greene representing himself in the playwright Roberto.

appear either in Henslowe's list of playwrights (though these are not named before 1597) or borrowers. Shakespeare was himself a loan broker and he and Burbage were members of the Lord Chamberlain's Men, producing plays first at the Theatre and later at the Globe, neither attached to Henslowe's activities. Henslowe held plays as surety for loans, and the loans he made seem intended to tie playwrights to his own theatres. That Watson is not on the list of playwright-debtors suggests he was employed more formally than Marlowe, and did not need loans to bind him to Henslowe. Below Henslowe and the Allens would be local gangsters who collected on their employers' behalf, as well as their own. Among these, judging from their activities, it looks as if Thomas Watson and Christopher Marlowe are numbered.

The most notable incident we know of between Watson and Marlowe is the curious fight with William Bradley on 18th September 1589, betwen two and three in the afternoon. In *Christopher Marlowe* John Bakeless is convinced that William Bradley, the son of the innkeeper of the Bishops Inn on Grays Inn Lane, had matriculated from St John's, Cambridge, in 1580 [13] It is far from impossible. Tradesmen of the middling sort were sending their sons to grammar school and to the universities. Virtually all the members of the University Wits were the sons of tradesmen,

---

13   Bakeless, J., *Christopher Marlowe*, p154. I can find no evidence that supports Bradley being at St. Johns, Cambridge, where both Greene and Nashe studied, and would have been contemporaries, nor can I find anything that specifically denies it. He certainly felt great enmity towards Watson, saying 'Art thou now come!' a use of the familiar that, as Raleigh said at his trial in 1603, implies the person spoken to is an inferior.

just like Marlowe, the son of a shoemaker.[14] Bradley is also described as a thug. Graduate and thug are not incompatible, and Bradley shows himself to be quite happy to engage in a brawl in the middle of the day, and clearly knows Watson well, addressing him with 'thou'.

The brawl in Shoreditch seems to have been started by Bradley on meeting Marlowe in Hogg Lane. If Marlowe was a brawler then many would suppose that little provocation was needed to start a violent fight, especially if both antagonists were drunk. Like any such event it drew a crowd and there is a description given by witnesses as to what occured.

It is reported that on 18 September 1589 Marlowe was met in Hogg Lane by William Bradley, who was either an innkeeper's son or an innkeeper himself. Bradley is said to have started the fight, so presumably challenged Marlowe. They then began to fight presumably using sword and dagger, as was the custom. At some point during the fight Thomas Watson arrived, as if by chance, and the fight changed to one between Bradley and Watson. Watson was driven to the ditch and wounded, how badly is hard to tell, and then, apparently in self-defence, Watson ran Bradley through with his sword. Bradley probably died within a few minutes. Only at this point did the local watch come out to do anything about the affray. Bakeless gives the bare outline above, with quotations from the court roll.

Bradley is dead. The coroner's jury heard this description of events. That Bradley had 'insulted, wounded

---

14 A shoemaker, like a glover, was near the top of the trade pyramid, only really surpassed by workers in precious metals, and grocers. Both sorts of tradesmen were producing high order goods.

and ill-treated' Watson - 'verberauit, vulnerauit and male tractauit'. That Watson 'fled from the aforesaid William Bradley for the salvation of his life as far as to a certain ditch in the aforesaid (Hogg) lane' – 'a predicio Wellelmo Bradely pro saluacione vite sue usque ad quoddam fossatum in venella predicia fugijt' - Watson could go no further, the ditch blocked his flight. Then, 'beyond this certain ditch Thomas Watson could not flee without peril of his own life' - 'ultra quodquidem fossatum idem Thomas Watson absque periculo vite sue fugere non potuit' - beyond the bank (fosse) Thomas Watson could not safely retreat. Not until this extremity did Watson strike at Bradley, 'giving him a mortal wound in and upon th eright part of the breast...near the nipple, of the depth of six inches and the width of one inch, of which injury the same William Bradley...instantly died'.[15] There is no mention here of Watson being hurt.

Riggs is of the opinion that the fight was a put up job between Marlowe and Watson, because Bradley was reneging on a loan. It seems that Bradley owed Thomas Watson's friend John Allen money, was avoiding re-paying it, and using the support of another friend, Captain George Orrell, to continue to avoid paying. Riggs suggests that Watson was acting as a debt collector and that Marlowe was helping him.[16]

But there are other implications of the fight between Marlowe, Watson and Bradley. The area around Hogg Lane, Norton Folgate, is 'publand'. It is full of inns, taverns (the haunt particularly of Watson), theatres and brothels[17], and all

---

15   Bakeless, ibid, pp 159-160.
16   Riggs, The World of Christopher Marlowe, p250.
17   Emilia Bassano's tenement might well have been one of these brothels.

that comes with such a collection of enterprises: young men bent on diversion and trouble. Bear baiting and cock fighting, both the focus of gambling, take place in the theatres, before and after play performances, and inns - Edward Alleyn, for example, makes his fortune out of these activities at his pit on Bankside. Both William Bradley and John Allen are innkeepers, liable therefore to be involved in bear baiting and cock fighting. Watson himself is a frequenter of taverns, most likely using them as a source of low level information to pass on the Walsingham, but also as a base for petty swindles and protection rackets. Bradley himself was a known brawler. So was Christopher Marlowe.

And everyone knows Marlowe and Bradley fight, but it is highly unlikely that either would fight the other. For what we are seeing in Norton Folgate, on Hogg Lane, surrounding the theatres, actors and playwrights is gangs, and gangs have their own psychology and their own rules. A chief feature is that well-known and successful fighters do not fight each other. There is no match for supremacy, they do not want it, for it is likely to result in the death of one of them and a re-arrangement of the local balance of power. Thus, if Marlowe and Bradley are well-known and successful in their fighting they would infinitely prefer not to meet. So why do they? What makes Marlowe fight Bradley? And if they are fighting why does Watson intervene?

Conventionally, Watson is attacked by Bradley who leaves off fighting Marlowe. Neither expect Marlowe to continue to attack once they start fighting. But this is odd. First, two alpha males decide to fight each other, and then one stops. And Marlowe seems to stop, not Bradley. If Riggs is correct then Marlowe was simply having a go at Bradley on Watson's behalf, and when Watson arrives he ceases fighting. Riggs suggests that the reason for this is that the whole thing has been concocted between Watson and Marlowe in order to murder Bradley who owes Allen money. This makes little sense, for if Bradley dies Allen is unlikely to get his money back, especially if either Marlowe or Watson end up accused of murder (as Watson is). It makes more sense if Watson is a debt collector and Marlowe is his enforcer - except that Marlowe gives up the fight and allows Watson to come in, as if Watson is the enforcer. And finally, it makes more sense if we are talking about rival gangs and the teaching of consequences to anyone who stands against them.

For this fight has the hallmarks of a gangland brawl, and the local constable, Stephen Wyld, a tailor, would really not want to intervene if he could avoid it, especially if he was being protected by one of the gangs, which is probable. He waits until the outcome is certain and Bradley dead, before coming out to bring the force of the law against the combatants. Therefore, a reasonable scenario is that both Watson and Bradley are running protection outfits, and are rivals. This is most probably a turf war, with Watson likely muscling in on Bradley's territory. In which case Riggs is correct, this is probably a put-up fight by Watson, and Bradley will not have been expecting to see him. Whether it was Watson or Marlowe who was originally intended to kill Bradley is not clear, but one possible interpretation of events is that the plot goes wrong because Marlowe is *really* not winning, and Watson *has* to show up and intervene. He was perhaps watching from a nearby tavern.

Further information might shed some light on the fight. William Bradley made an application for Thomas Watson and Hugh Swift, (who appears to be John Allen's lawyer, and Bradley is trying to stop Swift taking him to court for his debt), and also John Allen, to be bound over to keep the peace. Nothing actually comes of this and at the inquest on Bradley's death no-one says that Bradley had said he was in fear of his life from Watson and his friends and asked for them to be bound over; indeed Bradley's name is missing from the charge sheet[18]. Added to Wyld's slow reaction to a brawl in broad daylight, this looks suspicious, as if money has changed hands and the authorities are not supporting Bradley. On the day of the fight Marlowe seems to be fighting to wear Bradley out before Watson arrives, making the affray look like a put up job to murder Bradley and make it appear as self-defence. In the theatre both Marlowe and Watson are said to be used to setting up fights, brawls and tricks. Setting up a theatrical set piece to conceal a murder as a brawl gone wrong would be well within the compass of both. The scene requires Marlowe (or Shakespeare) to fain losing, so that he can back off without it appearing odd, once Bradley is tiring. Both Watson and Marlowe would be fitter than Bradley because they are practising setting up fights, even though Bradley is known for a brawler and hot tempered, and within minutes Bradley would be verging on exhaustion. Ten minutes of constant fighting would be exhausting for most men, but Marlowe, and possibly Shakespeare, would probably have more

---

18   Kuriyama - ibid p83. The magistrate, Sir Owen Hopton left the space for the victim's name blank. Wyld possibly did not know who had been killed and Watson did not mention the name, presumably as it would link him to Bradley's attempt to have a restraining order put on him, as Bradley was in fear of his life. Wyld might also be in Watson or the Allens' pay.

stamina from either enacting such fights on stage or demonstating how to set them up.

As part of the fight's consequences Thomas Watson allows himself to be backed against a ditch and appears to be injured by Bradley - and this is his main evidence that he killed in self-defence. But though he is supposedly in jail for several months, in conditions that might be thought to encourage gangrene, no further mention of the wound is made. These are men who set up fights and provide make-up which makes an actor look wounded.[19] Was the blood that witnesses saw pig's blood in a bladder? This could be pierced by Watson, it does not need Bradley to actually hit him. Were both Marlowe and Watson so armed, so that whichever killed Bradley would appear to be wounded? And at the inquest did Watson in fact display a painted on wound, as would be used on stage, and as beggars were commonly known to do? Any witnesses watching what is actually a theatrical set piece will see Watson bleeding and agree that he was indeed wounded. There is no suggestion that Watson was examined by a doctor. What is actually happening is that Watson is taking out Bradley to gain control of his territory in Norton Folgate, probably under the aegis of Alleyn and Henslowe.

In which case both Watson and Marlowe are guilty of murder. But so successful is the ruse that Watson is able to plead self-defence, and Marlowe is released almost at once, on surety of two men who seem to be connected to Lord Burghley, Richard Kitchen, a lawyer of Clifford's Inn, and

---

19   'What bloody man is that?' Macbeth Act 1, scene ii. The make-up would need to look realistic for this scene, which is the opening one, and needs to grab the audience and pull them straight into the story.

Humphrey Roland, the horner.[20] That Watson's pardon is delayed for several months, until 18 February 1590, does suggest that someone in authority was not happy with the story and thought it was murder, but was unable to prove it. Watson was almost certainly not in jail for all of that time, however. Kusiyama reproduces the documents that outline the case in 1589, and against Watson's name is the word 'bailius' - bailed.[21]

So in summary, on 18 September Watson draws attention to himself so that Bradley will turn his attention away from an apparently vulnerable Marlowe. If Marlowe is really in trouble after ten minutes or so of the bout, Watson may be wondering why he is in trouble, and possibly worried that the put-up fight is not going according to plan. He would not guess that Marlowe is two people and the wrong one is on the street. It suggests that not Marlowe but Shakespeare is fighting here, and there is never any suggestion that Shakespeare is a brawler. Watson may not know the reason for a possible misadventure, and goes in to apparently stop the brawl, just as Romeo really intervenes between his enemy Tybalt and his friend Mercutio.

And to bear out the supposition that Shakespeare is fighting Bradley, it looks as if the man who wrote the fight between Tybalt and Mercutio must have had first-hand

---

20   But that Burghley put up sureties for Marlowe is only surmise. One surety is a lawyer, and may instead be either a friend of the Allen brothers or Henslowe, or the enterprise's lawyer. Roland might be someone who is 'protected' by Alleyn and Henslowe.

21   Kuriyama, ibid, 81-90, and p.203. That Watson was not in jail for the whole five months must preclude his dying in September 1592 from the effects of his imprisonment. There is some other cause, so far unexplained.

knowledge of the fight in Hogg Lane, so closely does the pretended version match the real one. Mercutio intentionally baits Tybalt who returns with an insult concerning Mercutio's relationship with Romeo, which Mercutio chooses to assume is suggesting that he and Romeo are not gentlemen but common players as 'consort' means both to spend time together, and to be a band of musicians. 'To consort' also contains a sexual innuendo, and there is an undertone of homosexuality as well.

Angrily then, Mercutio says: 'Consort? What, dost thou make us minstrels?' (Act I, scene 3). Mercutio attacks Tybalt, who retaliates; Benvolio tries to stop the fight but it is Romeo who intervenes to break it up, trying to put up their swords. Mercutio dead, Romeo attacks and kills Tybalt - just as Marlowe retires and Watson attacks and kills Bailey. Though not exact, the details of the double fight against one man, who is provoked into brawling in the street, closely mirror the events of 18 September. The way in which Mercutio starts his fight with Tybalt also suggests a premeditated fight - Mercutio wants to fight before Tybalt insults him, the insult is an excuse, which echoes the Bailey fight. Then, Romeo's intervention includes drawing his sword, while Tybalt runs off and then returns, as Bailey turned on Watson, and they fight, death intended on both sides.

Shakespeare wrote *Romeo and Juliet* somewhere between 1591 and 1594, basing it upon Italian tales that had existed for centuries, but culminated in Luigi da Porto's version set in the Verona of Bartolomeo II della Scala (who becomes Prince Escalus in Shakespeare's play[22]) a version which da Porta may have taken from the Decameron.

But what is the evidence for such a claim as Shakespeare being present in Hogg Lane and its aftermath and using the knowledge in his work? Not just from the fight. The original story of Romeo and Juliet says nothing of the nature of gang warfare in Verona. Those details of how gangs work and how they interact look like they are based on personal knowledge. Knowlege that Shakespeare has gained in the 'liberties' of London, where the stews, theatres, inns, bear gardens and cock pits are run by gangsters who appear respectable men and entrepreneurs. The liberties of London were outside the control of the city, and were much more lawless places where the underworld of sixteenth century London plied its trades. Shakespeare's knowledge marks him out more clearly as participating in gangland than does his supposed knowledge of courts[23] or ships - he has a finger on the beating pulse of how gangsters work. On honour, on revenge and on making sure members of each gang know where their loyalties lie and what happens when they try to change that loyalty or betray it. Tybalt wants to fight Romeo for honour's sake, just as would any mafiosi or modern gangster in London today.

---

22 The della Scala (sometimes Scaliger) badge was a ladder. The name Escalus, for the Prince of Verona, is built on the Latin root 'scala' a ladder, flight of stairs or steps. (The same root gives us escalator, for a moving staircase, very close to the name 'Escalus' in form and sound.)

23 In fact Shakespeare shows little knowledge of the complex workings of a sixteenth century royal court - his courts are more like the workings of a small aristocratic household such as that of Alexander Hoghton.

Not only is gangsterism knowledgeably portrayed but the plot of *Romeo and Juliet* involves the seduction and marriage of a fourteen year old girl, to an unsuitable suitor, organized by a Catholic priest, who throughout the play acts as a fixer, rather like Watson in the scam on the Cornwalis family. At no point are we given Romeo's age (and modern versions such as Zeffirelli's or Baz Luhrmann's make Romeo just a little older than Juliet, about sixteen) but we are told Juliet is 'not fourteen'. Romeo, thinking of marriage, is could be in his early twenties. [24] Paris is also considerably older than Juliet. This mismatch of ages in a marriage was not so obnoxious to an Elizabethan as it seems to us. For some time it has been thought that Marlowe's sister, Joan, was married to an older man at fourteen.[25] Watson and his brothers-in-law, Hugh and Thomas Swift, were engaged in arranging an unsanctioned marriage between an unacceptable suitor and Frances Cornwallis, who was fourteen in 1591. Thomas Swift had been employed in her father's household for some years. How long Watson had been there is not clear, but long enough to have been grooming a young girl for what Watson and Hugh Swift call a 'jape' but which her father considered in no such light. So there, in the Cornwallis scam, is the plot for Romeo and Juliet's love.[26] An event Shakespeare already knew about

---

24   It is a truism that most marriages took place between a bride of around twenty-five and a groom a few years older, but this is a mean average, which shows much of the population was older or younger than this.

25   See Appendix II for an examination of the age of Joan Marlowe at marriage. It is much more likely that the Frances Cornwallis incident is the source of Juliet's age than the marriage of Christopher Marlowe's sister.

26   From the Elizabethan point of view, the tragedy of Romeo and Juliet

when he came across Da Porto's story. In the play Romeo refuses to fight Tybalt, who challenges him because of the insult to the Capulet family by Romeo's sneeking into their ball, but Mercutio takes up the challenge. If Marlowe (or Shakespeare) is fighting on behalf of Watson and then Watson intervenes ot stop it, and kills Bradley, we have the complete Act III Sc.i action, though distilled to meet the needs of Shakespeare's plot. This interpretation leads to Bradley representing Tybalt in Shakespeare's play, and Marlowe Mercutio. And the character of Mercutio, which is Shakespeare's own invention, not copied from the sources, thus reflects the irrelevance, the bawdry and the homoerotic nature of Christopher Marlowe himself. When we hear the Queen Mab speech in Act I, Sc.iv, we may be listening to an echo of Marlowe himself, punning, sexually explicit and irreverent, particularly of lawyers and priests, and people who thought too well of themselves. This is a Marlowe that Shakespeare clearly knew well:

In 1672 John Dryden wrote: 'Shakespeare show'd the best of his skill in his Mercutio, and he said himself, that he was forced to murder him in the third Act, to avoid being

---

stems from their fault in disobeying the rules of their society. Juliet - and Romeo - should follow the advice and wishes of their parents when choosing a spouse, not rush off and marry who they liked. The play is about the consequences of disobedience and secret love affairs. not, as we now tend to see it, as an indictment of parents and society trying to force young people to marry against their wishes. The Elizabethan point of view fits exactly with the behaviour of Frances Cornwallis and what her father thought, and did, about it., taking legal action against Watson and Swift. It is also about the problems caused by feuds and gangs, and the love plot is used to illustrate the results of such violence.

killed by him.'[27] If Shakespeare did indeed say this then he is actually saying that he needed to kill Marlowe who was killing him. Shakespeare sees his role as Marlowe coming to an end. Marlowe must go because Shakespeare is being sucked dry by the impersonation, the double life. Marlowe, the Marlowe of the plays and the University Wits, must die to allow Shakespeare to live.

Cumulatively, the evidence presented by the fight in Hogg Lane, Watson's dealings with Frances Cornwallis and Shakespeare's identification of Mercutio as his Nemesis who must be killed, point to Shakespeare being the man in the fight – not playing at being exhausted, but actually played out, necessitating the intervention of Watson, who thought he was working with Marlowe, an experienced fighter, and found himself with Marlowe's shadow, a young man unable to cope with a fighter like Bradley. This suggests that Shakespeare and Marlowe, when he was in London, were in the habit of simply swapping, Shakespeare going off to do the sort spying that did not involve being a Catholic priest, for example 'reading with' Arbella Stuart. No-one but Marlowe and Shakespeare would know of this – but its danger was that the wrong one would get involved in something like the Bradley incident.

After the fight in Hogg Lane Marlowe is in prison for a short time, in Newgate. Here he meets John Poole[28], who, Baines says, gave him 'certain knowledge' of coining, which later features at Flushing (Vlissingen) when Marlowe is accused of counterfeiting. And it is to Flushing that it is now

---

27   Scott, Mark W.; Schoenbaum, S. (1987). Shakespearean Criticism. **5.** Detroit: Gale Research Inc. p.415.
28   A recusant, involved in ferrying Catholic priests into England and, according to Baines, knowledgeable about coining.

necessary to look to see if Shakespeare might be Marlowe, for it is another place where the 'wrong' Marlowe appears to be.

Chapter Twelve

Vlissingen and the Philosophers' Stone

At the beginning of 1592 Baines avers that Christopher Marlowe met 'one Poole', actually John Poole, recusant (and relative by marriage to the Stanleys), in Newgate Prison whilst incarcerated for the killing of William Bradley. Baines also says that Poole was a counterfeiter and that he explained this art to Christopher Marlowe in the few weeks – actually roughly twelve days - they were imprisoned together. This meeting and discussion is the basis for Baines accusing Marlowe of counterfeiting in Flushing in January 1592.

It is at Vlissingen, called Flushing[1] by the English, where Baines finally shows his hand clearly in his attempt

---

1   Flushing is the English name for Vlissingen. The town had been ceded to the English by the Dutch in return for support in their war with

to put an end to Christopher Marlowe's career. Vlissingen was an English enclave, a nest of spies, supporting several factions, and possibly sending spies onwards to the rest of the Low Countries and to other countries with the intention of disrupting Philip II's plans to maintain Catholic power in Northern Europe. Sir William Stanley was in the vicinity at Nijmegan with a regiment of about 700 men fighting on the side of Catholic Spain and also supporting the removal of Elizabeth from England's throne. Richard Williams, who had robbed Winchester Cathedral in August 1591 and then joined Stanley, said that he himself had offered to carry out the assassination of Elizabeth for a suitable amount of money. The candidate preferred or hoped for in English Catholic circles at this time was Ferdinando Stanley, Lord Strange, the heir of the Earl of Derby. He was later to be the focus of the Hesketh 'plot' - more likely a plot set up by Burghley to trap Stanley as many of the letters involved, especially that carried by Hesketh to Stanley, which purported to be from English Catholics living in Prague, look like forgeries. That Stanley took about ten days before he reported the letter Hesketh had brought to him, suggests that he might not be entirely averse to the premise that he be king in Elizabeth's place. He died suddenly in 1594; some

---

Spain.

thought that he was the victim of poison, possibly administered by his groom, who suddenly disappeared.

Sometime late in 1591, or very early 1592,[2] Baines and then Marlowe and a man named as Gifford Gilbert are residing in Flushing. They must have had passes as it was impossible to leave England officially without one. No-one knows who was employing Gilbert, Marlowe or Baines, nor why they were in Flushing. In outline, at the end of 1591, or maybe in January 1592 (NS), Marlowe crossed to the Low Countries. He lodged with Richard Baines, and Gilbert, apparentlly a goldsmith, and remained with them for several weeks. At some point Gilbert minted a false Dutch shilling. This was seen to be of such poor quality by Richard Baines (who describes it as being made of pewter[3]) that he decided to report the operation to the governor of Flushing (after this one shilling had been put into circulation), Sir Robert Sydney.[4] Sydney felt somewhat

---

2   Some confusion may be caused by the use of the Old Style calendar, which calls January 1592 January 1591.

3   Pewter is a mix of tin and lead.

4   Robert Sydney was Philip Sydney's brother, and brother-in-law to Frances Walsingham, who was by 1591 Countess of Essex. His other brother-in-law was the Earl of Pembroke, married to Mary Sydney. The First Folio of 1623 was dedicated to Pembroke's sons, William and Philip. Lord Pembroke was also patron to the acting company Pembroke's Men, which performed Marlowe's Edward II as well as Shakespeare's Henry VI, part III

burnt, it would seem, by his castigation two months earlier over the treatment of Michael Moody,[5] another secret agent who seems to have worked with Robert Poley, and so was unwilling to deal with the matter himself. He sent the three conspirators back to Lord Burghley: Marlowe and Gilbert in chains and Baines as a witness, though Marlowe had counter-accused Baines of counterfeiting.

Sidney sent a letter with his consignment of prisoners, which is remarkably lacking in detailed evidence of the charges made.

'To the right honorable my lord of Burghley *Lo*rd Treasurer of England.

Right Honorable Besides the prisoner Evan Flud, I have also given in charge to this bearer my anciant[6] twoe other

---

and and probably part II (Riggs p. 280). The Earl of Essex was beheaded in 1601, following the Essex Rebellion (Shakespeare and Burbage were involved here, performing Richard II on the eve of the rebellion, apparently being paid £2 per head to do so). Nicolas Skeres, a witness to the events in Deptford, was on Essex' payroll and accompanied him to the Low Countries in August 1591, along with William Richards who had been part of the 'gang' which raided Winchester Cathedral in August 1591, taking £1800 worth of plate for William Stanley's cause and who then joined Stanley. (Riggs p 276) Among his co-conspirators was Edward Bushell, a 'servant' of Lord Strange (Riggs p 270).

5 Investigating the Stanley Plot, of which Burghley was well aware.
6 Ensign.

prisoners, the one named Christofer Marly, by his profession a scholer, and the other Gifford Gilbert a goldsmith taken heer for coining, and their mony I have sent over unto yowr Lordship: The matter was revealed unto me the day after it was done, by one Richard Baines whome also my Anciant shal bring unto yowr Lordship: He was theyr chamber fellow and fearing the succes, made me acquainted with all. The men being examined apart never denied anything, onely protesting that what was done was onely to se the Goldsmiths conning: and truly I ame of opinion that the poore man was onely browght in under that couler, what ever intent the other twoe had at that time. And indeed they do one accuse another to have bin the inducers of him, and to have intended to practis yt heerafter: and have as it were iustified him unto me. But howsoever it hapned a dutch shilling was uttred, and els not any peece: and indeed I do not thinck that they wold have uttred many of them: for the mettal is plain peuter and with half an ey to be discovered. Notwithstanding I thowght it fitt to send them over unto yowr Lordship to take theyr trial as yow shal thinck best. For I wil not stretch my commission to deale in such matters, and much less to put them at liberty and to deliver them into the towns hands being the Queens subiects, and not required neyther of this sayd town I knowe not how it would have bin liked, especially since part of that which they did counterfet was Her Majesty's coine. The Goldsmith is an eccellent worckman and if I should speake my conscience had no intent heerunto. The scholer sais himself to be very wel known both to the Earle of Northumberland and my lord Strang. Bains and he do also accuse one another of intent to goe to the Ennemy or to Rome, both as they say of malice one to another. Heerof I thowght fitt to advertis yowr Lordship leaving the rest to their own confession and my Anciants report. And so do humbly take my leave at Flushing the 26 of January 1591[7] Yowr honors very obedient to do yow service

R. Sydney

Endorsed: 26 Jan. 1591 (4) Sir Robert Sidney to my Lord. He sendes over by this bearer his Aunteint one Evan Lloyd, and 2 others Christofer Marly and Gifford Gilbert a goldsmithe taken for coynage, to be tryed here for that fact. There hath bene only one dutch shilling uttered, the mettall playne peuter.' [8]

What is going on here? If Marlowe and Gilbert wanted to counterfeit coinage either to prove to William Stanley that they were viable coiners, or to export the coins to England for their own monetary advantage, why did they

---

7   1592, New Style.
8   PRO SP 84 / 44 / 60 - Discovered and transcribed by R. B. Wernham, and first published in English Historical Review (1976) Vol.91 pp.344-5.

only make one, according to Baines, very poor quality, coin? Why go to Flushing at all, if the purpose was personal gain?

There is a considerable amount of unpicking to be done to decide what 'Chrisofer Marley' is doing in Flushing, and why he is 'chamber fellow' to Richard Baines. Moreover, Richard Baines is presented as 'fearing the succes' of the enterprise and thus must surely be a fellow conspirator, but he is not charged nor listed as a prisoner, only as a witness.

Sidney has been told about the counterfeiting by Richard Baines, who said he feared for the success of the operation of counterfeiting as part of his accusation of 'Marley' and Gilbert. Sidney does not include Baines as a prisoner but as a witness, so either he is giving Baines some 'witness protection' or he has no real evidence that Baines was actually counterfeiting, only that he was worried about the operations' success. Baines' meaning is unclear, and Sidney chose to think Baines was worried the operation would succeed and therefore revealed it to the authorities.

The first thing to look at is what Sidney says about Baines: 'The matter was revealed unto me the day after it was done, by one Ri*chard* Baines whome also my Anciant shal bring unto yowr Lo*rdship*: He was theyr chamber fellow and fearing the succes, made me acquainted wi*t*h all.' Calling Baines Marlowe's chamber fellow may simply mean they are staying at the same inn. It may also be – and this is likeliest – that the place both Baines and Marlowe are staying is a safe house for agents who are in Flushing on official business. Evidence for this is that Baines does not seem to be working with Marlowe; that Marlowe will succeed in counterfeiting coins and that this will be to Marlowe's credit or gain, and he wishes to put a stop to this by reporting the event. Thus, Sidney is simply saying Baines and Marlowe are at the same establishment.

Witness protection is the likeliest reason Baines is not sent back to London in chains. But all the time it must be remembered that Sidney has only what Baines says to go on.

At no point does Sidney explicitly tell Burghley what Baines actually said about the counterfeiting – he leaves this to be teased out by questioning in England. But what can we discern about Baines' testimony? Sidney says that neither Marlowe nor Gilbert denied they had counterfeited a coin, but that they said they did this because they were testing the goldsmith's skills. Sidney appears to agree with this assertion: 'and truly I ame of opinion that the poore man was onely browght in under that couler, what ever intent the other twoe had at that time'. Sidney believes Gilbert to be innocent of counterfeiting and that he has only been asked by Marlowe and Baines to show his skill by producing a coin. Sidney then says he does not know what the purpose of this test actually was – but he does not believe Marlowe and Baines when they say it was *only* a test of skill. Quite the contrary, Sidney thinks they were doing something else but he does not know what and will not make any suggestions.

Sidney also says 'The men being examined apart never denied anything'. This is odd because counterfeiting was a capital offence and the authorities in Flushing took a very poor view of people who did this because the port was being used as a clearing house for exporting counterfeit coins – Sidney comments on the town's reaction thus: 'I knowe not how it would have bin liked'. Not denying they were counterfeiting puts all three in danger at the very least of torture, and possibly of death. You would expect at least Marlowe and Gilbert to deny the crime if they could. Indeed, Gilbert can deny the crime for Sidney believes he was duped with a false story from Marlowe and Baines – he says they have 'iustified him unto me' and '(t)he Goldsmith is an eccellent worckman and if I should speake my conscience had no intent heerunto'. But no-one denies the crime. Sidney mentions only one dutch shilling and says it was 'uttered', which means put into circulation. Unless Baines went out and retrieved this coin to show to Sidney then no-one but Baines, Marlowe and Gilbert have seen the coin.

Then Sidney says: 'a dutch shilling was uttred, and els not any peece: and indeed I do not thinck that they wold have uttred many of them: for the mettal is plain peuter and with half an ey to be discovered.' This looks as if Sidney has seen the coin but if so, does he send it to Burghley? He says he sends 'twoe other prisoners...and their mony'. He does not say it is counterfeit coins – and he surely would not call counterfeit coins 'mony' because in a real sense it is not money, not legal tender. Sidney looks as if he is going on Baines' word about the 'dutch shilling' and has not actually seen it. He is accepting that this coin is made of pewter and would not pass muster as legal currency.

That no counterfeit coins were sent is reinforced by the comment written in London at the end of the letter: '(t)here hath bene only one dutch shilling uttered, the mettall playne peuter'. This is merely repeating what Sidney has said, rather than a comment on the actual coin.

Nor is any equipment apparently sent over. There could be two reasons for this. The first that being a goldsmith Gilbert might legally have with him instruments to smelt gold and silver and also make these metals into objects; these items would not be evidence of counterfeiting unless moulds or stamps for coins were among them.[9] The

---

9   Milling coinage was not frequent and Elizabethan coins only seem

second reason could be that no equipment was found. If this were the case it suggests that any equipment was destroyed which means that Marlowe and Gilbert, having 'uttered' their shilling,[10] were leaving Flushing having been unsuccessful in their enterprise – whatever it was. And it looks impossible to work out what Marlowe, Gilbert and Baines were doing in Flushing.

Riggs suggests that Marlowe was really investigating Sir William Stanley and that counterfeiting was a guise in order to enter into dialogue. Stanley was always short of money, getting only moral support from Spain, and was always looking for ways to finance the enterprise through theft and counterfeiting. But he had his own counterfeiters, why would he entertain more, and that dubious people such as Marlowe, a member of a very suspect profession: playwrighting? As for Baines, his reputation among Catholics was that of an untrustworthy person, for he had

---

to have been milled between 1561 and 1571. The process required a screw press, much too involved for a counterfeiter such as Marlowe or Gilbert appeared to be, so such equipment need not be assumed present. Source: *The Milled Coinage of Elizabethan England*, D.G.Borden and I.D. Brown and *The Coinage of Britain*: 7 Early Milled Coins: Mestrelle's Coins, Ken Elks. 2001. Mestrelle produced milled coins with machinery driven by a horse drawn mill, Seaby, *The Coins of England*, p139.
10   'uttered' – published or put into circulation.

confessed to intending to murder students and teachers at the English College in Rheims by putting poison in the well.

They might of course be spying on events in Flushing, or even spying on each other or on Sir Robert Sidney.

Sidney comments that Marlowe and Baines intended to counterfeit again, so it looks as if they are in Flushing as this is a good place for coining where it is possible to pass false coin and get it to England. In which case everyone is there for personal gain. But they had to have passes to leave England, so must have had a cover, though Gilbert was probably able to travel as a merchant. Since both Baines and Marlowe are employed by the secret service it is likely that the Stanley plot is their cover. Moody had been baulked so Burghley sends more spies. But Baines seems no friend to Marlowe. He goes to Sidney with the tale of counterfeiting as soon as he sees the fake coin. And Marlowe does not seem to recognise Baines and Baines does not appear to know that Marlowe is an agent just as he is. He seems to think that Marlowe is just a counterfeiter. This argues that Baines is not in partnership with Marlowe and Gilbert and that Marlowe's counter-accusation of Baines is nothing more than an attempt to shift blame. That Sidney seems to take no notice of the accusation, besides recording that 'they do one accuse another', seems to bear out Baines having nothing to do with the actual coining.

The first thing to emerge from Marlowe not seeming to recognise Baines is that this is not Christopher Marlowe at all, but William Shakespeare. Marlowe, as Baines' betrayer, would recognise him from Rheims and be wary. (He might also recognise him as someone he had seen at Seething Lane[11] as well, even if Baines has not seen him there.) Shakespeare has never met Baines and would know nothing about Rheims except what Marlowe might tell him.

If the Stanley plot is the cover and making false coin is the real object, why is Baines present? He may also be investigating the Stanley faction, or he might be spying on spies – but not on Marlowe as he does not recognise him as a fellow spy. It has been suggested that Marlowe might have been using a false[12] name in Flushing, and it is possible both he and Baines were disguised in some way, and that Baines also was using a false name. Baines might be spying on Sidney, of course, which Sidney might be bearing in mind, especially after the incident with Moody.[13] But it does not seem that Baines is really part of the counterfeiting project and he does not know much about it – or why does Sidney

---

11   Walsingham's headquarters.
12   Ayres, R. Evidence that Christopher Marlowe was the 'Ghost' of William Shakespeare. Online blog 2014, Ayres on Environment, Exergy, Economy and Growth.
13   Sidney would have been aware of this possibility, and accordingly acted circumspectly, not to alert London, or Baines, to his suspicions.

not raid the workshop that Gilbert must have had, since smelting and working metals could not be carried out in an inn room without being noticed?

What emerges is that Baines has seen something which he interprets as counterfeiting and reports it to Sidney probably as a way of attacking Marlowe. Marlowe for some reason does not deny the charge even though there seems to be no physical evidence. The 'dutch shilling'[14] is somewhere in circulation, there is no clear evidence that Baines showed it to Sidney. All we know about the coin is that it is made of pewter and Baines says it will not pass as a real coin.

Added to this Marlowe claims he is known to the Earl Northumberland, the Wizard Earl as well as Lord Strange. Also both Baines and Marlowe accuse each other of going over to Rome. This is a repetition of the 1587 rumour from Baines, and a standard accusation of proposed treason for Marlowe. It also bears out that Baines has no idea Marlowe is a secret agent, and that Marlowe may be unaware of Baines' role too. The accusation suggests that the cover of contacting Stanley in order to spy on him is correct. Such

---

14   Sidney writes: 'part of that which they did counterfet was Her Ma*jesty's* coine.' This looks as if more than one coin was struck, but that need not be the case. It is more likely that the 'dutch shilling' might have been an English coin and the word 'dutch' refers to origin not type.

accusations together with Marlowe returning to England in chains would much increase his credit with Catholics.

But whatever is happening why is only one dutch shilling minted? And why, if it is made from pewter, does Baines say it will not pass muster as a real coin? Pewter is known as poor man's silver because it shines just like silver, especially when new. If the coin is pewter and new it will be just as shiny as a silver coin. It would pass as silver by sight. But Baines says it will not pass by sight, which suggests that it is discoloured in some way (Sidney says that Gilbert is a skilled goldsmith so that we do not need to entertain the idea that the coin's appearance apart from colour was not good). Pewter holds its shine for some time which suggests that this coin is not pewter, but Baines thought that it was. The inference is that pewter was not the metal the coin was made of and that silver was not the metal that Gilbert and Marlowe were trying to make.

Pewter is an alloy of lead and tin. Lead is one of the metals thought by alchemists to be transmutable into gold. The search for the means to change base metals into gold was a pre-occupation of alchemists in the sixteenth century and was believed to be possible. Modern science proves that it is possible to transmute lead, which has an atomic number of 82, into gold, which has an atomic number of 79. (The atomic number represents the number of protons an element has, and this defines the element.) However, lead is a stable element and making it release three protons takes a great deal of energy, far more than possible to produce in the sixteenth century. To remove protons in order to transmute lead into gold would need a particle accelerator.

***

There are modern reports that transmutation has been completed twice, once in 1972, by Russian scientists, and once in 1980, by Glenn Seaborg. It is possible that Seaborg did not transmute lead but bismuth.[15] Further, nuclear scientists at the Lawrence Berkley National Laboratory, California, were able to produce small amounts of gold from bismuth. In doing so they found it much easier to retrieve the gold particles produced than if they had used lead. This is because bismuth is more homogenous than lead, having only one stable isotope as opposed to lead's four, according to David J. Morissey, of Michigan State University, who took part in the experiment.[16] This experiment appears well attested.

15	Source: ThoughtCo, Lifelong Learning. *Transmutation Definition and Examples*: 'For example, Glenn Seaborg made gold from bismuth in 1980.

16	Scientific American: Fact or Fiction? Lead Can Be Changed into

Bismuth has an atomic weight of 83.[17] It is also a silvery coloured metal when first produced. However, it oxidizes quite rapidly to a pinkish colour.[18] Bismuth has been known for many thousands of years but has often been mistaken for tin and lead with which it shares some properties – all are transition metals. By the mid sixteenth century the Latin name bisemutum was in use for bismuth. In modern times bismuth has 190harmaceutical uses, such as bismuth subsalicylate. Thus, bismuth fits neatly into the alchemists' toolkit, being a metal like lead and also having medicinal properties, cures and medicines being another area of research alchemists pursued.

From Baines assertion that he feared the success of the operation, and Sidney's saying that the coin would not

---

Gold. Particle accelerators make possible the ancient alchemist's dream – but at a steep cost, John Matson on January 31, 2014. The date the article puts the bismuth to gold a reaction in 1984, thirty years previous to 2014.

17   Bismuth is also diamagnetic – that is it is repelled by a magnetic field. It is also a poor conductor of heat.

18   *Greenwood, N. N. & Earnshaw, A. (1997). Chemistry of the Elements (2nd ed.). Oxford: Butterworth-Heinemann. ISBN0-7506-3365-4. Krüger, Joachim; Winkler, Peter; Lüderitz, Eberhard; Lück, Manfred; Wolf, Hans Uwe (2003). "Bismuth, Bismuth Alloys, and Bismuth Compounds". Ullmann's Encyclopedia of7Industrial Chemistry. Wiley-VCH, Weinheim. pp171–189. doi:10.1002/14356007 .a04_171.Suzuki, Hitomi (2001). Organobismuth Chemistry. Elsevier. pp1–20. ISBN-978-0-444-20528-5. Wiberg, Egon; Holleman, A. F.; Wiberg, Nils (2001). Inorganic chemistry. Academic Press. ISBN-0-12-352651-5.* Summary from Wikipedia.

deceive, I believe that Marlowe and Gilbert were working not with pewter (lead and tin) but bismuth. A coin made from bismuth would quickly discolour through oxidation and become unusable as silver. It looks very much as though Gilbert and Marlowe were attempting to perform alchemy, not counterfeiting.

Further, it is on Baines own testimony that we know that Marlowe was instructed by John Poole in counterfeiting. Looked at dispassionately Baines' claim that Marlowe knew all about counterfeiting cannot stand – though Baines may have believed it. It takes more than a few weeks of talking to someone in order to learn how to counterfeit. One may understand the procedure and the process, the steps to be undertaken and how to produce a result. But that is not the same as having carried out these things under supervision as an apprentice. That Gilbert is present at Flushing, a goldsmith not only by his own word but also on the word of Sir Robert Sidney who says he was a good gold-worker, makes it clear that if Marlowe knew anything about counterfeiting it was theoretical only. A real practioner was needed. That the practioner is a skilled goldsmith is both remarkable and interesting – surely a man who knew about minting coins, like the Frenchman Mestrelle who had worked at the English mint (and had also been a counterfeiter[19]) would have been a better choice. Goldsmiths do not routinely mint coins.

But they do know about alloys, and, in so far as such a thing can be said to exist in the sixteenth century, were chemists, with a knowledge of the properties of metals, their melting points and the mix of alloys needed to strengthen them. A goldsmith therefore could also be an alchemist because they were dealing with metals in the same fashion. And so we can surmise that what Marlowe and Gilbert were doing in Flushing is not counterfeiting, but the transmutation of bismuth into gold. Neither Baines nor Sidney recognise this, because they are both fixated on counterfeiting. Baines shows no knowledge of the difference between bismuth and pewter, all he notices was the discolouration. There is no suggestion he saw the equipment used by Gilbert, but if he had it is unlikely he would have known the difference between that needed for making coins from pewter compared with alchemical equipment and materials for making gold coins from transmuted bismuth.

Lastly, if Gilbert were an alchemist it might well be that he saw bismuth, a white metal, as the Philosophers' Stone, sometimes called 'white stone' and that it was for this reason that he chose the metal over lead in this experiment.

---

19   For which he was hanged in 1578 – ibid.

That Marlowe, and indeed Shakespeare, knew nothing of counterfeiting now becomes irrelevant. They did know of Giordano Bruno, who, in addition to his other activities, was at least a theoretical alchemist. It is very likely that he was the source of Marlowe's knowledge of alchemy whilst Gilbert, goldsmith and alchemist, had the necessary skills. But we do not know who Gilbert was.

-0-

A summary of the evidence for this makes things clearer. Little or nothing is known about why Baines, Marlowe and Gilbert are in Flushing, which is not only close to Sir William Stanley's camp but also a clearing house for counterfeit coin. Baines is sharing a lodging with Marlowe and Gilbert. He accuses them of counterfeiting after seeing a 'dutch shilling' which he says will not pass muster as a silver coin, it being 'playne peuter'. No-one seems to have seen this coin except Baines, who says it was put into circulation. No-one reports seeing Gilbert's workshop nor his tools. No evidence of these things, nor the counterfeit coin, seem to go to London. London seems to think, from the endorsement put on Sidney's letter, that this is a matter of small account, and nothing happens to Marlowe (Sidney seems to exonerate Gilbert) – which suggests that ostensibly (and as far as we can tell Burghley knew) he was on secret service business to do with Stanley while in Flushing.

As his defence against any accusations Marlowe – or rather, as it appears from the lack of recognistion of Baines, Shakespeare, – lists among his contacts Henry Percy, Earl of Northumberland.[20] Northumberland, along with Henry Brooke and Sir Walter Raleigh, were named to James I and VI by Robert Cecil (Burghley's younger son and first Earl of Salisbury) as being interested in occult practices. It is possible Shakespeare simply lists all the important people he is acquainted with as Marlowe, in the hope that this will divert Robert Sidney from charging him, without realising the implications of naming the Wizard Earl. A more understandable reason might be the bravado of hiding a secret in plain sight. Mentioning Lord Strange, a connection of Poole's, could be being used in this context to point Sidney in the wrong direction, whilst obliquely showing him the right one. This suggests the truth is alchemy, not counterfeiting.

Next, Baines thinks the coin 'uttered' by Marlowe and Gilbert is pewter. But he says it will not pass as a silver coin. Pewter would pass. But bismuth would not since it quickly

---

20   Northumberland is a possible patron of Marlowe's. Kuriyama, ibid, pp90-91. That he also lists Ferdinando Stanley, Lord Strange, suggests a signal that he is in Flushing on official business. This looks like a distraction technique. Lord Strange was also under suspicion because of the Catholics' preference for him to be king in Elizabeth's place. The recusant John Poole was a connection to Strange by marriage. Northumberland was not in high favour either, having been suspected of plotting to marry Arbella Stuart.

oxidizes to a pinkish colour; it follows that the coin is not intended to pass for silver. If Gilbert and Marlowe are coining then two questions must be answered: why do they only, apparently, make one coin and why do they use a metal which will not pass for silver?

That they are alchemists, trying to transmute bismuth into gold is the only conclusion that fits the facts stated and also explains why neither Marlowe nor Gilbert deny the charge of counterfeiting. Alchemy was not illegal in England, indeed the Queen had her own alchemist in Dr Dee, though she employed him as an astrologer. Notwistanding this, alchemy is pretty close to being witchcraft, for which the proofs are much easier than for counterfeiting, and witchcraft carried the death penalty if proved. Given that there was no proof of counterfeiting – only Baines' word – it was much safer for Marlowe and Gilbert to admit to this to Robert Sidney and get sent back to London to be questioned, than to say they were actually alchemists, which might result in a trial for witchcraft, possibly in a hostile Flushing. For example, the alchemist Thomas Charnock believed that he was able to discover the Philosophers' Stone, and wrote to Elizabeth I, in 1565, offering wealth and health provided by it;[21] whatever

---

21   History Today (August 2005).

Elizabeth I thought about alchemists, Charnock's neighbours feared him. That he kept in a continuous fire and carried out experiments they could not understand made him suspect in their eyes. It was difficult to distinguish, for people like Baines and indeed Sidney, the difference between alchemy, which could be called good magic (and alchemists such as Paracelsus were beginning to call themselves magi or mages), and the bad magic practised by people such as Johannes Faustus[22], which might be termed witchcraft or wizardry. Marlowe had by 1592[23] written the play *Dr Faustus*, and this coupled with an admission of being an alchemist might be enough for a court to find him guilty of witchcraft. Better accept an accusation of being a counterfeiter with no evidence for it, than be convicted of witchcraft and almost certainly hang.

Thus, not counterfeiting, but alchemy is being performed in Flushing. It fails and Marlowe and Gilbert prepare to go home, only to be accused of counterfeiting by Richard Baines and handed over to Sidney to be sent to England in chains. A sad end to what they had hoped might be a highly lucrative venture.

---

22   Source: Sixteenth Century Europe, blog of Bromley Adult Education College, created by Dr. Anne Stott.
23   Shakespeare would later write *The Tempest*, which, in addition to its political themes, features a powerful magician.

But there is more. Poole, like Alexander Hesketh, is from Lancashire, and a Catholic, and also part of the circle of people connected with the Stanleys – and the various plots to put Ferdinando Stanley on the English throne. Possibly also known to Poole is Edmund Kelley also from the Lancashire circle and also known to Hesketh, in 1591 a resident in Prague (the home of many English Catholics) and in such favour with Emperor Rudulph II that he was knighted and made a member of the emperor's Privy Council. This would not concern us overly, despite the Poole and Stanley connection, except that Kelley is in receipt of letters from Lord Burghley, carried by Matthew Royden (another associate of Marlowe and Northumberland), some of which concern alchemy. For Edmund Kelley was an alchemist, and also associated with Dr. Dee. Burghley was corresponding with Kelley in May 1591, and at some point asked him for 'essences' used in alchemy in order to help English finances.[24]

This looks like the final piece of the jigsaw in the puzzle of what Marlowe was doing in Flushing, and may give some insight into who Gifford Gilbert was, for there is no trace of him in England and he did not necessarily sail to the Netherlands with Marlowe. It is possible they met in

---

24   Nicholls p.310.

Flushing and that Gilbert had travelled from somewhere in Germany to meet Marlowe, who had come to carry out alchemical experiments on the orders of Burghley, and armed with information gleaned from Kelley. Gifford Gilbert could have been an alchemist called Tankard, known to Kelley, or it is just possible to suppose that we are looking at Bruno, travelling from Frankfurt (where he had attended the Book Fair) before going back to Italy. Though this might be a very fanciful idea, Bruno had, apparently, worked for Francis Walsingham, and could have known Marlowe. The question comes down to how the man named as 'Gilbert' came to be in Flushing with Marlowe. Since Burghley was corresponding with Kelley, contacting Tankard would have been entirely possible, but Bruno would have been difficult to contact. This leaves Tankard as a good possibility, even to the name Gifford Gilbert, a reverse of the name of the English agent and later Catholic priest, Gilbert Gifford (1560-1590), and perhaps signalling Tankard's allegiance to the Catholic cause. Whoever he was, Gilbert disappears from the record, (though Tankard re-appears in 1593 as a debtor to a money lender known as Wolfall (who Skeres[25] worked for), along with Matthew Royden) and Marlowe is certainly free of any constraint by May 1592, which

---

25   Skeres was involved in a case against Wolfall, described as a 'skinner' - money lender and confidence trickster.

suggests that Burghley was fully aware of the trip and that Marlowe was not free-lancing[26] on this occasion by attempting to spy on Sir William Stanley. A failed alchemy experiment was not something Burghley would want to advertise, suggesting as it does desperation to fill England's coffers by any means, so Marlowe would likely be released without charge and the whole matter put aside. That explains another reason why Marlowe would not admit to being an alchemist in Flushing, because it might lead to revealing Burghley's involvement, and led him instead to admit to counterfeiting as a lesser charge. Only Sidney and Baines' involvement would be a problem for Burghley, but there was no physical evidence of wrong-doing (or none survived its arrival in London) and the whole episode could therefore be passed off as simply an intelligence operation that had been de-railed by Baines' reporting Marlowe, because they did not know they were both working for the Privy Council. That they seem to be at odds may be because Marlowe was working for Burghley while Baines was working for Achbishop Whitgift and Lord Keeper Puckering (to whom he seems to have meant to address his note concerning Marlowe's atheism, in May 1593). What does

---

26 Free-lancing, in order to get information for sale, was not uncommon. Poley's contacts with Mary Queen of Scots and her supporters was entirely free-lance work, for example.

emerge is Baines continuing hostility to Marlowe, one that can only be explained by an abiding hatred on Baines' part, generated by acts of Marlowe that could not be forgiven. The events at Vlissingen/Flushing allowed Baines, unrecognised as a threat because Shakespeare did not recognise him as an enemy, yet again to attempt harm on Christopher Marlowe.

***

Once returned to London, Marlowe, that is Shakespeare, distances himself as much as possible from magic and alchemy in the plays *Edward II* and the first of his works concerning the Wars of the Roses, *Henry VI part III* [27] (listed by Henslowe as *Harey Vj*).

---

27   Though in Henry VI part II (probably in the repetoire of Pembroke's Men in 1594) the Duchess of Gloucester is accused of and punished for using witchcraft against Henry VI and Margaret of Anjou.

Chapter Thirteen

Richard Baines – Priest and Spy

Richard Baines was some years older than Marlowe and was a former Catholic (though this cannot be seen as particularly significant since much of the population were former Catholics even in the late 1570s when we first hear of Baines). Although there has been some dispute as to who Richard Baines was, Boas first put forward the idea that he was not, as had originally been thought, a rather shady lawyer who attended Lincoln's Inn and was later hanged, but another man who came from or went to Lincolnshire and who in the late 1570s went to Rheims to train as a priest, not in order to re-convert the English but in order to spy upon English Catholics, and who later was given a living in Lincolnshire – thus resulting in the confusion of this man with the Richard Baines of Lincoln's Inn. Current thought suggests that the Richard Baines who wrote the Note was hanged in December 1594, having been accused of a theft which was, in fact, set up to trap him. The theft of a valuable cup, and the trick used to catch Baines, is included in *Dr*

Faustus. Some suggest that the cup trick was added after Baines' death[1] but were it to have been added after Baines was hanged it does not prove anything other than that the author of *Dr Faustus* was connected to Baines' arrest for stealing a cup. It is possible that hanging and story are linked and that Baines was the victim of a plot to cause his death and that following his death someone - the perpetrator of the plot, perhaps – added the story to the play, as a sort of codicil to the real life events. If so, it suggests that the shady lawyer and the recusant priest turned Anglican vicar were the same man because the man at Rheims is certainly the author of Baines' Confession, and the man in London writing the Baines' Note uses many ideas and accusations contained in the Confession.

Baines was in Rheims from 1578[2] and beforehand went to Christ College Cambridge, a college from which people tended to be ordained as Anglican priests, and then to Caius. Baines was therefore probably already ordained when he went to Rheims and he went as a spy, sending information back to England. But having given his confidence to an apparently like-minded colleague he was betrayed and found himself imprisoned by Dr. Allen.

Eventually, after months of imprisonment and torture, he made confession of his intention to betray his fellow students and the whole English college and was freed to return to England by 1585. In 1593 Richard Baines wrote his Note condemning Marlowe for atheism; the Note went to Privy Councillor John Puckering who showed it to

---

1   In which case Shakespeare added it.
2   Chapter Six.

Elizabeth I sometime late in May 1593 – the version Elizabeth saw is dated 26 May.

Baines says in his Confession (this is the published version put out by Dr. Allen) that he delighted in profane writers, that he 'began to mock at the lesser points of religion' moving on to 'utter divers horrible blasphemies in plain terms against the principle points of religion', and tried to work on the ideas of his colleagues at Rheims by 'arguments...and communications'. He confessed that such thoughts and actions were 'the highway to heresy, infidelity and atheism, as to my great danger I have experience in mine own case'.[3]

Baines also says that 'Arrogantly I made examination of the mystical ceremonies...and in secret conversations I said that they were no more than pretty gestures performing which even a Turk would look holy, and that without them the rest of the mass was nothing but Bale-worship...'[4]

Accusations of heresy and blasphemy are made against Marlowe in the Baines Note, and there the comments are given. So Marlowe is accused of calling Moses 'a Jugler', that 'Crist was a bastard and his mother dishonest' – this last is probably a reference to the ancient heresy that Mary was raped by a Roman soldier.[5] This statement alone

---

3 *A True Representation of the Late Apprehension and Imprisonment of John Nichols.* Cardinal Allen edited and introduced it and there is a copy in the British Library. It contains Baines' confession. Cited by Nicholls, ibid, p.150. Honan also quotes Baines' Confession.
4 ibid p.446.
5 This ancient blasphemy is even more graphically given in *'Jerry Springer, the Opera'*, where in the BBC version the script has Mary say she

is enough to condemn anyone as a heretic and blasphemer, suggesting as it does that God has prostituted Christ's mother. If Marlowe had been in trouble with the Privy Council this accusation of repeating a horrible blasphemy would have been damning.

The Baines note makes a reference to counterfeiting as well, accusing Marlowe of saying 'he had as good a right to coine as the Queen of England and that he was acquainted with one Poole in Newgate'.[6]

Baines was tortured at Rheims, before making this confession. That he was tortured is confirmed in a report of 2nd May 1582[7], from an agent in Paris, which tells Walsingham 'Banes has had the strappado and is often tormented'. The report also makes clear that Baines was one of Walsingham's agents, as no explanation of his identity is included. Thus it seems that at least in 1582 Baines was working for Walsingham at Rheims. Who he was working for in 1592 is unclear, as is what he was doing in Vlissingen/Flushing. He might be on Burghley's business, but if so, then Baines must have come under some displeasure over the events at Vlissingen/Flushing – perhaps his Note is an attempt to re-ingratiate himself with his spymasters.

***

---

has been raped by God. Even Baines will not go this far in his accusation, but the implication is clearly there.

6   Kuriyama, ibid, p. 221, *Transcriptions and Translations*

7   Questier, M., *English clerical converts to Protestantism*, Recusant History 2,, 1991, 455-77. PRO SP1 5/27A, f 120.

Because of the Baines Note, Baines has been called Christopher Marlowe's Nemesis, but why this should be has been unclear. In Chapter Six is detailed a possible cause between Marlowe and Baines originating in Rheims, to do with Baines' betrayal to Dr. Allen by Marlowe, who was working as a spy like Baines. This chapter will expand on that theory.

For reasons which are currently unclear, twice Richard Baines traduced Christopher Marlowe. First at Vlissingen/Flushing when he accuses Marlowe of counterfeiting for the Catholics, along with one Gifford Gilbert, and then in May 1593 when he accuses Marlowe of atheism and says that such a dangerous man as he is should be eliminated, leading to Elizabeth I requiring pursuit of the matter to the utmost vigour. Why does Richard Baines, who hardly seems to have known Marlowe although they were both secret agents, want to discredit him so? The interesting point at Vlissingen/Flushing is that Marlowe seems not to recognise Baines, although Marlowe has been thought to have met him at Walsingham' headquarters in Seething Lane. One plausible reason, discussed above in Chapter Twelve, is that it is not Marlowe in Vlissingen/Flushing, but Shakespeare, which is why he does not recognise Baines as a fellow agent and does not see the danger of listing the Earl of Northumberland as someone to whom he is known.

Nicholls supposes that Baines met Christopher Marlowe, at that time a newly recruited member of the Privy Council's spy network, some time in 1585.[8] In that year Marlowe, or Shakespeare, had just completed his BA and

---

8   In *The Reckoning*.

was proceeding with MA studies. There was no question that he would not receive his BA, but he came quite low on the list of candidates. It is also the year of the supposed portrait of Marlowe, with its enigmatic motto. Nicholls suggests Baines met Marlowe at Seething Lane, but it is just as likely the meeting took place at Cambridge, where Baines would possibly find a welcome as a former student. And when he met Marlowe there, perhaps in those circles where both might be spying on possible recusants, Baines was entirely confused because he thought he had met the young man before. Baines does not recognise Marlowe as a fellow agent at Vlissengen/Flushing because he did not see him at Seething Lane but at Cambridge, and was unaware of any connection to secret agent networks. If Baines was not working for Burghley in 1592, then it must have been for some other network, possibly that of Essex, who had his own stable of agents, and there was no communication between the different 'secret networks'. And because Shakespeare had perhaps seen Baines, maybe only fleetingly, at Cambridge he did not realise that he was a threat. Indeed, at Cambridge, Baines may have been at pains to conceal himself from 'Marlowe', so that Marlowe would not recognise his danger at being recognised by Baines as a student at Rheims.

If Marlowe, whether he had swapped places with Shakespeare at the instigation of Walsingham or one of his employees or by his own arrangement, went to Rheims he would have arrived sometime in 1581, depending on how long it took him to get from Calais, if that was the route he took via Dover, rather than sailing from London. He would have met Richard Baines, then two years into his course. Marlowe would have been very anxious to be in the good books of Dr. Allen and also to prove that he was a genuine seminarian, intent on the re-conversion of England, because this is what his spymasters would want of him. Baines, well into his own spying activities, clearly confided in someone whom he thought was a fellow spy perhaps to increase his importance among the younger students whom he wished to undermine or possibly convert to the English cause. If he confided in Marlowe he may have made his first mistake. Marlowe may even have suggested that he was a fellow spy, or let it slip (something he would later be at pains to conceal). Then it was that Marlowe betrayed Baines to Allen in order to ingratiate himself and gain information or influence in the college and later when on his mission in England. If, in this case, Marlowe had told Baines that he was also a spy then it would make explicable Baines' confidences, but also leave Baines in the position of being unable to betray his betrayer who would certainly have posed as an agent provocateur acting to draw out an enemy of Doctor Allen and loyal Catholics. The betrayal and following imprisonment partially ruined Baines' life, and though he continued to work for them it is possible that he was never again entirely trusted by Walsingham, Burghley and the Privy Council, Thereafter Baines was probably always wanting to prove his usefulness and loyalty while also holding a grudge against the man he felt had led to his imprisonment, during which he had been tortured and been in fear of his life, and which had led to his consequent loss of status in the English spy network. Baines definitely tries twice to get Marlowe executed – the penalty for coining was death, as it was for atheism – and his second attempt appears to succeed, except it is not clear whether the entire Privy

Council saw his deposition on Marlowe before the end of May 1593, or only Puckering.

***

But are these two incidents the only times Baines attempts to damage Marlowe? Where did the rumour that Marlowe was going to Rheims surface from in 1587? It was enough to make the authorities at Corpus Christ reluctant to hand over Marlowe's MA – and his absences from college overall are not enough to justify this as many scholars were absent, on study leave, or studying away from the university[9] – so that the Privy Council intervenes on his behalf, saying he has done unspecified work for the Queen, presumably in the thirty-five weeks he was absent from Cambridge that same year. That the rumour was heeded is interesting in itself. It suggests that the student called Marlowe was consorting with Catholics or Catholic sympathisers at Corpus Christi, and that this was well known, despite being a Parker Scholar and so presumably a staunch Protestant. But Marlowe had no intention of going to Rheims, and was intent instead on going to London, something which he must have mentioned to his colleagues, because all students talk about what they are going to do when they graduate. As far as anyone knows he was not intending to be any sort of priest, let alone a Catholic one. So whence comes the rumour?

If Richard Baines met Marlowe at Cambridge rather than at Seething Lane he may well have recognised his betrayer from Rheims – though it was probably Shakespeare he was actually seeing. Cursory enquiry would have shown

---

9   Christopher Marlowe at Corpus, 1580-87 ibid.

that the Marlowe at Cambridge, a man he recognised by looks not name, had been there on and off since 1581, and therefore could not have spent unbroken lengths of time at Rheims between 1580 to 1585. Baines must have had a double take. What was going on? Had the man he recognised left Rheims and gone to Cambridge with the intention of returning after getting his MA? What he would not have guessed was that there were two Christopher Marlowes – one in Rheims and one at Cambridge. It would have been inconceivable to Baines, and Walsingham would have been at pains to conceal this information outside his office, or may even have been the only person who knew it (with difficult consequences for his protegées after his death in 1590). To destroy his betrayer as he had been destroyed by torture and humiliating confession, might have been a prime directive for Baines, given the opportunity. He may have given the name of his betrayer as a seminarian at Rheims who would be coming to England in due course – but if he did, his accusation would have had no traction with Walsingham. What could he do? He could set up a rumour that Christopher Marlowe of Corpus Christi was intending to go to Rheims once he had his MA – almost a death warrant and certainly good reason for the authorities to withhold a degree. Thus, Baines is the likeliest source of the rumour about Rheims, and because of its source the Privy Council pounced on it at once and squashed it flat – probably on Walsingham's orders. And it was a rumour without any truth in it. Marlowe was not intending to go to Rheims for he had already gone and was now on his way home with the identity of a Catholic priest and entry into every Catholic household in the country; a man competent and willing to spy on those who trusted him.

If the rumour about Rheims set about in 1587 is included in the attempts by Richard Baines to do Marlowe harm then there are now three incidents: at Cambridge, at Vlissingen/Flushing and finally with the Baines Note in 1593. But other events of 1593 might also involve Baines. The Dutch Church Libel verses were meant to incriminate Marlowe by signing the name of his most famous character, Tamburlaine, as their author. Whose idea might that have been? The likeliest people behind the Dutch Church Libel are thought to be Baines and Drury, though they were not the writers of the verses – that was someone with the ability to produce iambic pentameters. This would make the Dutch Church Libel Baines' fourth attempt to traduce Marlowe and cause him trouble, even if id it did not lead to execution. Verse was obviously chosen because Marlowe was to be the target, and was able to write the type of verse used in the Libel.

Four attempts to cause Marlowe's death look very like a vendetta, only explained by a real sense of injury. Baines' betrayal at Rheims is such an injury, so that including all these incidents supports the argument that Marlowe was at Rheims in 1582, not at Cambridge, and did betray Baines, who thereafter did all he could to cause Marlowe injury.

But it was not Baines or Drury who wrote the Libels. The Privy Council decided that they were looking for a playwright and it was Thomas Kyd who was arrested for the crime and found with heretic papers in his 'bundle'. What was the reason for the arrest of Thomas Kyd and why was Marlowe to attend on the Privy Council for most of May 1593?

Chapter Fourteen

The Strange Arrest of Thomas Kyd

Why was Thomas Kyd arrested on 12th May 1593? This question is usually answered by saying that he was a friend or colleague of Christopher Marlowe, but, as a playwright battling to make a living in the London theatre companies, he was Marlowe's rival, and there is no evidence that they were friends, except that Kyd says in his deposition made after his arrest, that they shared a room. Even if they shared a lodging it does not mean they were friends, and Kyd is adamant Marlowe is not the sort of man he would befriend on any terms whatsoever. Also, Kyd is the only person who says they did share a lodging, or rather that he and Marlowe were writing in the same room. So why did the Privy Council, deliberating on the Dutch Church Libels on 11 May, light on Thomas Kyd?

Thomas Kyd was slightly older than Shakespeare and Marlowe, having been born in 1558, the year of Elizabeth I's accession. He was the son of a scrivener and attended Merchant Taylors school. He did not, however, go on to one of the universities, and therefore was not accounted by such as Greene (and no doubt, Marlowe) as one included in the society of the 'university wits'. Greene would have seen Kyd as a lesser playwright because he did not have the education that he, Greene, and also Watson and Marlowe had enjoyed.[1] Thus, Kyd, from the point of view of such playwrights as Marlowe, was inferior because he did not have the requisite level of education.

But Kyd was a popular playwright. His Senacan-style[2] play *The Spanish Tragedy* was immensely popular throughout Elizabeth's reign, and Kyd's plays were performed across Europe. He was no small figure on the Elizabethan dramatic scene. On the contrary, he was successful and well-known.

It is not clear how he began writing plays, but it may be that as a scrivener he was employed to copy plays for theatre companies. It is not a huge step from reading and copying plays to writing them, for familiarity with form and method would both be acquired, and one of the features that Kyd is said to have had is a strong knowledge of how a play needs to be staged; perhaps you could say he was an actor's playwright. (Nothing is more frustrating for an actor than a play that does not give time for costume or scene changes, or lacks an understanding of how a play is staged.) But

---

1   This lack comes to light in his accusation that Marlowe said that Jesus Christ was homosexual - a possible misreading of the Arian heresy and the Gnostic idea of 'Homoousion', the same in essence e.g. as the Father and the Holy Spirit.
2   Seneca's tragedies were popular, and contained revenge plots, violent deaths, witches and ghosts. They also contained long soliloquies.

beyond his fame Kyd's life appears to be blameless, giving no reason for the Privy Council to decide to arrest him, certainly not for atheism.

What had exercised the minds of the Privy Council in early 1593 was a set of verses put on the door of the Dutch church, in London, railing against the incursions of immigrants, who were favoured by the government, and their taking of English jobs. The feeling of the Privy Council was that these verses were inflammatory and would cause riots. Who posted the verses is unknown, but they were signed 'Tamburlane' a direct reference to Christopher Marlowe's play *Tamburlaine*, and they used words and ideas from two other plays, *The Jew of Malta*, and *The Massacre at Paris*. The last had been performed in January, and would still, presumably, be well known to Londoners.

It looks as if Kyd has been arrested in order to locate Marlowe, but this cannot be the case since the Privy Council and their agents are unlikely to know that Kyd is intimate with Marlowe. Far more intimate with Marlowe is Thomas Walsingham. Why does the Privy Council not arrest him, or search his house, where Christopher Marlowe has actually been staying? They certainly knew he was likely to be staying in Walsingham's house because this is where he is fetched from on 21 May, and the address is included in the instruction.

It was the Dutch Church Libel that lead to the arrest of Kyd, but Marlowe was not arrested because of this – indeed, he was not arrested at all. He was fetched in to attend the Privy Council, for reasons unknown. The court was at Greenwich in May 1593, and that would be where the Privy Council would sit, since it convened close to the sovereign. Marlowe is required to go to Greenwich every morning between 21 May (the day John Penry appeared before magistrates) and until whenever the Council could see him. They had not seen him by 30 May, when he apparently went to Deptford at the invitation of Ingram Frizer, a man employed by Thomas Walsingham. Since Marlowe and Frizer's party arrived at about 10 a.m. it is fair to suppose that Marlowe did not attend upon the Privy Council on 30 May, simply because there probably was not time – or perhaps there was not the need.

The evening before, John Penry had been hanged at St Thomas-a-Watering, having been rushed from his dinner at around midday, and told to prepare to die. Not inexplicably wherever he was buried was not bruited abroad for fear the place would become a shrine or gathering place for Separatists. Even so, there is no record of any sort of his burial upon 29 May.

Penry had been arrested before the Dutch Church Libel appeared and has no connection with it. Marlowe's being requested to attend on the Privy Council the day of Penry's committal to trial may be a coincidence (his trial was actually on 25 May). Marlowe was pointed to by the Dutch Church libelist's comments. So why was Thomas Kyd arrested and not Marlowe or Walsingham?

Thomas Kyd said that he was informed on[3]. He explicitly says so in his letter to Sir John Puckering. He writes: (if) 'some outcast *Ishmael* for want or of his own dipose to lewdnes, have with pretext of duetie or religion, or to reduce himself to that he was not borne unto (,) by enie

---

3   Kuriyama -Christopher Marlowe A Renaissance Life, p. 230: Kyd's letter to Sir John Puckering.

waie incensed your l(ordshi)ps to suspect me'. Kyd is saying that someone betrayed him for money or advantage, pretending it was duty or support for religion. He believed this was why he was arrested and his rooms searched. But Thomas Kyd seems to have led a blameless life, writing and selling plays, and attached to a patron and a theatre troupe. Among the throng of poets and playwrights filling London Kyd was remarkable in that he was not engaged in espionage and seems to have had nothing to do with the gang violence, prostitution and gambling that took place in the Liberties. He seems utterly innocent of harm.

Yet he says someone informed on him. Who and why?

To give any answers then the question of Thomas Kyd's arrest must be turned on its head. It was not Marlowe who was the target of the Privy Council. It cannot have been. It looks as if Kyd did not make his disposition until after 30 May[4] (and also that Puckering and the Privy Council did not see the Baines Note until after 30 May either). With this in mind, Marlowe cannot have been the target of the Privy Council. They arrested Kyd, so Kyd must have been their target – this is the simplest explanation. It was his rooms they searched and his papers. They were clearly looking for something that Kyd had done, not Marlowe. The Arian papers turned up as a bonus – but were not associated with Marlowe. It is Kyd who is accused of atheism, unjustly, he says in his letter to Puckering.

---

4   Kyd's Letter to Puckering c. June 1593 quoted in Kuriyama - *Christopher Marlowe A Renaissance Lif*e. Transcriptions and Translations, p.229..

I think what the Privy Council was looking for in Kyd's rooms was proof that he was the author of the Dutch Church Libel. This is what Kyd says he was suspected of: 'I was first suspected of that Libell that concerned the state'.

The verses were in pentameters, which Kyd could easily write, and were an indictment of the government for supporting foreigners over English people, as well as a rallying call for Londoners to attack the immigrants.

'Ye strangers y^t doe inhabite in this lande
Note this same writing doe it vnderstand
Conceit it well for savegard of your lyves
Your goods, your children, & your dearest wives.'

And:

'In Chambers, twenty in one house will lurke,
Raysing of rents, was never knowne before
Living farre better then at native home
And our pore soules, are cleane thrust out of dore.'

In these lines the Dutch Church Libel is not significantly different from some of the writing of the English Defence League, and the sentiments expressed and complaints made are similar, especially the lines about renting out property, and immigrants being squeezed into poor accommodation. And they are incitements to social unrest, which could not be tolerated by the Privy Council.

The Libel also implies that Marlowe is the author of the verses. They are signed with the name of his most famous character and refer to some of his recent plays.

Thus:
'Your Machiavellian Marchant spoyles the state
Your vsery doth leave vs all for deade
Your Artifex, & craftesman works our fate,
And like the Jewes, you eate us vp as bread.'

These lines can be clearly read as a reference to *The Jew of Malta*, performed in London the previous January.

And again, the last few lines, indicting the aristocracy and then suggesting a possible author of the verses:

'Nobles said I? nay men to be reiected,
Upstarts yt enioy the noblest seates
That wound their Countries brest, for lucres sake
And wrong our gracious Queene & Subiects good
By letting strangers make our harts to ake
For which our swords are whet, to shedd their blood
And for a truth let it be vnderstoode
Fly, Flye, & never returne.
per. Tamberlaine'[5]

    There is a clear and instantly recognisable reference to Christopher Marlowe in the signature: by Tamberlaine, implying: by Christopher Marlowe.
    If Kyd were the author of the Libel why would he implicate fellow playwright and room mate Marlowe? Perhaps because the relationships in 1590s London, among

---

5   Bodleian Library, MS.Don.d.152 f.4v, and transcribed by Arthur Freeman in his article *'Marlowe, Kyd, and the Dutch Church Libel'*, English Literary Renaissance 3, 1973.

playwrights, were not particularly harmonious. There is no reason to suppose Kyd and Marlowe were friends. As playwrights they were rivals, and Kyd, whose *Spanish Tragedy* had been an early success, was probably on the way down in popularity, whilst Marlowe was still on the rise. It is more likely that Kyd, like Greene in a similar position, felt jealousy rather than admiration for Marlowe. Having a rival arraigned on a charge of treason (or atheism), would certainly slow, and maybe even stop[6], his rise in popularity, leaving space for other playwrights. Thus, it looks as if Kyd has good reason to suggest that Marlowe is the author of the Libel, as, apart from shifting suspicion from himself and whoever he was working for, it eliminated a potent rival.

Two problems flow from the realisation that Kyd is the real suspect, arrested for what he is supposed to have done, not as a conduit to Marlowe. The first is why Kyd published the Dutch Church Libel. The second is who informed on him.

Kyd had a patron in the theatre world. But we are not sure who that patron was. The choices are Lord Pembroke, Lord Sussex[7] or Lord Strange. Of the three the most consistently found as a patron is Lord Strange, a supporter of the arts all his life, and so he is likely to be Kyd's. And in his letter to Sir John Puckering in June 1593, Kyd says that his acquaintance with Marlowe 'rose upon his bearing name

---

6   Kyd never recovered from being charged with atheism. He could get neither patron nor theatre troupes to take his work, and died in poverty in August 1594.

7   Kyd's last publication was dedicated to the Countess of Sussex.

to serve my Lo(rd)...in writing for his plaiers'.[8] Marlowe wrote plays for Lord Strange's Men from 1591. Kyd might also have worked for Strange in another capacity, for example as a secretary. As the son of a scrivener and a pupil at Merchant Taylors he would have a good hand, (Kuriyama describes Kyd's letter to Puckering as being in an elegant secretary hand) and be used to copying documents. Indeed, it has already been suggested that it was as a copyist for actors that Kyd made his way into playwrighting. And Kyd must know Strange well, for he says of him that he 'does not know Marlowe except for writing plays for his players'.

At the beginning of 1594 it took Lord Stanley (by then Earl of Derby) ten days to decide to tell Robert Cecil he had been approached from Prague, by Richard Hesketh (a member of a well-respected Lancastrian family, which was aligned with the Stanleys), with a view to putting Stanley on the throne of England. It is possible that he did have ambitions to become king (his mother certainly did not want herself displaced in the succession by Elizabeth's marriage and possible motherhood, as she was accused of speaking against the Queen's suggested marriage to the Duc d'Alençon in 1579, and, like Shakespeare's Duchess of Gloucester, was even suspected of using sorcery to poison the Queen[9]). In his middle thirties, Stanley possibly had time to act, but unrest in London perhaps coupled with

---

8   Kyd's Letter to Puckering c. June 1593 quoted in Kuriyama, ibid. Transcriptions and Translations p229.

9   Lawrence Manley, "*From Strange's Men to Pembroke's Men: 2 "Henry VI" and "The First Part of the Contention"*, Shakespeare Quarterly, vol. 54, No. 3 (Autumn, 2003), pp. 253-287.

dissatisfaction with the religious and political situation – as exemplified by Greenwood, Barrowe and Penry – might have suggested a method of making his way clear to a throne. He also had the support of Catholics who saw him as a better replacement for Elizabeth than the Presbyterian James VI. Causing riots with anti-foreigner propaganda was not unknown, and unrest in London (as Essex hoped eight years later) could lead the government to fall, and with it the Queen, who was not as popular as later generations believe. Elizabeth was in any case getting old and there was a general worry about the succession, which, for example, Shakespeare exploits in his history plays running from *Henry IV* to *Richard III*, showing the consequences for a realm that an uncertain succession brought. James of Scotland was the favoured candidate, backed by Burghley and Cecil (who were positioning themselves for his succession), but he was actually debarred both by Henry VIII's will and the Third Succession Act as well as by Edward VI's letters patent to the same effect. The descendants of Margaret Tudor were debarred as 'foreigners' in favour of the descendants of Mary Tudor from her marriage to Charles Brandon, Duke of Suffolk. This legal settlement, in default of Katherine Grey's sons whose legitimacy was uncertain until after Elizabeth's death, left Ferdinando Stanley and his daughters (the eldest was Anne Stanley) as the heirs presumptive to the English throne through Stanley's mother, Margaret Clifford (d.1596). Since neither Cecil nor Burghley were likely to back the Stanley claim the only way forward for Lord Strange was to ferment rebellion. The Dutch Church Libel might well have been put up at his instigation.

If so, then Kyd would most likely have been in Strange's pay for the actual text, and his arrest was an attack by the Privy Council on Lord Strange, not on Christopher Marlowe.

But if that is the case it still does not explain who it was informed on Kyd in the first place. Who does Kyd mean by 'some outcast *Ishmael*'[10]? It seems Kyd does not know. Yet there is one clear candidate for this rôle, a person who had been called by the Privy Council as a witness, and who had been implicated as the writer of the Libels by the inclusion of his work. Christopher Marlowe (and his alter ego William Shakespeare), agent for the Privy Council, is the person most likely to have informed on Thomas Kyd, for he is perhaps the only person in a position to know who the author was, having contacts both in the world of playwrights and the world of spies, and probably the world of court intrigue. He is also attached to Lord Strange through his work as a playwright and claims acquaintance with him in Flushing, where his meeting with Gilbert could have included early arrangements for the Hesketh plot[11] as well as alchemy, through the agency of Gilbert, if he was the alchemist Tankard. Lord Strange repudiates the claim he

---

10   Ismael, the eldest son of Abraham, was outcast before he was born. God said that he would be a contentious person and that every man's hand would be against him. Kyd is suggesting someone on the fringes of respectability has betrayed him, someoe he sees as an outcast.

11   The Hesketh Affair seems to be another of Burghley and Cecil's plots to discredit English Catholics. The most well known of these attempts are the Babbington Plot, in which Robert Poley was involved, and the Gunpowder Plot, which seems entirely a government fabrication.

knows Marlowe, suggesting he does not want to be associated with whatever Marlowe is doing in Flushing, or possibly that he is worried that admitting acquaintance might lead to uncomfortable revelations about his own activities.

Marlowe is also the most likely person to have put the Arian heresy papers into Kyd's bundle of work, firstly as it is likely he had access to such a piece of writing[12] and secondly as retribution for implying that he was the author of the Dutch Libel and thus being put in danger of arrest. As a government agent, breaking into property, picking locks and planting evidence convincingly would have been skills he possessed as well. That Kyd had no idea the Arian papers were in his bundle seems evident; he says he handed them over willingly. It is most unlikely, as a working writer, that he had not looked through his papers in two years, but he can think of no excuse for heretic writings among them except that he and Marlowe were writing in the same room two years earlier and that Marlowe's things must have got mixed up with his own. There is no evidence except Kyd's deposition that he and Marlowe ever worked together, and socially they are poles apart. Marlowe is a university wit, Kyd is a grammar school boy who never went to university. They would scarcely be friends, let alone share a room. That the Privy Council seem to have thought much the same and took no notice of the imputation of Marlowe's guilt is clear,

---

12   The text was from John Proctour's *Fall of the late Arrian* (a refutation of the Arrian heresy), a copy of which was held at the King's School in Canterbury. It had belonged to the schoolmaster, John Gresshop.

since they did not have him arrested; instead they seem to have called him as a witness, probably against Kyd, rather than accusing him of heresy.

In implying that Marlowe was the author of the Dutch Church Libel it is likely that Kyd was unaware that Marlowe/Shakespeare was a government agent. He was not a spy himself, and by his own admission to Puckering, he did not know Marlowe well, indeed they were not friends – 'That I should love or be familiar frend, with one so irreligious, were verie[13] rare'. It is doubtful Kyd would have asserted he was not friends with Marlowe if someone, for example Lord Starnge, or some other playwright or actor, could have come forward to contradict him. He was also clearly unaware that Marlowe, or rather Shakespeare, was under the protection of the Privy Council, which had seen him escape consequences of his actions before – the Council was not likely to damage its own agent in this case either. That his choice of victim lighted on Christopher Marlowe/William Shakespeare was thus unfortunate for Kyd, and shows he really did not know Marlowe well, since Marlowe/Shakespeare had the easy means of informing on him – and would do so without a second thought, just as would have Poley or any other in the service of the Privy Council. Had Kyd any inkling of this it is unlikely he would have accused Marlowe, for his own safety's sake.

Kyd's arrest and Marlowe's being called to attend on the Privy Council now appear to have nothing to do with the

---

13   Here 'verie' would appear to have its old meaning: 'truly', rather than modifying rare in the more modern sense of 'extremely'. Kyd is emphasising that he is telling the truth.

events at Deptford Strand. Marlowe is not in danger of being tried for treason or atheism and no-one appears to want him dead. Indeed, he looks as if he is a valued witness in the prosecution of Kyd. So why, on 30 May is he dead?

Chapter Fifteen

The Three Musketeers?
Robert Poley, Ingram Frizer, Nicholas Skeres – and Eleanor Bull

On 30 May 1593, nine days after he has been asked to attend on the Privy Council, Marlowe is lying dead at a house in Deptford Strand, surrounded, according to the coroner's report, by his three friends, Robert Poley, Ingram Frizer and Nicholas Skeres. These three were accepted as reliable witnesses by the inquest, but as noted in Chapter Two, they were all, in various ways unreliable.

Robert Poley, who presumably bore witness to the affray in Deptford, was a spy, or rather, a government agent working for the Elizabethan secret service which was centred around Francis Walsingham, Lord Burghley and Sir Robert Cecil. As in any age there were many spies but the Elizabethans were particularly worried about foreign and particularly Catholic plots against the sovereignty of Queen Elizabeth. Catholic Europe considered her a bastard with no right to rule England, and promoted in various ways her replacement by her rival, Mary Queen of Scots. Elizabeth had finally agreed to Mary being executed in 1587 but this did not abate the fear of foreign invasion.

Robert Poley had been involved in several unmaskings of anti-government plots, most notably the Babington Plot, where he had become a confidant of Anthony Babington, inveigling himself into the inner circle of this plot and finally revealing it, leading to the arrest, torture and execution of the main participants.

Poley entered the service of Walsingham via Sir Philip Sydney's household. Sydney had married Walsingham's daughter, Frances. The year before Poley entered this service he had been imprisoned for alienation of affection – he had seduced another man's wife and continued to see her after he had been sent to gaol. He became involved in the Babington plot by posing as a Catholic – a role he must have used for some years for it to be convincing. Anthony Babington did not entirely trust him and yet did not cast him off either. Poley went to prison as a plotter as a result of his investigation of Babington – there is some suggestion he was actually an agent provocateur – and once he was released his cover as a Catholic was blown. Thereafter he served a more administrative role. However, in 1592/3 he was engaged by Burghley on work in Scotland and was under government contract until June 1593, thus covering the period when Marlowe was arrested for heresy and the events at Deptford. By the time of Marlowe's death Frances Walsingham had been widowed (Sidney died in 1586) and had married Robert Devereaux, Earl of Essex, the then favourite of Queen Elizabeth.

Ingram Frizer, the man who actually claimed to have killed Marlowe, was an employee, but not a servant, of

Thomas Walsingham. He was probably born in Kingsclere, Hampshire in 1561, the son of Stephen Ingram; at least there is a baptismal record listed in the International Genealogical Index for a female Ingram Frizer for 26th September 1561 and a parish record for a son of Stephen Ingram, Ingram Frizer. He seems to have been a property speculator and commodity broker as well as what might be termed a 'fixer' for gentlemen of 'good worship'. His deals were not always honest as was the one he arranged with Drew Woodleff in 1593. Woodleff signed a bond for £60 in exchange for some guns which Frizer had, which Frizer then claimed to have sold on Woodleff's behalf, but for only £30, thus leaving Woodleff £30 in arrears. Eventually Woodleff signed a bond to Thomas Walsingham offering a forfeit of land in order to be free of Frizer's bond. This seems like complete double dealing, for Woodleff at no point was in possession of either the guns or the money for which he gave Frizer a bond – but ownership was so muddied by the end that the bond was impossible to refuse. Nicholas Skeres was also implicated in this particular trickery and he and Frizer may have made a living luring young men into borrowing money which they had to pay back at high interest. The profit on the Woodleff deal was one hundred per cent.

After Marlowe's death Frizer continued in the employment of Thomas Walsingham, and his wife Audrey, and received favours from them and from James I. Some have thought that this suggests that either Walsingham or his wife Audrey arranged for Frizer to murder Marlowe as he had become a dangerous encumbrance to them because of his atheism and suggested homosexuality.

The third witness to the murder of Marlowe was Nicholas Skeres. He was born in London in March 1563, the son of a merchant tailor, like Kyd. His father died when he was three, leaving him money and property. Instead of attending the merchant tailors' school he joined Furnival's Inn, one of the Inns of Court, and so must have received some education – if so he may be the Skeggs who accompanied Thomas Walsingham to France in 1581. However, he may later have fallen somewhat down the social scale as he may be the Nicholas Skeers listed by William Fleetwood, in a letter to Lord Burghley in July 1585, as a cut-purse and masterless man, engaged in robbing gentlemen's chambers and artificers' shops. In 1586 Nicholas Skeres was employed by Francis Walsingham, Burghley's associate, in uncovering the Babington Plot. He is noted by Walsingham's people as one of Babington's associates, along with Henry Dunn (who was executed for his part in the plot) but disappears from the record, presumably because he was a government plant.

Whilst in government service Skeres continued with his other activities, acting as a lure for a skinner (a moneylender) called Wolfall[1], accused in the Court of Star Chamber of obtaining money under false pretences in April 1593. Wolfall was clearly a moneylender preying on young men and Skeres admitted working for him (under duress, he claimed) for ten or twelve years. If he was under duress to Wolfall it is odd that he is carrying out the same scam with Ingram Frizer in the same year. Skeres, however, continued in the employ of Francis Walsingham, carrying letters from him to the Earl of Essex in 1589. By 1591 he is employed

---

1 Tarrant, who might have been Gifford Gilbert the goldsmith and possible alchemist, was indebted to Wolfall by 1595.

by Essex and goes to France with him. There seems to have been some falling out between 1593 and 1596, as Skeres petitions Essex's secretary to get him back into favour – this might have to do with the death of Christopher Marlowe but is more likely to be connected to the arrest of Nicholas Williamson for treason in 1594. Skeres was among those arrested as being in Williamson's house, but was released as having given a reasonable account for his being there – he was probably spying on Williamson. Whatever the cause of Skeres' rift with Essex he was among those arrested in 1601 when the Essex Rebellion ended in failure. He probably died in the Bridewell, to which he was transferred from Newgate. At any rate he disappears.

These then were the three men who witnessed to the death of Christopher Marlowe on 30 May. All three were liars, confidence tricksters and the type of man who would say anything to save their own reputation or life. They are not reliable witnesses.

But what of Eleanor Bull, who ran the house in Deptford? She was a widow, and a relative of one of the Queen's intimates, Blanche Parry, Chief Gentlewoman of the Queen's Privy Chamber (and therefore a woman who controlled access to the Queen), who had left her a legacy. She might have been distantly related to Lord Burghley, who was a friend of Blanche Parry, and perhaps could call in that direction for assistance. She might also have been someone the court could call on for aid. It may be that her house, where she let out a room and use of the garden to gentlemen, was actually a government safe house or meeting place, where agents could freely go, assignments could be given, a lover met with, or where someone might lie low if their activities had got them into trouble with the authorities as had Marlowe's in 1587 when Corpus Christi refused to give him his MA because he had been continuously absent. If the house at Deptford was such, then Marlowe was there for a reason, either to be rescued or to be killed. If murdered, then why and by whom? If rescued, then why and by whom? And then, in the case of rescue, whose body was substituted for Marlowe's?

Twenty-four hours before Marlowe's death John Penry was taken from prison and hanged privately – that is with no witnesses, and without the presence or knowledge of his wife and family. There is no record of his burial, no body. So now there are two deaths within twenty-four hours, geographically quite close to each other, of two men who were a thorn in the establishment flesh, but only one body, which is rather hastily buried in St. Nicholas's churchyard in Deptford. So who was John Penry and what happened to him?

John Penry was a protestant preacher. He had been at Peterhouse, Cambridge, in 1580 and knew the preacher John Greenwood, who was hanged in March 1593. It was at Cambridge that he probably converted from Catholicism to Protestantism. He may have been the man behind the Marprelate pamphlets that scourged the Elizabethan clergy and particularly Archbishop Whitgift, who was the first signatory on his death warrant. Certainly he was associated with secret printers such as Waldegrave and John Hodgkins, who was arrested in 1589. Penry escaped to Scotland but returned by 1592, becoming involved in Puritan circles but taking no public role. He was arrested on 22 March 1593 and accused of sedition. A petition among his private papers was used as proof of guilt and he was sentenced to death.

John Penry's body has frequently been cited as the likely substitute for Marlowe's body. But this is impossible, for Penry is supposed to have been hanged, and the jurors would have seen the signs of hanging on the body, rope marks and stretching and a broken neck, the face discoloured – they would not have accepted such a body as a stab victim. So Penry's hanged body cannot have been substituted. But what of Penry's stabbed body?

Penry's death merits closer look. It is said that on the evening of 29 May he was summarily removed from the Poultry Compter prison, while at *supper*, and taken to St Thomas-a-Watering, where he was hanged at about four in the afternoon – an unusual time of day for a hanging, the execution having been put off from the 28 May.

This is odd. Odder still is that there is no contemporary account of these events, but only one written several years later by a person not present at Penry's death. From what is known of Penry he was an itinerant preacher, and perhaps the first protestant preacher in Wales (he was born in Brecknockshire between 1559 and 1563, and was thus similar in age to Marlowe and Shakespeare) and, after his sojourn in Scotland, a Puritan separatist, having spent his time there writing tracts in supporting the Scots church against its critics. He was wont to disguise himself as a gallant when seeking to escape his persecutors – a disguise also frequently used by Roman Catholic priests.

Why was Penry's execution put off and then so hurriedly and inhumanely carried out without an opportunity, usually given to condemned men, for him to take leave of his wife, Eleanor, and their four daughters? Such haste argues some plot or intrigue being involved. Penry had been interviewed by Burghley and was known to the state's intelligence service. He journeyed into Scotland, a safe place for Protestants but also a destination taken by men (for example the poet Royston) wishing to throw their allegiance behind the candidacy of James VI as Elizabeth's heir , and a place where spies of the Privy Council, such as Poley, were sent to gather information. Penry was contacting the Scottish church. When he returned he became intimate with extreme protestant preachers, including Greenwood, who has been shown to be acquainted with Marlowe, and Henry Barrowe, who were both hanged during the time when Penry was associating with them. He himself was arrested on the word of a local vicar at Ratcliffe, who recognised him. He had a personal interview with Lord Burghley. His execution is put off and then he is hurried away. No-one saw the execution on 29 May.

Chapter Sixteen

John Penry – Like Macavity, he's not there!

John Penry is the final actor in the drama at Deptford. As we have seen, John Penry was a Welsh preacher who showed remarkable ability to get from under persecution by the state. He is also almost certainly one of the authors of the Marprelate tracts, along with Job Throckmorton. It has been suggested, by the style of writing, that another one of his co-authors was Christopher Marlowe.[1]

Penry was a true radical. One of those who gave no tolerance to people with other beliefs. In this he is a precursor of the Pilgrim Fathers, who left for the Americas not so much to flee persecution as to flee lack of persecution of those with whom they disagreed, and the Puritans and Parliamentarians who took arms against Charles I and

---

1   Other researchers do not think this to be the case, though the double 'mar' in Martin Marprelate is tempting as a pun on Marlowe's name.

absolute monarchy. They would all very much agree with Jesus in saying 'he who is not with me is against me'. [2]

Very little is known about John Penry's origins. He was born in Wales, on a prosperous farm near Llangammarch – at least Cefn Brith is his traditional birthplace – between 1559 and 1563,[3] and he seems to have been roughly the same age as Marlowe and Shakespeare, thus about twenty-nine or thirty in 1593. Like Marlowe he went to Cambridge in December 1580, to Peterhouse, but then moved to St Alban Hall, Oxford for his M.A. He seems to have started out life as a conventional Welsh Catholic but been influenced by Protestantism and Puritanism at Cambridge. He remained within what was becoming the Anglican Church, however, until his sojourn in Scotland from 1590 to 1593 after which he joined the London Separatist group to which also belonged Marlowe's Corpus Christi colleague John Greenwood[4], and Greenwood's friend, Henry Barrowe,[5] who had matriculated from Clare College (Hall) and taken his B.A. in 1570. Penry was a licensed preacher and not ordained. In this he differs from

---

2   Matthew 12:30 - Authorized Version.
3   1559 is the date given by the 1911 Encypaedia Britannica, 1563 by Llangammarch Wells own web page.
4   He entered Corpus Christi as a sizar in March (Lent term) 1577 (NS 1578) and commenced his degree in 1581. He uses Marlowe's buttery allowance on one occasion. Greenwood, John (GRNT577J) A Cambridge Alumni Database. University of Cambridge.
5   Horne, C. Silvester. "A Popular History of the Free Churches", Fifth Edition, James Clarke & Co., London, 1903 Barrowe was also hanged 6 April 1593.

other players on this stage, many of whom were ordained, for example John Greenwood, though he repudiated his ordination as 'unlawful', and some, such as Richard Baines, ordained as both Protestant and Catholic priests.

Beyond those bare details little is known of Penry's early life. However, he was clearly a charismatic preacher and was known for the beauty and melliflousness of his voice, actually called 'Telyn Cymru', 'the harp of Wales'.[6]

More than that, Penry appears to be a passionate man of many faces. His disguise mirrors that frequently used by Catholic priests travelling about England for he would dress himself on his journeyings as a gallant, in a long sky-blue cloak, trimmed with gold and silver lace, his costume finished off with a soft, light coloured hat. He also carried a sword, but this would not be unusual in the sixteenth century – any gentleman was entitled to one, and Penry, as a graduate of Oxford and Cambridge, counted as such. His passion seems to have extended to his marriage, for not only does his wife travel with him to Scotland, but they have four children in four years. This suggests a close and happy relationship, for the natural interval between births is generally two years, and it seems Penry and Eleanor had been in love for many years whilst he was a lodger in her father's house, before they were able to marry.

Penry's historical importance rests in his connection with the Marprelate Controversy. Those who seek to find a body to place at Deptford look also at his hurried, and

---

6   Source: Powys Digital History Project.

unrecorded execution, and the lack of a burial place for his body.[7]

One thing to note about Penry is that association with him leads to arrest and imprisonment. The printer, Hodgkins, loses his livelihood – his press is smashed – thanks to working with Penry, who got away scot free while Hodgkins and his associates were arrested.[8] Others, such as Greenwood and Barrowe, lose their lives, and other associates like Mistress Crane are heavily questioned about the activities of Penry's press.

Penry first comes to notice in 1587 when protesting to Archbishop Whitgift that there are too few Bibles in the Welsh language, only just enough for each parish to have one. His pamphlet, *The Aequity of an Humble Supplication*, brought forward a request that provision be made for preaching the Gospel in Wales, pointing out that the printing of Welsh Bibles in 1567 was in insufficient numbers to provide every parish with a copy. In the tract Penry was very careful to distance himself from criticising the Queen, the Supreme Governor of the church, as being associated with the actions of her bishops, thus avoiding the charge that he was attacking the Queen herself. This was an important distinction, since criticising Elizabeth herself would have attracted a possible charge of treason. However, Archbishop Whitgift saw the pamphlet as a personal attack

---

[7] The Welsh Independent Chapels in West Carmarthenshire asked that the Church of England apologize for the death of John Penry, who they regard as 'the father of their faith', in 2008. BBC Online News 15/5/2008. Penry is regarded as a Puritan martyr.

[8] Honan, P, in *Christopher Marlowe, Poet and Spy*.

on him and the church and imprisoned Penry for twelve days, although he was actually held for a month – and tortured.

On his release Penry married Eleanor Godley the daughter of Henry Godley of Northampton, and then lived in Northampton, his wife's home town, for a while. After 1588 the Marprelate tracts begin to appear, as well as Penry's own work. The Marprelate tracts are definite attacks on episcopy, singling out particular bishops (such as Bishop Cooper) for especial condemnation. It is episcopy and its trappings that Penry, and his co-conspirators, object to, believing it to be unnecessary in a Protestant church.

Though the theological aspects of the Marprelate tracts look as if they may be Penry's input, the humourous style of the writing does not match Penry's style in his other works, as pointed out by enquirers at the time. A more likely candidate for authorship is Job Throckmorton, a friend of Penry's and in whose house Penry set up his printing press at one time. Matthew Sutcliffe, a pamphleteer on Whitgift's side, accused Throckmorton of being the author and Throckmorton vehemently denied this, in 1595, unsurprisingly as admission could have led to his arrest and imprisonment. However, the authorship of the pamphets is not the main interest here (even if they were written by Christopher Marlowe), but rather the history of Penry's movements and the assaults upon his press and printers.

These events are interesting as, until his arrest as a Separatist in 1593, Penry avoids capture each time and is able to escape, whereas his companions are often taken.

In February 1588 one Robert Waldgrave's printing work was severely restricted by the Court of Star Chamber. Waldegrave took his type and moved out of London, where he had been publishing near the sign of the Crane[9] in Paul's churchyard. He moved to the house of Elizabeth Crane in East Moseley[10]. Mistress Crane was the widow of the Cofferer of Elizabeth's household, a member of the Board of Green Cloth which controlled the household finances. There he seems to have met Penry who had with him a press he had purchased from a Dutchman (according to evidence given to the Court of High Commission[11]). Waldegrave and Penry remained at Mistress Crane's over midsummer, for the three weeks around 21 June and returned at Michaelmas, around 29 September. In November the press was removed to Northamptonshire, to the house of Sir Richard Knightley (who was later arrested on charges of printing the Marprelate tracts and other separatist literature) at Fawsley Hall. Penry paid the large sum of 50/- to have the press carried from London to Fawsley Hall by Master Jeff of Upton, a tenant of Knightley's son. Within weeks Martin

---

9   During the 1580s Waldegrave was at Without Temple Bar in The Strand, near Somerset House, and briefly in Foster's Lane in 1583. Later he was printing from the Sign of the Crane, in St Paul's Churchyard and also at the White Horse in Cannon Lane.

10   According to Elizabeth Crane's servant, Nicholas Tomkins, during his interrogation, Giles Wiggington, later involved with William Hacket, was at East Moseley. Wiggington was questioned about his involvement in December 1588, refused to take the *ex officio* oath (Burghley likened this oath to the Spanish Inquisition) and was imprisoned. Examinations of Nicholas Tomkins (February 15, 1589; November 29, 1589) The Martin Marprelate Press: A Documentary History. UMASS, Document 9.

11   Perhaps Vound Hoēl, whose name was given to the Court of High Commission by Nicholas T(h)ompkins. Source: doc 19, The Martin Marprelate Press: A Documentary History. UMASS.

Marprelate's *Epiphany* was published. Another move took place in January 1589 (NS), to an empty farmhouse belonging to Knightley, near Daventry. The stay here was brief (it seems to have been a hiding place the farmhouse was empty) before everyone was again on the move to White Friars, a house belonging to Knightley's relative, John Hale, who later claimed he only took it in at his wife's behest, and found himself heavily fined for 'obaying' his wife. A third Martin Marprelate tract was printed and distributed from here, along with Penry's *A View of Some Parte of Public Wants.* A fourth Marprelate tract followed, *Hay Any Worke for a Cooper,* (an attack on Bishop Cooper) which took approximately three weeks to print. Penry moved into Job Throckmorton's house at Hasley while it was being printed.

    At this point Waldegrave seems to have decided to quit. Penry reported that the printer had taken himself to La Rochelle, but there is little evidence of this. However, he eventually arrived in Edinburgh and set up in business, later becoming the King's printer. Waldegrave's place was taken in July by John Hodgkins. There is no mention of him in at the Stationers' Office, so where he learned his craft is uncertain – perhaps abroad. He does not seem such an expert printer as Waldegrave, but was assisted by Valentine Simmes and Arthur Thomlyn[12] who were. While they remained the Marprelate printers the press moved to Roger Wigston's home, Wolston Priory[13]. Later the press was

---

12   They printed the tracts known as *Martin Junior* and *Martin Senior.*
13   Possibly then known as Priory Farm - the printing was done in the cellar.

moved again, this time finally, to Manchester. And in August 1589 the press was seized there by agents of Lord Derby[14], and Hodgkin was ruined. But Penry seems to have been warned of the raid on his press and he escaped capture. He fled to Scotland where he remained, to all the intents and purposes of the government, until 1593.

So, much to-ing and fro-ing, whilst the press was pursued at every turn and those who supported it marked for arrest. The Marprelate tracts caused controversy and anger. The church looked for writers who could produce as witty and amusing tracts as Marprelate to counter his influence. Among those chosen for the work were Greene and Nashe [15]- and perhaps Christopher Marlowe. If Marlowe did have a hand in the Marprelate tracts this would be ironic.

Once the printers were found in Manchester all was finished as far as Marprelate went. The printers were tortured, and the distributor of the tracts, Henry Sharpe, was identified and arrested. He was able to name all those involved, but could not identify who had been Marprelate. By October Elizabeth Crane (now Carleton, as she had remarried), Sir Richard Knightley, John Hale, Roger Wigston and his wife were all arrested, to be interrogated and fined. (The fines were later remitted by Whitgift's order. Whitgift wanted to find the tracts' perpetrators and was little interested in the minor backers.)

But Penry escaped, just as he had during the raid on his house in Northampton. He and his wife and two daughters fled to Edinburgh, where Penry had more

---

14   Ferdinando Stanley's father, Henry Stanley.
15   Nashe wrote the pamphlet *An Almond for a Parrot*.

pamphlets printed. However, despite the risk to his liberty, some suggest that Penry chose to journey back to London in the spring of 1591 when the Hackett-Coppinger plot[16] erupted, despite a Privy Council warrant being out for him since 1589.

William Hackett was a convert to Separatism and proclaimed himself first John the Baptist and then Jesus Christ. He was aided in his preaching, which drew huge crowds but also caused him to be whipped out of York and Leicester and jailed in Northampton, by his friends Edmund Coppinger and Henry Arthington (who seem to have met each other on 19 July 1591), and their mentor, Giles Wigginton. Giles Wigginton[17] had been at Mrs Crane's house while the first Marprelate pamphlets were printed, and was also known in Northamptonshire, where he seems to have converted Hackett from a dissolute and disorderly life during which he spent his time drinking and fighting – biting an opponent's nose off on one occasion.[18] Wigginton can be considered one of Penry's circle, at least while at Mistress Crane's.

The Hackett-Coppinger conspiracy's popularity seems now to be a completely inexplicable. Hackett

---

16   Winship, Michael P. (Univ of Georgia) *'Puritans, Politics and Lunacy.' The Coppinger-Hackett Conspiracy as the Apotheosis of Elizabethan Presbyterianism.* The Sixteenth Century Journal: The Journal of Early Modern Studies, Vol. 28 (2007)/2 (Summer) pp 345-346.
17   Ibid, The Martin Marprelate Press: A Documentary History. UMASS., Document 9.
18   Apparently this happened in a tavern quarrel, and the victim was a schoolmaster.

preached the dethroning of the Queen and of the Anglican episcopy, which was a to some extent in line with Separatist ideology, though most Separtists tried to avoid suggesting harm to the Queen because it would be seen as treason or sedition. However, Hackett added that he, William Hackett, was to becom king of Europe as he was Jesus Christ. Apparently Job Throckmorton heard Hackett preach and said he was on 'a wild goose chase'. However, it is unsurprising that once Hackett began to talk of revolutionary activity such as removing the Queen and bishops, the state took an interest in his apparent ravings, especially as he had acquired such a large following. The crisis came for the government when Hackett preached the coming judgement in Cheapside – the main shopping centre of London. There was a riot and Hackett and his co-conspirators hid in the Mermaid Tavern. The Privy Council felt the need to take action and Hackett, Coppinger and Arthington were arrested, and were locked up in the Bridewell. On 26 July Hackett was tried at Sessions House, near Newgate, found guilty and then hanged on 28 July. Coppinger was not hanged but is described as having starved himself to death, dying in the Bridewell on 29 July – this seems a little quick for starvation, so the manner of Coppinger's death remains unknown, and rather suspicious; possibly he died from torture. Henry Arthington appealed to his friends at court (he was a minor courtier) and was eventually released, having pleaded that he was 'bewitched'. Wigginton was also reprieved.

Penry had hoped that Hackett's preaching was the beginning of a new revolution. Since Wiggington and Penry knew each other Hackett can be seen as Penry's disciple, explaining why Penry should risk his life coming back to

London to oversee the rebellion. Penry was soon disabused of the idea that Hackett's preaching could lead to a Separatist revolution and returned to Scotland the same day Hackett was hanged, having spent some three months in London, arriving around Easter (14 April) and leaving at the end of July.

In Edinburgh Penry continued his work, though Elizabeth had asked James VI to expel him, and James said that he had complied , when he had not. The Scottish Puritans protected Penry from interference and extradition. Penry repaid their favour by writing a rebuttal of Richard Bancroft's[19] 1589 aspersions on the Scottish Presbyterians which said that they were disloyal to the crown, an accusation that Penry had been at pains to distance himself from in his writings in England. Penry wrote *A briefe discovery of the untruthes and slanders against the true governement of the church of Christ*, a pamphlet that was published anonymously by Penry's former associate, the printer Waldegrave. However, despite his warm welcome in Scotland Penry himself decided to return to England in September 1592, emboldened by the pardon given to Greenwood that year. Unfortunately for Penry he decided to join a Separatist group led by Barrowe and Greenwood and was caught up in the events that led to their arrests and deaths in March of 1593.

---

19   Richard Bancroft, future Archbishop of Canterbury. His speech at St. Paul's Cross denounced many presbyterian practices, and in particular he rejected the idea of private judegement of religious experience. (Encyclopedia Britannica).

Penry, who was still sought by the Privy Council, was recognised by the vicar of Stepney, the Reverand Anthony Anderson[20], while riding through Ratcliff, on his way to address a large Separatist meeting in Islington. He was arrested on 22 March, apparently in Ratcliff, at the bidding of Anderson. However, he seems to have escaped from the original meeting in Islington woods, although large numbers of Separatists were arrested there, and been taken up later. Arraigned for treason, Penry appealed to Lord Burghley, well-known for his dislike of hanging religious dissidents. It appears that Burghley, having signally failed to rescue Barrowe and Greenwood from Archbishop Whitgift's designs, made an attempt to get Penry released, but without success, possibly because the Queen herself was set against Penry, as was the majority of the Privy Council.

And here the story gets very confusing. On 21 May Penry appeared before magistrates. He was tried on 25 May 1593, before the Queen's Bench, for treason, but not as the writer of the Marprelate pamphlets. There was no clear evidence to link him to the pamphlets[21] that had so annoyed Whitgift, and none of the conspirators questioned by the Commissioners had ever said who Marprelate actually was. Given that the evidence was questionable Penry was indicted on writing that could actually be ascribed to him. For these writings, and not for the Marprelate controversy, he was found guilty of treason, and condemned to death,

---

20   Dictionary of National Biography, 1885-1900, Volume 44.
21   Arthur Hildersham (1563-1632) reported that Penry admittedd misleading 'souls' into not attending church, but maintained he was not Marprelate.

even though Penry himself said the writing were drafts containing other people's ideas, not his own. He admitted he had misled some souls by encouraging them not to attend church, but not the rest.

Penry appealed to Lord Burghley on 28 May, who said he could do nothing to stop the execution, which seems to have been set to take place on that day; but it did not take place. Penry wrote to his wife and four small daughters, giving his last advice to them before he died. He probably expected to have some time to reflect, and no doubt (as was usual) see his family before he was executed, but something very peculiar happened. At about dinnertime (*not* supper as previously said) on 29 May - so between eleven and twelve in the day - a warrant arrived, reportedly brought by the Sheriff, and signed by Archbishop Whitgift, Sir John Puckering, the Lord Privy Seal, and Sir John Popham, the Lord Chief Justice, saying Penry must be delivered into the hands of the bearers, who were to take him to be hanged. At between four and five o' clock that same day he was hanged at St Thomas-a-Watering[22], a few miles from Deptford Strand. There were few if any witnesses and who had come to fetch Penry to his hanging is unclear. Penry was not allowed to make the traditional speech, and his wife and children did not visit him before he died. His burial place is not only unknown, but no suggestion of a burial or burial place is recorded.

Waddinton, writing in 1854, says:
'... in the midst of his meal, Penry without ceremony was hurried on to his hurdle and dragged to St. Thomas-a-

---

22   Now part of the Old Kent Road.

Watering, where a gallows stood waiting its next victim. Having arrived there, Penry found no friend among the sprinkling of people who saw the grim cortege pass, and were drawn to the scene by their morbid curiousity. It was part of [Whitgift's] mean design to have none of the condemned man's friends present; and in any case, peremptory orders were issued to deny him the ordinary courtesy of the times, an opportunity at the gallows to bid farewell to the world, profess his innocence and loyalty.'[23]

But there was no report of his being seized and hanged until *Aerius Redivivus* by Peter Heylin[24] which was published posthumously in 1670. According Heylin[25] (who was a Royalist), as Pierce writes: 'Recording that Penry was executed at St. Thomas-a-Watering, he (Heylin)[26] then says, "that he was executed with a very thin company attending on him, for fear the Fellow might have raised some Tumult, either in going to the Gallows, or upon the Ladder".'[27]

And such a long gap before any real description of the event does seem a little odd, when Penry had been such

---

23 "Penry would have spoken, but the sheriff insisted, that neither in protestation of his loyalty, nor in the avowal of his innocence, should he utter a word. His life was taken, and the people were dispersed. The place of his burial is unknown". Waddington p204.
24 Peter Heylin, Royalist, sub-Dean of Westminster, 1599-1662.
25 *Aerius Redivivus : A History of the Presbyterians*, p. 325.
26 My addition.
27 Pierce, W., *John Penry, his life, times and writings*, p480.

an important figure in the Separatist movement and had been arrested and executed for treason. That he had been hanged was certainly made common knowledge - there are some popular rhymes celebrating his death - since there was no advantage in concealing his execution and great advantage in putting it about, but there is no contemporary account of who took him from prison or who witnessed the hanging. Additionally, St Thomas-a-Watering was a place where those accused of similar matters as Penry were likely to be hanged, which makes the 'thin company' unusual, but also raises questions as to why the place execution was known but the execution has no contemporary description. One must ask, what then happened at St Thomas-a-Watering, and who fetched Penry from prison to be hanged there? One might also ask, why was Christopher Marlowe in attendance on the Privy Council from the day of Penry's trial, but never seen?

Chapter Seventeen

Who Died in Deptford?

The inquest at Deptford on 31 May is deeply suspect. We have the testimony of only three witnesses, and although the killing of Christopher Marlowe is within the verge (as confirmed by Frizer's pardon on 28 June) there is only one coroner present, when there ought to be two. Although, as has already been explained, the lack of the second coroner does not make the inquest illegal, it does make it questionable.

When examining the inquest into the death of a gentleman at Deptford Strand in 1593 we must not imagine anything like a modern, or even a late nineteenth century, coroner's court. Coroners (originally crowners) were first appointed to investigate crimes, including sudden, unexplained deaths, during the reign of Richard I. In setting up crowners' courts the state's interest was not only justice but also financial reward. Until 1887 inquests into sudden deaths (other crimes had been removed from the coroners' jurisdiction by the late nineteenth century) involved the crown receiving much of the estates of those identified as perpetrators. Both murderers and suicides, and their families, faced confiscation of all their property[1]. Thus, the coroner and his jury were open to pressure from the state to get a verdict favourable to the crown, and pressure from those called to the inquest to decide against murder and suicide. Such pressure might be in the form of bribes, or political pressure.

Nor is this the only difference from a modern inquest. True, witness statements were carefully recorded. However, close examination of the body was not a feature of a coroner's investigation. A wound was shown in the eye of the dead man, and this was claimed to be the cause of death. The witnesses were men of good employment and character as far as the jury and coroner were concerned. An employee of the Privy Council and Lord Burghley, a member of Lord Essex's household, and a member of Sir Thomas Walsingham's menage, who knew the victim as one of Walsingham's protégés. It seems strange to us that men we

---

1   Hogarth, in the final painting from the sequence 'Marriage à la Mode', shows the Countess's relatives removing her jewellery as she is dying, having committed suicide, as everything of which she died possessed became the property of the crown.

know to have been spies and confidence tricksters, and in Poley's case probably an àgent provocateur, would be accepted by a coroner's jury as respectable, but they would have been. No-one would suggest that the Privy Council, the Earl of Essex or Sir Thomas Walsingham, would employ rogues and cheats, thus impugning the honesty and probity of the state. So, their testimony was accepted without much question. Frizer found himself in prison for a month, but doubtless he was quite sure he would receive the Queen's pardon – after all, she had wanted Marlowe dead.

So there would have been no close questioning of the witnesses and no close examination of the body – this the more so as it was June, warm, plague was in the air (supposed to be carried by 'bad airs' indeed) and the body was now a day old, with no refrigeration, so it would have begun to smell unpleasantly sweet of its corruption.

Thus, the identification of the body as Christopher Marlowe is distinctly suspect. No-one looked too closely, the room would likely have been dim, and none of his friends had been summoned to identify him – only his killers were there to do that. It could have been any young man, and my suggestion is that it is the body of John Penry, who had supposedly been hanged on 29 May, although there are no contemporary witnesses to this event. There is no record of the burial of his body either. What is also odd is that his family were not informed of the execution and were not present, and there is no record of his last words at the scaffold. One must ask: why not? And the answer is almost certainly that he was not hanged on 29 May.

And even more odd - and certainly more suspect than the question of whether Danby should have been presiding alone or whether Deptford was within the verge of Greenwich (as the contemporary account says it was) where the Queen was - is the burial. Why was a well-known playwright, with patrons and friends, shoved into an unmarked grave, even if it is summer and plague is about? For the plague is not in Deptford, and a whole day passes when messages could have been sent. Thomas Watson had been properly buried, as had Greene, so would Shakespeare be, in the fullness of time. Why not 'kind Kit Marlowe'?

Apart from the identification of Ingram Frizer as the person who carried out the killing, and the identification of the body of Christopher Marlowe we have very little to go on. The central question is not whether someone was killed in Deptford, but who it was. Since the account of the inquest was discovered many people have doubted that the victim was Marlowe. What is the evidence for this? Very little in point of fact. It is total supposition, based on the idea that Christopher Marlowe is William Shakespeare. The entire argument of this book has been that William Shakespeare is, for the most part, Christopher Marlowe, and that these two young men were used by the secret state that was

Elizabethan England as a very effective spying duo. With Marlowe a Catholic priest with access to Catholic households and the recusant priests that Dr. Allen was continually sending across the Channel, and Shakespeare inside the theatrical world with its contacts both with vice and the aristocracy, the state had a remarkable machine for generating information.

There are three possibilities as to what caused what happened in Deptford. Firstly, Lord Burghley, or Robert Cecil, decided that Marlowe needed to disappear, because he had evidence of atheism against members of the Privy Council, or members of Elizabeth's court – this might mean murder or rescue. Second, the Allen brother wanted Marlowe dead, as a warning to other challengers of their power in the Liberties and the theatre. And lastly, Thomas Walsingham wanted his friend to disappear, either to appease his future wife, or to remove him from the danger of murder by the Allens.

Once the problem of Kyd's arrest for the Dutch Church Libels is explained, showing that this act did not in any way incriminate Christopher Marlowe, there is no reason to dispose of Master Marlowe – unless someone else wants him dead. It is unlikely the Privy Council, or the Cecils, wanted an effective secret agent eliminated. But there is evidence that Elizabeth herself wanted Marlowe dead, possibly because the Earl of Essex did not like him, or more probably because Essex saw Marlowe as connected to his rival, Sir Walter Raleigh, and wanted him dead as a signal to Raleigh that there was no way for him to come back into favour with the Queen. If this is so, then the Privy Council were in a difficult position. They could not continue to use the services of a man the Queen disapproved of and wanted eliminated. Certainly, they could have arrested the man they knew as Marlowe for atheism – for he does seem to have expressed heretical and atheist opinions quite freely, or so we are told. However, they do not do this. But on 31 May we see that an inquest is held on Marlowe's death, and the witnesses are three secret agents, two of whom we know are confidence tricksters, and the third a man who would say anything to save himself. There is thus a possibility that events were ordered by someone on the Privy Council.

But it is equally possible the Allen brothers wanted Marlowe dead as well, as he seems to have fallen out with Edward Alleyn over the play *Tambercam*, but they seem at first unlikely to have access to secret agents to carry out their wishes.[2] But this fails to notice that Alleyn was the most important actor of the Admiral's Men, the acting troupe whose patron was Howard of Effingham, Lord Admiral,

---

2   The Allen's wishes, though, are a powerful reason for Marlowe and Shakespeare to want to remove Marlowe from theatreland.

member of the Privy Council and head of the Navy Board. He also owned property in Deptford, one tenement of which was leased to Wolstan Randall,[3] one of the jurors at the inquest on 31 May, as noted by Peter Farey. Indeed, several of the jurors are men of Deptford and tradesmen who might have been employed or traded with the dockyard, which was under Howard's jurisdiction. Alleyn, as a leader of a gang in the Liberties, would see Marlowe's accusations of plagiarism as a matter of 'respect' and want him removed to show others that even those who enjoyed some protection from the Privy Council (as Marlowe undoubtedly did) were not immune from attack by Alleyn's people. Marlowe is also among Henslowe's list of borrowers. Bradley and Greene, who owed the Allens money, both died. If Marlowe still owed money then this was yet another reason for Alleyn to pursue him to death. However, it still seems unlikely that Alleyn employed Frizer, Poley and Skerres; but what proof is there that any of these men were actually involved in the events on 30 May at Eleanor Bull's, except their word? The connection to Lord Admiral Howard is tenuous but it is not impossible the jury included men who would favour a self-defence verdict so that Frizer was not charged with murder and no further investigation would be made. Wolstan and the other jurors would almost certainly not know Marlowe,

---

3   Farey, P. *The Deptford Jury,* 2008

they are there to make certain the verdict puts a stop to a murder investigation, not identify the victim. But why substitute Frizer for the real murderer? Especially as part of the point of a gangland killing is that everyone knows what has happened. And if Frizer is the agent, then what is the connection between him and Alleyn? The only one is knowing Christopher Marlowe, but there is no evidence that Ingram Frizer had anything to do with theatres, or any connection with Marlowe outside the household of Thomas Walsingham. One point to note, however, is that having fallen out with Alleyn, Marlowe's career as a playwright in London was over – just like Greene, he would find demand for his work disappearing. He needed to find another source of income, or take-up that source for which he had trained at Rheims: a Catholic priest. So Marlowe has good reason to disappear, which have nothing to do with atheism or the Privy Council. And Shakespeare also has reasons for wanting Marlowe to disappear.

Also included on the jury is Nicholas Draper, gentleman, identified as being from Leigh, in Kent,[4] where a son born to him is baptised in 1588. But, according to Peter Farey, Nicholas Draper is also listed as having a

---

4   William Urry, *Christopher Marlowe and Canterbury*, 1988 (pp.93-4). Data from *Archaeologia Cantiana* Vol. 31, 1915, *Extracts from some lost Kentish registers*, by Leland Duncan.

lodging in London and also one in Chislehurst, Kent in *Collectania Topographica Et Genealogica* by Frederic Madden et al[5], using material from the Burghley Papers.[6] Listed are all the names of non-citizens with lodging in London in 1595, that is persons who also had a lodging elsewhere. Nicholas Draper of Bromley, in Kent, is listed for the Wallbrook ward. Bromley, in Kent tallies with Nicholas Draper marrying in Bromley in 1587. And half a mile from Master Draper lives Sir Thomas Walsingham, of Chislehurst in Kent, in the Tower Street ward. This does add another possibility. That Thomas Walsingham had arranged the murder, through his employee Frizer, and wanted to make sure a verdict of self-defence was brought in, rather than murder, which would have involved a trial and the probability his name would have emerged as instigator of the crime. If Draper is known to Walsingham he might have known Marlowe, and identified him accurately, and if he is foreman of the jury (as he might well be as his name is first on the list) then he could lead the jury to deciding a self-defence verdict. But Walsingham has no real reason to kill Marlowe, who seems to have been his friend, and therefore we may be looking at a rescue not a murder. If we are looking at a rescue attempt and the victim is not Marlowe

---

5   Frederick Madden, Bulkeley Bandinel and John Gough Nichols *Collectania Topographica Et Genealogica,* p.205.

6   BL *Lansdowne* MSS.78, No.67.

then Draper can confirm that the body *is* Marlowe, at Walsingham's request, thus leading everyone to accept that the playwright is dead.

Which of these possibilities is it? The Allens look less likely because the nature of gangland killings is publicity. But it could be Walsingham helping Marlowe 'disappear' from the ambit of the Allens, and using his man Frizer and his neighbour Draper to facilitate this. That Burghley might want Marlowe out of the picture is also a possibility, if the Baines Note might come to the notice of the Queen.

In sum, so far, we have Marlowe dead at Deptford, or rather, we have a body identified by Poley, Frizer and Skeres as Marlowe, but these men are experienced liars. The body has also possibly been identified by Draper as well, a man possibly known to both Danby and Walsingham. All these men have reasons to lie about the corpse and we also have possible reasons for their lies. However, if it is not Christopher Marlowe (either the real man born in Canterbury or his alter ego, William Shakespeare) then who is the dead body?

Various suggestions have been put forward, two of which carry weight. I intend to add a third. The first suggestion is that the body shown to the coroner and jury was one picked up off the streets of London, a dead sailor perhaps, or some vagrant, or an unlucky reveller at an inn.

Dead bodies were not infrequently found and this is a possibility. The body does have to be reasonably fresh; even though it is early summer and a body would begin to smell after twenty-four hours; a very decayed body would not have passed. There is also another difficulty. The body had to look as if it belonged to a 'gentleman', not a vagrant or a sailor, or manual worker, so it had to be dressed. Dressing a dead body is no easy task, and might have required the assistance of someone experienced in laying out the dead – someone else to consider as a possible source of unwanted and dangerous testimony at a later date, for a bribed person does not necessarily stay bribed. Even dressed, a vagrant or sailor is not going to look very like a gentleman without a great deal of work. When British Intelligence invented the Man Who Never Was it took a great deal of skill and effort to produce a body that would deceive. Although not suggesting that such lengths as were used during World War II to deceive Germany were needed to disguise the body of a sailor, or vagrant, or simple unfortunate to make it appear to be Christopher Marlowe, yet the deception would have taken time. True, Poley, Frizer and Skeres (if they were actually present) had from the morning of 30 May till the morning of 31 May, but would they have had the skill to carry such a deception forward? Others must necessarily have known. From the point of view of simplicity, the replacement of Marlowe with any dead body is difficult. It would be much better to secure a particular dead body, preferably of similar age, condition and height.

Which leads to the second suggestion. Both Frizer and Skeres were confidence tricksters and one of their most common means of making a living was persuading gullible young men to take out a loan and then sign a bond which allowed Frizer and Skeres to not only keep the money they had apparently loaned out, but also put the debtor in the position of owing more than they had borrowed, because Frizer and Skeres said they could not recover the debt by the means set out in the bond. The precise method was to have the target signing up to a loan that would resolve itself into selling items that Frizer owned for less than the value of the loan, thus landing themselves in more debt.

If the fourth man at Eleanor Bull's house was not Marlowe (or Shakespeare) then it might have been one of Frizer's victims, a young man, perhaps not long resident in London, who had been invited out to a feast in order to finalize his loan. Such a person would be of the right sort, a gentleman, and could easily have been in his late twenties – a recent university graduate might have been a good choice. It would not be impossible to produce such a young man, and even persuade him to use the name Christopher Marlowe – perhaps being told that this will mean the eventual loan falls on Marlowe and not on himself, quite an incentive. But finding such a man, and at quite short notice, poses many of the problems of acquiring a random body from the London streets – or carrying out the more risky operation of murdering a likely subject outside an inn. There is a better solution.

At the beginning of this enquiry it was noted that two well-known young men were said to be dead at the end of May 1593, but that there was only one body. The other man supposedly dead by the end of May was John Penry, a man roughly the same age as Marlowe (or Shakespeare), a gentleman, who tended to dress as a gallant, and who was condemned to death for treason – therefore a dead man walking. And the execution of John Penry is, as we have already seen, very odd, and also has no contemporary accounts describing it.

The greatest stumbling block to suggesting that John Penry is the victim at Deptford is that he is supposed to have been hanged. Even in a dim room the marks of strangulation would be on his face, and strangulation could not be passed off as self-defence, which is what Frizer averred was the cause of his killing Marlowe. Even a lax coroner would have been hard put not to notice, and draw conclusions as to the causes of death and the likelihood that the accused defence was true. Penry can only be the body if Penry was not hanged on 29 May.

It is possible that Penry was not hanged on 29 May, and that this explains why his family and friends were not present. There is also the fact that Penry was intended to be hanged on 28 May and on this occasion his family attended but Penry was not brought. Instead, Whitgift and Puckering rose early and signed a death warrant for the 29 May and this was taken, at about noon, to Penry's prison. He was taken away on a hurdle, and hanged at St Thomas-a-Watering around 5 pm. There are no witnesses to speak of – the description says a few people passed by. This is the official version.

But what if Burghley, annoyed that he had not been able to stop Whitgift hanging Greenwood and Barrowe, decided to rescue Penry? Or what if, in fact, Penry, with his gift for always escaping arrest, was actually an agent of Burghley's, providing information on the Separatists and also carrying messages to Scotland. In either of these cases might not someone waiting on the Privy Council have been told to persuade Whitgift's messenger to hand over the death warrant, which was then used to release Penry from prison and take him to Deptford with the intention of sending him either to the continent or to Scotland? Marlowe is attending on the Privy Council, and Poley has orders which cover his movements during the necessary period, allowing him to visit Scotland, so that either or both could have been instructed to rescue and remove Penry. Once out of prison

Penry's removal from England by ship could have been arranged from Deptford.

However, he would not have been able to take his wife and children with him, for the entire enterprise rested on the involvement of Burghley never coming to light. If Penry, in love with his wife, refused to leave without her or insisted that he would continue preaching as himself once out of England, this would have caused an enormous problem for his rescuers. And this could be the real quarrel over 'ye reckoninge', the reckoning that will come for Burghley, Marlowe and Poley if Penry is caught and questioned once he is out of their hands. They would have to kill him, for if he re-appeared then both they and Burghley were in very serious trouble indeed. Penry dies. Poley and Marlowe know that the Queen and Whitgift will believe that Penry was hanged, because the evidence they will get is that the death warrant was executed. They also know that Whitgift wants Marlowe dead, so the body of Penry is presented to the coroner as Christopher Marlowe and Marlowe uses the transport provided for Penry to leave the country. He might have had funds with him from the reward for whoever revealed the Dutch Church libeller, since he is the most likely informer on Kyd, but he also had a destination: most likely Valadolid, and the English school there for recusant priests.

An outlying alternative is that Job Throckmortone, who may have had access to Burghley and actually arranged for Penry to see him, realised that no help was coming from that quarter and arranged a rescue himself. It is then again possible that Deptford was the stopping place from which Penry was to take ship either to the continent or to Scotland.

Frizer and Skerres do not have to be present for any of these solutions. The entire Deptford story is clearly cooked and only their testimony puts them at the place. If instead, Christopher Marlowe and Throckmorton were there with Poley then Marlowe probably killed Penry. The most likely reason is again Penry refusing to leave his wife and children behind. They could never join him in exile except by a sham marriage or a sham death – which would involve yet more people in a conspriracy, with increased danger for everyone involved. If Penry became obstinate there was no choice but to kill him – otherwise Throckmorton was in desperate trouble and likely to lose life and property. Poley would not have put his life at risk for Penry and nor would Marlowe. There may have been a fight, and the blow to the eye is a standard fighting stroke from a skilled swordsman. Marlowe would fit this description and would be capable of the deed. He is indeed, of the four people named as being in Deptford that day, the only one with a history of violence.

These are possible scenarios but do not account for Marlowe's need to leave the country and appear to be dead.

There is a much simpler explanation of what happened in Deptford which does not involve either Burghley or Throckmorton taking unnecessary risks. It involves not a rescue but a murder.

In this final scenario none of the evidence given by Frizer, Poley and Skeres has anything to do with what actually happened at Eleanor Bull's house in Deptford. We already know that Marlowe was in no danger of being arrested for atheism, and was only wanted by the Privy Council as a witness against Kyd. We know that Elizabeth I wanted Penry dead. It is not entirely clear that she also wanted Marlowe dead[7], but she may have wished him removed, and some elements of the Privy Council, notably Whitgift, certainly had no issue with having Marlowe executed.[8] Certainly Baines wanted Marlowe dead, it is the real purpose of his Note. At this point the delay in Penry's execution from 28 May to 29 May is sinister. It looks as

---

7   Riggs, D. The World of Christopher Marlowe. "Then after all this there was by my only means set down unto the Lord Keeper (and) the Lord of Buckhurst the notablest and vilest articles of Atheism that I suppose the like was never known or read of in any age all which I can show unto you they were delivered to her highness and command given by her self to prosecute it to the full..." Letter from Thomas Drury to Anthony Bacon, 1st August 1593. It is generally thought that the 'vilest articles of Atheism' refers to Richard Baines' accusations in his Note. This seems to be the sole evidence that Elizabeth I wanted Marlowe dead.
8   Whitgift had Marlowe's translation of Ovid's *Amores* burned.

though some means of escape has been provided to Marlowe (or Shakespeare - we do not really know at this point) because though he is not arraigned for any crime yet there are those who would like him to disappear permanently, and that it is arranged for 30 May – and Marlowe may well fall in with this arrangement because his future in London, as a writer, is now over; he has fallen out with the main impressarios: Henslowe and Alleyn, and will find getting sales difficult. He will also know that Greene fell out with Alleyn, and Greene is dead from food poisoning. Marlowe needs to be dead for the escape plan to work, and for him to continue as an agent abroad. Thus, Burghley needs a body of a gentleman to show at the inquest on 31 May. And John Penry is condemned to death. Instead of a rescue on 29 May there is a murder. Penry is removed from prison under Whitgift's death warrant, and he is collected, most probably by Robert Poley. But Penry is not taken to St Thomas-a-Watering, nor is he hanged. There are no witnesses and no body. It is not clear where he was taken but sometime between noon on 29 May and the evening of 30 May he was murdered, probably by Marlowe, aided by Poley. The means to do so was a mimicking of a swordsman's death stroke to the eye, which would partially disfigure Penry. He may already have been persuaded to change his clothes, as part of what he may have been told was an escape plan, so he was dressed in the same way that Marlowe might appear.

He may have actually been killed in Deptford, for it is easier to transport a living victim than a dead one, and the murder indeed have taken place in Eleanor Bull's parlour, in which case she will have been told that Penry is Marlowe - if she is present at all, for the most obvious reason for her not to have been called to the inquest is that she was not present on 30 May and thus had no information to give. Frizer and Skeres may or may not be present. Marlowe and Poley may have acted on their own and then called them in as witnesses. They must have been in the vicinity but I think Poley would have preferred not to have unnecessary witnesses to the murder of Penry.

Which of the four versions is the truth is perhaps beyond finding. Firstly, Penry as Burghley's agent is possible. He goes to Scotland and James VI does not repatriate him when requested, which suggests that Penry is under some sort of protection from the court and that Elizabeth's request has been subverted by someone in London with reason and authority to do so. He reportedly returns to London during the Hackett Plot, and escapes arrest again, whilst everyone else associated with it is arrested. As a useful agent Penry has value, as has Marlowe. Keeping them working, especially in the fraught 1590s when the succession was heavily in question, might have been a priority of Burghley's.

The Throckmorton solution also has merit. It may be that Throckmorton affects a rescue, but in that case he has to know Poley. If Marlowe has been working on some of the Marprelate pamphlets then there is a connection. But it is unproved that Marlowe had any hand in Martin Marprelate, or knew Throckmorton. If Penry was an agent it is possible Marlowe knew him, but their acquaintance is not necessary to the plan for an eve of hanging rescue. So far this scenario is not proven, however.

The Allens may not have had the ability to murder Marlowe at this range. There is no connection to Poley, Skeres or Frizer, only to Marlowe and Thomas Walsingham as a patron of the theatre. If the Allens are involved, it is through Thomas Walsingham's agency.

And Thomas Walsingham has often been put forward as a candidate, possibly in order to eliminate Christopher Marlowe, who is becoming something of a liability with his brawling and his dealings with the Privy Council. Walsingham's involvement would account both for the presence at the inquest of Ingram Frizer, his employee, and for the advancement Walsingham later gives him - such favour is unlikely if Frizer had murdered Walsingham's friend, which points to Marlowe's removal rather than his death, since Walsingham seems sincere in his patronage of Marlowe.

Finally, that Penry, a dead man walking on 29 May, was simply provided by Burghley as a convenient body to impersonate Marlowe, who was a valued agent, is quite persuasive, if Marlowe was indeed a person that the Queen wanted dead, whilst the Privy Council, or the Cecils, wanted to continue using him as a secret agent. This solution, put together with the ending of Marlowe's career in London's theatres because of the enmity of Alleyn and Henslowe, is the most likely.

Whichever explanation is the truth, the inquest on 31 May is presented with the body of a gentleman, about thirty, appropriately dressed, his face disfigured by a wound straight through his upper eye. Three men swear he is their friend Christopher Marlowe and the jury and coroner accept this. In his evidence Frizer shows a superficial scratch that he says Marlowe inflicted using Frizer's own knife, taken from his belt. This is his main argument for a plea of self-defence, along with still being present. Neither of the other people supposedly present stopped the fight between Marlowe and Frizer though they could have done so. No evidence comes from Eleanor Bull nor from any servants. Other coroners report all the evidence given – this suggests they actually did not give evidence.

Frizer is sent to prison to await pardon, as he has claimed he acted in self-defence when attacked by Marlowe in a dispute over the bill (ye reckoninge) and he has remained on the premises to show that he is telling the truth. It is summer, and Marlowe's body is quickly buried, in the local churchyard because it is hot and there is no-one present except his friends Poley, Frizer and Skeres and no-one else to pay for an elaborate burial. His London friends are not applied to because they would recognise that the body is not Marlowe's.

Four men are supposed to have been at the house in Deptford. There is a dead body and three witnesses, who appear to be lying. The entire story looks like a fabrication. We only have Frizer's word that he invited Marlowe to a feast and that they dined, and walked in the garden and only Vaughan reports that they played backgammon. None of this needs to have happened. Marlowe may never have been in Deptford but if he was then he was very likely a murderer by the end of the day.

The most likely cause of the argument between the four men, that would be accepted as entirely possible by a coroner's jury, was a dispute over a game of chance rather than the dispute over a bill. A game of chance was far likelier to arouse passion and also involve a substantial sum to quarrel over. Only Vaughan mentions backgammon, but, as pointed out in Chapter Two, he was a connection of Essex's, and may have had his information from Nicholas Skeres. The account of the inquest found by Hotson does not mention playing backgammon. It reports that Frizer said he was caught between Skeres and Poley at the table and could not get out. The account is written in Latin, and is a translation of the statement spoken in English by Frizer. There is no word for backgammon in Latin, the game did not exist. But in the sixteenth century backgammon was called 'tables' (as it still is in Spain, for example) and is a game played on a board that has two sides, or tables, with a bar between upon which the counters can be trapped because they have been taken off by opponents. Gettng off the bar becomes increasingly difficult as the game progresses, it being necessary to throw a precise number to get pieces back in the game,whilst avoiding opponents' pieces and becoming a 'blot' - a sole counter on a point, vulnerable to taking. As the game nears completion, and opponents' counters are on all the points of the first table in order to 'bear off' or escape the table, moving from the bar becomes virtually impossible, so that the player so hemmed in cannot get his counters out, he cannot escape his opponent, who will now win the game. If Frizer is playing at 'tables' with Poley, Skeres and a fourth person (playing in pairs), then it is quite possible for an argument to erupt. Frustration at not being able to get counters 'out' because they are marooned on the bar and cannot be moved because Skeres and Poley's counters are blocking the first table, along with the probability that the doubling cube has been used heavily, so that the stakes are now very high, would very likely be the cause of an argument over 'ye reckoninge'. If everyone is slightly drunk because they have been drinking all day then Frizer will not want to pay out a large sum to his opponents because he is unsure about how the stakes have been raised. A trickster himself, he will be quite aware that surreptitiously upping the stakes is something that Skeres, at least, is likely to do. Indeed, both he and Skeres may be habitual cheaters at backgammon in order to win money off unsuspecting young gentlemen visiting London.

Danby's report says the following on the moments before the attack, as presented by Kuriyama in *Christopher Marlowe: A Renaissance Life*:

'…praedictus Cristoferus Morley prope lectum vocatum nere the bed sedens & cum anteriori parte corporis sui versus mensum & praedicti Nicholaus Skeres & Robertus Poley ex utraque parte ipsius Ingrami sendentes tali modo ut idem Ingramus Frysar nullo modo fugam facere…'

'…the aforesaid Christopher Morley then lay, near the bed, that is sitting nere the bed and with the front part of his body towards the table and the aforesaid Nicholas Skeres and Robert Poley sitting on either side of the same Ingram so that the same Ingram Frysar could in no way flee…'[9]

---

9 Text and translation Kuriyama ibid pp 223-225.

Hotson's version reads:

'... the said Christopher Morley was then lying, sitting near the bed, that is *nere the bed*, and with the front part of his body towards the table & and the said Nicholas Skeres and Robert Poley sitting either side of the said Ingram in such a manner that the same Ingram ffrysar in no way could take flight...'[10]

Thus Poley and Skeres are described as being on either side of Frizer so that he could not escape from whoever was holding him on the bar. This might be Penry, or could be Marlowe who had given his place in the game to Penry and is watching from behind. We know Poley would lie to save his life. Frizer and Skeres, given their reputations, would as well. What happened may have been a general brawl, or it might have been a pretext to murder. Strewing confusion as to what actually happened, and who had died, would have been an object for all three men at the inquest. Backgammon seems to be the likeliest cause of an argument over the reckoning, and to an audience not familiar with backgammon it is easy to obscure the events, and just as easy to obscure who had actually died. Unfamiliarity with backgammon would also explain why later investigators have not picked up what was being said at the inquest about

---

10   Hotson, ibid, p 32.

the cause of the quarrel, despite the fact that Vaughan mentions the game quite clearly. Vaughan is hearsay, of course, but putting his phrase (Ingram) 'was then playing at tables,[11] together with the words: 'corporis sui versus mensum', - body towards the table – and 'Nicholaus Skeres & Robertus Poley ex utraque parte ipsius Ingrami sendentes tali modo ut idem Ingramus Frysar nullo modo fugam facere…', Skeres and Poley were on either side of Frizer at the table and he could not take flight, then the game 'tables' can be inferred.

If Marlowe got involved in the fight between the players, or was at any point involved in the game, his hot temper may have led to murder. If Penry had been playing backgammon with the other three Marlowe may have intervened. He is the only one of the four men named who had a reputation for brawling, and had been in a fight with Bradley which put him in gaol, as well as having been involved two other affrays which led to being bound over to keep the peace, or requiring payment for his release.

None of the evidence given on 31 May 1593 may have any basis in fact. The entire story looks like a fabrication, which is then passed on to Vaughan via Skeres. If the plan was to rescue Penry, and that plan went wrong,

---

11 A longer extract of Vaughan's text is in Chapter Two.

or if the intention was to murder Penry in Marlowe's place, then the entire story about tables, backgammon, knives and reckonings bears no relation to the truth – though the game *might* have been set up to facilitate killing someone. What happened in Deptford was murder. The killing stroke is one used by experienced swordsmen to kill – it has no other use. The stroke is the 'roofguard' or 'vom tag' and is a German swordstroke, so called because it requires the wielder to raise his sword above his shoulder. Knowledge of it would have been available to Marlowe as it appeared in swordsmanship manuals from the fourteenth through to the eighteenth centuries. It is not, as sometimes been supposed, a stroke that would be used on someone held down; there is definitely a brawl using swords, as well as daggers. Using it meant the swordsman intended to kill, not wound and so the brawl was probably pre-meditated, a set-up, not arising from any argument. The story told to the coroner on 31 May was constructed, and intended to confuse, and it has confused for nearly five centuries.

And by the time of the inquest at Deptford Marlowe was probably half-way across the Channel, and William Shakespeare was beginning to emerge from his shadow existence, able to work as a playwright now being rid of his persona as Christopher Marlowe and his bad position with the Allens.

***

After 1593 there is ample evidence that Shakespeare was known as the author of the plays ascribed to him, and he has a presence in London as a well-known playwright as well as an actor and share-holder of the Globe. Jonson writes about him in his notebooks, which are later published.

Shakespeare buys and sells plays, and published revised versions of the works of others - this is something Jonson speaks of disparagingly. He is also well-known enough for publishers to put his name on plays they want to sell, which suggests he was a draw at the box office. In 1623 his colleagues, Heminge and Condell, published most of the plays we now have, in the First Folio. Jonson writes of him as the 'swan of Avon'. Somewhere around this time, but before 1623, a monument is put up to Shakespeare's memory in Stratford church, above his grave. It is the grave that now needs to be examined, for its cryptic messages have led to many suggestions that the man buried in the church of the Holy and Undivided trinity in Stratford-on-Avon is not who he says he is. It is the last stone in the wall of evidence that he is, and that he is also Marlowe.

Chapter Eighteen

The Burial Place And The Riddle of the Stones

The inscriptions on the monument and grave stone marking the burial of William Shakespeare have long been a temptation to the curious and those who wish to see anagrams (so popular with Elizabethans) or hidden messages that tell a tale the man buried as Shakespeare wished to intimate without actually telling it: that there is, indeed, a message hidden in plain sight for us to find. We have no inscriptions for Marlowe, nor do we know where he is buried, and much of what is written about Shakespeare in Stratford-on-Avon church belongs to standard eulogy, but it is possible that in the double inscription on the monument and ledger stone there is indeed a riddle, who's wise may read.

Much has been made of the peculiar inscriptions on Shakespeare's grave and gravestone. There are three inscriptions to examine. Two are on Shakespeare's monument, and one on his gravestone (which is discussed in section 2 of Appendix I). It is not at all clear when the monument was put up. Some think that Shakespeare's son-in-law, John Hall, commissioned it, and suggest it was put up as early as 1617, others prefer a later date. John Weever, an English antiquary (d.1632) transcribed the incription, but his manuscript is undated. He may have visited as early as 1617-18.[1] It was in existence by 1623 as a copy of it appears in the First Folio, published that year.[2]

These are the inscriptions:

> IVDICIO PYLIVM, GENIO SOCRATEM, ARTE MARONEM,
>
> TERRA TEGIT, POPVLVS MÆRET, OLYMPVS HABET

Both phrases rhyme internally and are in the accusative case. Translated they read:

> "A Pylian in judgement, a Socrates in genius, a Maro in art,

---

1   Duncan-Jones, Katherine, and H. R. Woudhuysen, eds. (2007) *Shakespeare's Poems* London: Arden Shakespeare, Thomson Learning, pp.438, 462.
2   And Leonard Digges' poem refers to it in the First Folio.

Thus the verses are comparing Shakespeare to Nestor of Pylus, the wise and aged king in the Odyssey who advises Telemachus, to Socrates, the Greek philosopher written about by Plato (so we could guess that Shakespeare was a Platonist[3]), and to Maro: Publius Vergilius Maro, the poet Virgil, who wrote the Aeniad which contains the story of Dido. In keeping with some of the rest of the verse (where Nestor is called by his title) Maro, Virgil's *cognomen*, is used rather than Virgil, though Virgil - Publius Vergilius Maro's *nomen*, or family name - was more usual. Indeed, Spenser is referred to as a modern Virgil, not a modern Maro - but there is a reason for this to be found in the English lines. In sum, the line suggests that Shakespeare was wise, intelligent and a great artist.

The earth buries him, the people mourn him, Olympus possesses him. [4]

---

3   If he was a Platonist it might be that Shakespeare was conversant with and also in sympathy with the idea of a republic or commonwealth with royal powers controlled by a legislature, as suggested by Richard Bacon (*Solon, his Folie,* 1594) and Thomas Smith (*De Republican Anglorum; A Discourse on the Commonwealth of England.* 1583) and Robert Cecil: in 1592, when Elizabeth I had been seriously ill, and there was no decision on who her heir was if she should die, Robert Cecil proposed that Parliament should be able to legislate without the monarch until a successor was decided upon and took the throne. Literally, a commonwealth – at least for a short interval.

4   Other translations are possible. For example the Oxfordian Alexander Waugh's translation uses the fact that the lines are in the ablative to produce:

(Though 'him' is not necessary since the subject of these words is considered to be obvious, and so the pronoun would not be needed in Latin.) The words are a pious sentiment, expressing sorrow, whether genuine or conventional, at the death of a famous man. This becomes clearer if the lines are reversed to read:

"The earth buries, the people mourn, Olympus possesses

A Pylian in judgement, a Socrates in genius, a Maro in art.

This man is mourned because he is all these things that have been listed, and he is honoured as such. The reference to Olympus suggests that Shakespeare is crowned

---

Pylius with his judgement, Socrates with his genius, Maro with his art,/The earth covers, the people mourn, Olympus holds. (This version does not make any change to the meaning of the words, except it is more explict that the person remembered has the qualities of the illustrious men cited.)

Waugh also suggests, using the names in the Latin inscription, that it refers to Francis Beaumont, often praised for his judgement like Nestor, Chaucer, frequently compared to Socrates, and Spenser who was compared to Virgil. All these poets are buried in the south transept of Westminster Abbey, Poet's Corner, which Waugh appears to identify with Olympus. Shakespeare is not - therefore, Waugh believes the point being made is that Shakespeare is not buried in Westminster Abbey because this man who lies in Stratford is not the writer of Shakespeare's works. Waugh is an Oxfordian (the Earl of Oxford died in 1603, whilst Shakespeare was an active playwright, and has a writing style nothing like Shakespeare's, which all make his attribution as the writer of Shakespeare's plays difficult). Waugh asserts that Oxford was secretly reburied in Westminster Abbey, along with Spenser, Beaumont and Chaucer, and that the monument in Stratford is obliquely saying this.

with laurel and among the gods - not a very Christian sentiment to find in a church.

STAY PASSENGER, WHY GOEST THOV BY SO FAST,

READ IF THOV CANST, WHOM ENVIOVS DEATH HATH PLAST

WITH IN THIS MONVMENT SHAKSPEARE: WITH WHOME,

QVICK NATVRE DIDE: WHOSE NAME, DOTH DECK Y^S TOMBE,

FAR MORE, THEN COST: SIEH ALL, Y^T HE HATH WRITT,

LEAVES LIVING ART, BVT PAGE, TO SERVE HIS WITT.

These words are written below the Latin inscription. Some, notably Peter Farley in a well-reasoned article,[5] suggest they are an acrostic revealing the name that decks the tomb as that of Christopher Marlowe. It might well be an acrostic as acrostics were a favoured conceit of

---

5   Farley, Peter. The Stratford Monument: A Riddle and Its Solution, 1999-2004.

seventeenth century graves, though its meaning is not certain if so. Certainly, the verse is worth investigation.

'Stay passenger, why goest thou by so fast'(?) - this is a standard sentiment[6] calling upon a passing visitor to stop and read, rather than hasten on and forget that we are mortal. It suggests that we should stop and contemplate the dead, who we will eventually join.

'Read if thou canst' - if you can read, read what is written. Since literacy was not universal it is possible a passer-by might not be able to read the inscription and would have to ask someone else. Or one might interpret this as meaning 'understand if you can, what is written'. But if the passer-by can read and understand, then read on and work out: 'whom envious Death has plast/With in the monument Shakspeare: with whome/Quick nature dide'. It is Shakespeare who lies here, placed (or literally plastered) on the monument in effect. We could read the sentence as: 'within lies the monumental Shakespeare', and one could then read 'Death has plast/with' as meaning that someone else is contained within the monument that is Shakespeare, or put with Shakespeare (though this stretches the sense a little after the words 'whom envious Death has plast'),

---

6   Romans put up roadside stones with this message, remembering the dead.

because that is what it says. So, who could be contained within the monument that is Shakespeare? The inscription tells us:

WHOSE NAME, DOTH DECK Y^S TOMBE,/FAR MORE, THEN COST:

If this is an acrostic then we are thinking of moving letters about. But first we need to look at whose name decks the tomb. In fact there are three: Nestor, Socrates and Virgil. Nestor is given his title, Pylium, Socrates and Virgil are both named, and Virgil's cognomen, Maro, is used. Only one of these people is a writer, the others are characters in someone else's books, Nestor a character in the Odyssey (and a legendary character also) and Socrates as the philosopher in Plato's Dialogues (and having some unknown relationship to the historical Socrates, whose philosophy was distinctly different from that of Plato). Only Virgil is a writer and inventor of characters - as was Shakespeare - and also a living person truly represented in what he wrote and said. Looking at what follows (and ignoring for the moment the odd word 'SIEH') we have 'HE HATH WRITT'. Virgil is the writer who decks Shakespeare's tomb. But it was not Shakespeare who clearly used Virgil[7] as a source, it was

---

7   Ovid is much more of an influence on Shakespeare, who may even seem to be avoiding connection with Virgil.

282

Marlowe, in *Dido of Carthage*. If we are pursuing the idea that Marlowe was Shakespeare then we could say that Virgil decking Shakespeare's tomb is a clue, since it is Marlowe, rather than Shakespeare, who is connected to Virgil in a literary sense. This could suggest that Shakespeare is also Marlowe, rather than that Marlowe wrote Shakespeare's work, and that it was Shakespeare, rather than Marlowe, who wrote the plays that bear Marlowe's name – at least as suggested in the most part of this investigation. Thus, the inscription is saying 'in this monument of/to Shakespeare is also Marlowe, because Shakespeare wrote the works attributed to Marlowe'. Since it is not proved that Shakespeare wrote this verse, it may mean just what it says: Shakespeare is a writer as great as the much-revered classical writer, Virgil. But let us suppose that Shakespeare did write it. In that case Shakespeare looks as if he is clearly indicating that he is also Marlowe.

'FAR MORE, THEN COST' further suggests that Virgil's name is worth more to have on the tomb than the actual cost of putting it up. One could see 'FAR MORE' as an anagram of sorts, as, by moving the vowels to the right one gets 'FR MARO E' - Maro, that is Virgil, and FR is short-form for 'father', which suggests both an inspiration and a person in orders. It is a pretty trick for someone who wants to play with words, and has another purpose in being close in letters to the name Marlowe, which is revealed later in the verse. The spelling of 'then' and 'than' were exchangeable in the seventeenth century, as spelling was not codified and, within reason or phonics, one could spell how one chose.

Which leads to the odd word 'SIEH'.

Sometimes this word is read as 'since' or 'sith' (meaning since), but this does not necessarily make sense. It cannot be a misprint, as one would not expect an experienced stone mason to make a spelling error on what was clearly a valuable commission.

SIEH ALL, Y^T HE HATH WRITT,

LEAVES LIVING ART,

Usually becomes: Since all, that he hath writ,/Leaves living art.

The new problem here, apart from the unlikely suggestion we have a misprint for 'sith', is the comma: since all what? This makes little sense and there is no reason to suppose the punctuation is not as intended. However, punctuation in the seventeenth century was different from modern usage. Commas were not only used to separate clauses, but used far more frequently than in the twenty-first century simply to divide the sentence up for reading aloud. They were sometimes used merely to show a line end or a breath, and having one does not always affect the sense –

frequently modern usage would not put a comma, indeed would see the usage here as a spliced comma, which is now a grammatical error. So, we would be better reading: 'Since all that he hath writte', no comma, and therefore no clue to acrostics or hidden meanings. But it still makes little sense to say 'since all' because we have already been asked to 'stay', which suggests that we should take a 'look'.

Much more sense is made if 'SIEH' is read as 'see'. Then the words read:

'See all, that (yt) he hath writte,/Leaves living art, but page, to serve his witte.'[8]

Which works even if the comma is allowed.

But how can we get 'see', meaning look, or notice, from 'sieh'? We can because investigation reveals that 'sieh' is a Germanic word, meaning see, look, check, watch. Putting 'see' instead of 'sieh' turns a cryptic sentence into a plain one. We are reading 'See all (the people reading this), (those things) that he hath writ, Leaves living art (he will write no more because he is dead), but page, (what is already written is all there will be) to serve his wit'. Which one interpretation will see as: whoever is reading this, look,

---

8   Or: See all, that which he has written now leaves living art, being but a page, to remind us of his wit. ('Leaves' and 'page' are puns on each other as well - a further example of seventeenth century wordplay.)

everything the person buried here wrote has now left living art, and we can only look at the pages he wrote in order to understand his wit (intelligence, great art). An alternative, perhaps even more persuasive, reading is that the words could be interpreted as: 'the leaves and pages of his still living art serve to show his wit', which chimes well with Jonson's poem to Shakespeare in the First Folio[9]. Either way, we have a sentence that makes more sense with SIEH recognised as a spelling of 'see'.[10]

But how do we get a Germanic word in an English sentence? The maker of the tomb was most likely the monumental mason, Gerard Johnson [11]. Gerard Johnson is the English version of Gheerart Janssen. The man who made the tomb was a second generation Dutch immigrant. Gheerart Janssen (Gerard Johnson) Senior seems to have

---

9   See below - 'monument without a tomb'
10   Even if we decide to interpret the words as meaning that Shakespeare's works outshine the work of artists yet to be born, or that it outshines the plastic arts, such as sculpture (comparing Shakespeare to a stone monument), the sentence continues to make sense.
11   Sir William Dugdale, *Antiquities of Warwickshire*, published in 1656, attributes the work to Johnson. It is possible that Shakespeare knew Johnson, as the Johnson workshop was near the Globe in London - (Cooper, Tanya, *Searching for Shakespeare*, National Portrait Gallery, 2006, p.51). Also Johnson had made a monument to Shakespeare's friend John Combe, which is also in Holy Trinity Church at Stratford, so he might well be an obvious choice to make one for Shakespeare.

come to England in 1567, and established himself as a maker of funerary monuments. [12] His son, Gerard Johnson the Younger, worked in the same business between about 1612 to 1623, and seems to have flourished. It is quite possible that Johnson the Younger wrote 'see' as 'sieh' without thinking about it; it was the way he spelled that word. He may, indeed, have supplied the verse; if not, he almost certainly took it down from someone who spoke it rather than having it written down for him[13]. Since there was no consensus on English spelling, no-one would see either a mis-spelling or a mistake. All we are seeing in the apparently odd word 'sieh' is an alternative spelling produced by a bi-lingual. Such spellings are sometimes considered to be 'interference' between a first and second language and appear frequently even now among bi-linguals. There is no mystery, nor is the word an anagram, nor a 'return' in the way of a cryptic crossword or acrostic. What we have is the simple: 'See all, that he has writte/Leaves living art, but page, to serve his witte', where, finally, 'but' can be understood as meaning 'only', or an elided version of 'nothing but', showing that only what is

---

12   White, Adam. *Johnson (Janssen) family (per c.1570-c.1630)* Oxford Dictionary of National Biography. Oxford University Press, 2004. Martineau, Jane. *Shakespeare in Art,* Merrell, 2003. p.21.
13   We also tend to see what we expect, so Janssen may have read 'seih' for 'see' even if he was given a written copy of the verse, and 'copied' it.

now written can be seen of the writer's work - there will be no more.

And is this all?

Once all the possible interpretations seem to have been made, a look at the ledger stone on Shakespeare's grave adds another layer. In the ledger stone the spelling symbol 'yt' is used twice. In the second usage it is usually read as 'that' to match the words above, but it could equally mean 'who' in both cases[14]: 'Bleset be ye man **who** spares these stones/And curst be he **who** moves my bones. If 'who' is substituted in the monumental inscription as well, we get: 'See all, **who** he hath writte' - and who is Shakespeare compared to? Virgil, or Maro as it appears in the Latin inscription. And now he, Shakespeare, leaves living art, and only the pages he has written (living art in the same way that Virgil's work is still living art) show his wit; not so much his intelligence but also his sense of humour and cleverness, and also his sleight of hand. It would appear, in this case, that the words mean: See **who** he hath writ: Look! he wrote the works by the playwright who followed Virgil, whose name,

---

14   Another example of 'that' also meaning 'who' is found in Davenant's In *Remembrance of Master Shakespeare*: "That reach the Map; and look' means 'who reaches for a map and looks', and 'who' can be substituted in the verse. The inscription on the ledger stone is further explored in Appendix I.

using - as already noticed above when discussing the Latin lines and the words FAR MORE - the closest version of it that can be got to Marlowe,[15] decks the tomb! Shakespeare has written Maro - that is, he wrote the works of the person who wrote about Dido. That is, Marlowe.

It can be written as a syllogism:

Shakespeare wrote Maro.

Maro wrote the story about Dido a modern version of which is attributed to a man called Marlowe.

In this instance Maro and Marlowe are therefore the same person, which is Shakespeare.

A truth Shakespeare concealed in life is revealed on his monument - but subtly, hidden. Who, after all, knowing how seventeenth century English was spelled, would read 'yt' as 'who' rather than 'that'? But it can be so read, not by eye - the symbols do not lie - but by brain, and that leaves Shakespeare laughing at *our* lack of 'wit'.

But also, as Jonson wrote at the beginning of the First Folio, echoing the words written on the Stratford monument, as well as answering the poem known as the Basse Elegy, which read:

---

15   Six of the letters in Maronem appear in the various spellings of Marlowe's name: **Marlowe, Marlin, Marley, Morley.** Though this point should not be laboured it is intriguing.

> Renowned Spenser, lie a thought more nigh
>
> To learned Chaucer, and rare Beaumont lie
>
> A little nearer Spenser to make room
>
> For Shakespeare in your threefold, fourfold tomb.[16]

And, from Jonson:

> Thou art a monument without a tomb,
>
> And art alive still while thy book doth live
>
> And we have wits to read, and praise to give.

Shakespeare needs no tomb, though he has one, for his work (like Christopher Wren's) is around us, in his plays and poetry, and if you seek his monument it lies in those works. Jonson is also saying that Shakespeare himself is a monument, as if his works and he were one. Compare Sonnet XVIII: 'So long as men can breathe or eyes can see,/So long lives this and this gives life to thee', and Sonnet LXXIV: 'The worth of that is that which it contains,/And that is this, and this with thee remains'. Both sonnets here have the idea that something written keeps the life of the writer in it, so that he lives still, which is the sentiment expressed also by the monument's verse: this same idea, in the end, is what those verses are expressing - as well as that Shakespeare was

---

16   The complete Basse Elegy is in Appendix V

Marlowe, and the writer of *Dido,* and *Tamburlaine,* as well as of *Romeo and Juliet, Macbeth,* and *Richard III.*

Conclusion

The Bones Assembled

At the beginning of this enquiry two questions were asked: first, what do we actually know about Christopher Marlowe and William Shakespeare, and second, what is known about the events at Deptford Strand on 30 May 1593. Investigation prompted more questions, to do with Shakespeare's education, his knowledge of gang-life, the references to the countryside in his plays. Marlowe's activities were also examined, particularly the rumour that he was going to Rheims in 1587, having been absent from Cambridge for thirty-five weeks, and the odd events at Vlissingen/Flushing, which made little sense as described. A third question was then asked: if Marlowe survived Deptford, where did he go and what was his source of income, as it was unlikely to be playwrighting, which was not sufficient to support him on the continent.

The death of Christopher Marlowe, in 1593 has been a thing of contention since almost the beginning. Inaccurate descriptions of his death, by contemporaries such as Gabriel Harvey have muddied the waters for centuries, as has William Vaughan's account in Goldengrove, which named the murderer as 'one Ingram'. Not until 1925 when Leslie Hotson discovered the records of the inquest on 31 May 1593 was the officially recorded story clear. Hotson's discovery while researching in the Public Records Office, was of the name 'Ingram Frizer' and Hotson himself states: 'I felt at once that I had come upon the man who killed ChristopherMarlowe. Vaughan's 'one Ingram' was instantly clear as an example of the same habit of nomenclature which referred to Gabriel Spencer, Ben Jonson's adversary: as 'one Gabriel'.[1] [2] Discovery of the full name of Ingram persuaded Hotson to continue his search, leading to the discovery of a pardon for Frizer, given four weeks after Marlowe's death, in the Chancery enrolments. What was needed now was the record of the inquest. But Hotson knew he had already

---

1   Hotson, J. L. *The Death of Christopher Marlowe,* London: The Nonsuch Press, Cambridge: Harvard University Press, 1925, p.23.
2   Gabriel Spencer was killed in 1598 by Ben Jonson - some have speculated that Spencer was Marlowe disguised.

searched the Chancery papers for an inquest on Marlowe, and had not found it.

'As a last resort,' he writes, 'I took up the (modern) manuscript calendar of the Miscellany of the Chancery. Here the documents listed, as the title gave warning, were highly miscellaneous both in nature and in date'.[3] They were also listed by county. Searching the records for Kent, he at last found the coroner's record of Marlowe's inquest. Hotson, by thinking sideways, had found what had been hidden since the 1590s.

Once this was found then most of the prior ideas about Marlowe's death became clearly at best fantasy and at worst lies. The inn or tavern was apparently a respectable house belonging to a woman connected to the court. Eleanor Bull let out rooms and provided food. There was no street brawl, and Marlowe was killed, not with his own dagger (as was averred by those who wished to see his death as a punishment dealt by God upon an atheist) but with Frizer's, which Frizer said was plucked from his belt whilst he sat at table, with which Marlowe attacked him as they quarrelled over the bill. Marlowe was killed by a thrust to the eye which only an experienced swordsman could have accurately given.

---

3   ibid p.25

Hotson is the first to question the veracity of the account given to the inquest by Frizer. Questioning of the honesty of the three men said to be present, Poley, Skeres and Frizer, has led to a re-animation[4] of the theory that Marlowe survived the Deptford incident, went abroad and there wrote the plays attributed to Shakespeare, sending them back to London and receiving remuneration in return.

But this scenario is unlikely. The money made from actual playwriting was not large, around £8 per play. Playwrights also had to keep up with current fashions, something that would be difficult to do whilst not in London, the hub of English Renaissance theatre. Sending plays from continental Europe to England is not impossible, and nor is sending money back, but sending money would involve other people in the transaction, and the whole argument for Marlowe being the author of Shakespeare's plays is that this remains secret to protect Marlowe's life. It is difficult to keep such a secret if money is being remitted abroad.

Compared to our knowledge of Marlowe our knowledge of Shakespeare's life before 1593 has proved to be extremely limited. Between 1564 and 1593 there is nothing known about Shakespeare except that he is baptised, his father John Shakespeare gets into financial difficulties

---

[4] The theory that someone other than Shakespeare wrote his work had surfaced in the USA in the nineteenth century.

and that Shakespeare himself marries and has three children. Before 1592 he does not exist in London; his identification as Greene's 'Shake-scene' and 'upstart crow' is not proven, and is more likely to refer to the actor, Edward Alleyn, who literally shook the scene with his stomping round the stage. But by 1594 Shakespeare is well-known in London and fairly rapidly becomes a successful entrepreneur. Where has Shakespeare been until then? We know he has not been in Stratford because there is no record of apprenticeship or employment there, only records of his marriage. The theory that he was at Hoghton Hall works well for 1579-1580, and gives him an income of £2 pounds a year from Alexander Hoghton's will, as William Shakeshafte, a recusant. Thereafter the conjecture that he was intended to go to Rheims in 1580, sponsored by the Hoghton family, rings true for a young man whose family had fallen on hard times, as Shakespeare's did after his father was caught avoiding tax on wool sales. A passage to Rheims was a gift that could not be rejected, even if becoming a seminary priest was not Shakespeare's ideal future. But Shakespeare clearly did not go to Rheims since he is in Stratford in August and November 1582. So, where did he go? We have seen that he could have joined a band of players, but how was he contacted by November 1582 to marry the pregnant Anne Hathaway? He has to have been somewhere that a message could reach him and bring him back to Stratford before her pregnancy could show. That could include being part of a band of players, if they regularly picked up messages from one point, but that would still not be reliable enough for the November wedding[5]. If, however, being a strolling player was Shakespeare's cover whilst he was at Cambridge, then messages could be sent to a permanent drop box where they could be reliably collected.

Returning to Marlowe's activities, in 1580 he had means to survive at Cambridge before he matriculated in March 1581. He also had extra money before 1585. His father could not have provided the extra and it looks, therefore, probable that he had money from another source. The Parker Scholars were a small group at Corpus Christi, and Marlowe in particular was associated with people suspected of being Catholics who were thought to be intending to go to the English School at Rheims. That Marlowe spent so much time with possible Catholics throughout his time at Cambridge suggests he was spying on them and that Parker Scholars were not only chosen for academic excellence but also Protestant zeal, and placed in the university to spy on fellow students, probably for the church authorities. This is supported by John Parker's financial and employment relationship with Whitgift. In

---

5   As, presumably, a first pregnancy Anne might not have been at all sure she was pregnant till sometime in mid-October.

1587 Marlowe is absent for thirty-five weeks, a long enough period for the university authorities to deny him his MA. At the same time a rumour arises that he intends to go to Rheims and this rumour cements the university's intention to deny the MA.

If Marlowe has been to Rheims, which the thirty-five weeks absence makes possible, why is there only a rumour that he *intends* to go to Rheims, a rumour for which there is no provenance? The suggestion is that the rumour was put about by someone who knows Marlowe and that he has been to Rheims, probably as a spy, but cannot reconcile this knowledge with the patent fact that Marlowe has a record of being at Cambridge for much of the last seven years. This suggests someone who was at Rheims himself as a spy, and who met Marlowe there. One person who had been to Rheims as a spy is Richard Baines, who was betrayed there and already known in Seething Lane when he is imprisoned by Allen. Events detailed in Chapters Seven and Fourteen suggested that Marlowe was the unnamed betrayer of Richard Baines and that this betrayal was the source of Baines' enmity, and that when Baines returned to England after his imprisonment, he recognised Marlowe at Cambridge. According to the Buttery and scholarship records Marlowe had been at Cambridge when Baines was betrayed. Thus, Baines, sure of his man but not his reception if he told his tale of betrayal, put about the rumour that

Marlowe *intended* going to Rheims because an accusation of having been to Rheims already was not just unprovable but could be proved false, as far as contemporaries were concerned. And for this reason, the rumour was easy for the Privy Council to deny, as in 1587 it was not true and provably not true. However, Christopher Marlowe is frequently absent from Cambridge, according to those same Corpus Christi Buttery Books and the records of payment of his scholarship. And during Marlowe's time at Cambridge the records are affected by the syphoning off of money to build a library for the Parker book collection. The records are not accurate and some are missing. The upshot of this is that Marlowe could have been absent at any time without it being recorded (so could be in Rheims when Baines was betrayed, for example). The repercussion of this discovery is that it is possible for someone else to be taking Marlowe's place at Cambridge and for them to maintain a continuing life elsewhere, meaning Shakespeare could have gone back to Stratford in November 1582 to marry Anne Hathaway, having received a message in his drop box. That not all absences are recorded allows us to believe the other dates will fit, but Marlowe is also absent from Cambridge during part of November in 1582, allowing the marriage to Anne. All the other of Marlowe's known absences allow Shakespeare to be in Stratford both in the summer of 1582 and the Easter of 1584, in order to father his three children.

But Shakespeare did not go to university. He tells Jonson his education is limited: the famous statement that he had small Latin and less Greek. Yet he quite likely went to Stratford grammar school and until the age of fourteen would have had a curriculum that was exclusively Latin and Greek. There is no evidence that Shakespeare did not have a university education, apart from what he told Jonson about his knowledge of Latin and Greek. In fact, the only evidence for this is Jonson's hearsay version of what Shakespeare said, and Shakespeare may have had a reason for telling lies about his education. However, many who dispute Shakespeare's authorship say he was completely uneducated and cite his daughters' lack of education. Because Susanna only signed her name and Judith made her mark some assume they were illiterate. But we have already seen that John Marlowe could only sign his name, but witnessed wills, which he could not do if he could not read. The ability to read was not always linked with being able to write; reading being considered more important so that one could read the Scriptures. Girls outside the aristocracy but of the middling sort were more likely to be taught only to read (by their mother) and to do household accounts, so their writing ability would be much more circumscribed, perhaps limited to signing their name and writing figures and short lists. Boys sent to school would have also learned to write because they had to make translations from Latin and Greek.

There is no reason to suppose that Shakespeare did not attend a university, because absence of evidence is not proof of absence, which is the grounds on which we tend to assume Shakespeare did go to grammar school. And although he retained his roots as a man of the middling sort, unlike some of his contemporaries, the evidence of Shakespeare's work, as opposed to his daughters' ability to write, is that it is the product of a man who was educated, and able to access knowledge from a variety of sources - not an ability available to someone of little education, since education itself allows the formation of schema to which knowledge can be added, and facilitates the gaining of new knowledge.

A mind already trained is apt to research, and Shakespeare did research his plots, using a variety of sources. The evidence for his education is that he writes plays based on stories from Ovid, Plautus and other classical authors. The argument is that he must have seen translations of the stories. But the choice of such stories argues an initial knowledge of them in order to want to write about them. It is well said that we cannot think about what we do not know, and the same can be said of writing: information looked up on a subject produces a much less plausible effect than embedded knowledge of it which allows manipulation and invention, and the addition of more knowledge over time. And Shakespeare had no urgent need of classical models as there were plenty of other subjects from English and Scottish history, from Chaucer (as in *The Three Noble Kinsmen*), and also from the Bible, as well as topical stories such as that portrayed in *Arden of Faversham* or from morality plays. But Shakespeare chooses tales from classical works, and from the Decameron (*Romeo and Juliet*) and the Arabian Nights (the tale of Christopher Sly in *The Taming of the Shrew*, and the *Shrew* itself). This suggests someone who is widely read not just in English but in other languages. This is one reason Marlowe, Oxford, Bacon and Emilia Bassano have been put forward as the writer of Shakespeare's works. But three pieces of evidence belie their authorship. First, Shakespeare shows a familiarity with the lives of ordinary people that Oxford, Bacon and Bassano[6] would not have had (and would not have written about if they had it) and second, his knowledge of court life – often put forward as showing the writer of Shakespeare's plays was an aristocrat – is inaccurate, royal courts being depicted much more like country houses than palace households; thirdly, the paper trail reveals Shakespeare's life in London and verifies the truth of it: Shakespeare wrote his own plays, which were attributed to him in his lifetime.

---

6   Marlowe would have such knowledge but it is Shakespeare who makes use of his tradesman's background.

Shakespeare's authorship is supported by contemporary accounts and by his friends, Jonson, Heminge and Condell. Shakespeare himself is found in both London and Stratford, as a business man, playwright, actor, play broker, theatre manager, and property owner. There is no doubt the man from Stratford is the playwright who worked with Burbage at the Globe. But it is quite clear that this playwright does not appear on the scene until after Christopher Marlowe has disappeared. That Marlowe influenced Shakespeare is clear, and many think one hand wrote the work of both writers.

Jonson does say that Shakespeare never blotted a line. 'I remember, the players have often mentioned it as an honour to Shakespeare that in his writing (whatsoever he penned) he never blotted out line. My answer hath been, would he had blotted a thousand. Which they thought a malevolent speech.'[7]

Oxfordians particularly see this statement as proving that Shakespeare only made a fair copy of someone else's text. But Jonson is not saying that Shakespeare produced a fair copy, but that his work was an unrevised draft -

---

7 *Timber, or Discoveries* (1630). Jonson on Shakespeare, Internet Shakespeare Editions, http://internetshakespeare.uvic.ca/Library/SLT/drama/reputation/jonson 1 html. Accessed 13/9/18.

something Jonson, who took great pains and time over his own work, thought careless and liable to cause errors.

And Jonson followed up his comment on unblotted copy with: 'Many times he fell into those things could not escape laughter: as when he said in the person of Caesar, one speaking to him, "Caesar, thou dost me wrong," he replied "Caesar did never wrong, but with just cause," and such like, which were ridiculous.[8] But he redeemed his vices with his virtues. There was ever more in him to be praised than to be pardoned', in order to show that he was not being malevolent. It also makes clear there is no suggestion at all that Shakespeare was not producing his own work. Jonson rather gives support to Shakespeare writing in a hurry, almost as if the actors are waiting in anticipation for the next scene so they can rehearse it, rather than that he is presenting a fair copy of someone else's work.

The Marlovian position, however, is that Shakespeare is not the author of his plays but a nom de plume for

---

8   Shakespeare appears to have changed the line. We now read: Know, Caesar doth not wrong, nor without cause/Will he be satisfied, with the second line short of the ten syllables. My own thought is 'Caesar did never wrong, but with just cause': makes perfect sense when you realise Caesar was a politician - he did wrong to people when he needed to do so because he had justified suspicions someone else was up to no good - perhaps using agent provocateurs - and Shakespeare was a spy with some understanding of politicians. Jonson was mistaken.

Christopher Marlowe. The suggestion is that William Shakespeare was only a play broker and theatre manager, not a playwright, because Shakespeare does not have the requisite education. But Shakespeare's plays touch on his life. Shylock's trial may mirror that of John Shakespeare, shamed by tax avoidance in his wool dealings. The Forest of Arden uses the family name of Shakespeare's mother. Shakespeare writes of the countryside as someone who knows it well, which would be likely for someone from rural Stratford-on-Avon, but much less so for someone from Canterbury, which was less rural by sixteenth century standards. This suggests that the man from Stratford wrote the plays that bore his name. The similarities to Marlowe's work is because between 1580 and 1592 Shakespeare and Marlowe were one person, and that person was mostly Shakespeare, working in London as Marlowe whilst Marlowe spied on recusants and fed the information to Shakespeare who passed it to Seething Lane.

It looks as if Shakespeare did receive a good education from somehwhere. His grammar school education to around the age of fourteen would have been heavily loaded with Latin and Greek so he would have the basic knowledge to attend a university, even without the further study Marlowe had had. Shakespeare might have gone abroad, or to Scotland, but the likeliest chance is that he went to either Oxford or Cambridge. Yet there is no record of him at either university. Unless he did not attend as William Shakespeare. If he took the place of Christopher Marlowe then he would not be recorded, and Marlowe could have been at Rheims to betray Baines to life-long emnity, and become a Catholic priest with access to Catholics in England, where he would be able to spy for Walsingham and Burghley.

In support of that supposition, in later in life, long after Marlowe has disappeared or died, Shakespeare makes a point of saying - in the teeth of the evidence of his work - that he has little classical education. Why? Because Marlowe and Shakespeare were interchangeable secret agents, but that by 1593 that world had become dangerous to one of them. Not necessarily for Marlowe, but possibly for Shakespeare. If Marlowe was in dispute with the Allen brothers then Shakespeare would have wished to disassociate himself as a matter of pure economics. As far as the Allens went Marlowe had a reputation that Shakespeare needed to be clear of, so their mutual identity had to end if Shakespeare was to succeed in London. Added to this problem was the proclamation of Marlowe's atheism and his possible connections to such people as Raleigh, as well as his connection with alchemy, suggested by the events at Vlissingen.

Once Marlowe was apparently dead then Shakespeare had to distance himself in every way from his fellow secret agent. He did this by changing his associates and changing the subject of his work, and even some of his writing style - but in this last he could not shake off mannerisms and phrases already embedded in his psyche, and like all writers he repeated himself. Thus, Marlowisms remain in the work of Shakespeare, and can be recognised as such.

-0-

Conclusions

The argument throughout has been that Shakespeare's is the major hand in Marlowe's plays and that after Marlowe disappeared Shakespeare attempted to change his style and subject matter to distance himself from earlier work. But writers repeat themselves and use stock phrases without thought, and Jonson confirms that Shakespeare did not revise, so it looks as though lines and thoughts that echo Marlowe's plays appear in Shakespeare's many years after 1593 because Shakespeare is repeating his own turns of phrase. This contention is supported by the Buttery records and the similarities between Shakespeare and Marlowe's work, is that it was Shakespeare who attended Cambridge as Marlowe, and that Marlowe went to Rheims either in 1580, with the connivance of Walsingham, or in 1582 (having intermittent attendance before that); both possibilities allow Marlowe to betray Richard Baines, and also allow

Shakespeare to marry Anne Hathaway and father three children.

Neither Richard Baines nor Christopher Marlowe have relationships with women and neither marry, unlike Poley, Frizer or Watson, for example, at least two of whom were originally Catholics, and one of whom also attended at Rheims (Douai). Not being married is unusual in the sixteenth century except within the church. We know that Baines was ordained as a Catholic priest, and went to a college where ordination into the reformed English church was expected. Married clergy were still not quite acceptable in England during Elizabeth's reign; Whitgift, Elizabeth's much favoured Archbishop, is not married, and Archbishop Parker, who was, was considered to be in breach of propriety by the Queen. The argument that Marlowe was homosexual does not explain his lack of marriage, as it was common in the past for men whom we would consider homosexual to marry and have children, whilst perhaps having relationships with men outside that marriage. Thus it cannot be sexual preference that stops Marlowe marrying (something his family would want and expect, and which would enhance his financial and social status), so it must be some other reason. That Marlowe did not marry supports the idea that he had been ordained and therefore was expected not to marry, and if he was ordained as a Catholic priest then marriage was out of the question if he was to maintain his cover in recusant households. Though his lack of marriage is is not conclusive evidence of ordination[9] it is indicative of a possibility.

Whilst Marlowe was supposedly at Cambridge, then, he has been training for the priesthood in Rheims. In which case someone else was at Cambridge, and that person has to have been capable of taking on a university course and spying on Catholics, and of writing the play *Dido* and making a translation of Ovid's[10] *Amores*. William Shakespeare fits that description if we accept he did attend Stratford grammar school.

A further salient point in the argument that Shakespeare took Marlowe's place at Cambridge is that Marlowe seems unaware that Baines is a danger during the sojourn in Vlissingen. Not until Baines reports that Marlowe and Gifford are counterfeiting does his presence emerge as a threat. The implication of Baines' approach to Sidney is that he, Marlowe and Gifford are working together, but that does not seem to be the case, even if they are sharing a chamber. Baines seems to know nothing of the whereabouts of Gifford's workshop and has no knowledge

---

9   Lack of a secure income would be another reason, but does not seem to have deterred Robert Poley, who saw marriage as a route to money, nor William Shakespeare and Thomas Watson.

10   Ovid is considered to be one of Shakespeare's main influences

of what is going on apart from reporting the defective Dutch shilling. Baines makes a straight accusation of counterfeiting and it is not denied, though Marlowe counter accused him. If Marlowe knew Baines from Rheims, then he would surely have recognised him. That Marlowe does not seem to know Baines suggests the person present in Vlissingen is not Marlowe from Canterbury, but his alter ego William Shakespeare from Stratford, carrying out a mission as Marlowe, on behalf of the Burghley, and furthermore a mission that Burghley wishes to keep secret. What appears to be happening is alchemy, probably at the behest of Lord Burghley who had been corresponding on the subject with a well-known alchemist in Prague. In this case it is not surprising that on returning to London the entire matter is dropped - attempting to use alchemy to bolster English funds would be seen as desperation, with probable dire diplomatic consequences, and possibly more tangible consequences such as renewed attempts at invasion. Marlowe/Shakespeare comes off scot-free, therefore, and continues his work as a secret agent and as a playwright.

It is Baines' consistent attempts to have Marlowe imprisoned and executed that point to a relationship between them that has roused Baines' enmity. It is this enmity that needs to be explained. The betrayal of Baines to Dr Allen at Rheims brings about a traumatic experience for him, including torture and the imminent threat of death. His betrayer seems to have been someone he trusted, a fellow spy, a lover perhaps. The betrayer is never named and yet Baines, once in England, uses every opportunity he can get to discredit Christopher Marlowe. A plausible explanation is that Marlowe has done some injury to Baines that Baines is unwilling to reveal, perhaps because it does relate to a homosexual affair, but wants to revenge. Getting Marlowe executed is a very satisfactory outcome. The reported killing at Deptford would also satisfy, though perhaps not as much as public humiliation and execution - things which Baines had experienced and feared whilst in prison in Rheims. It is also Baines' enmity that suggests Marlowe is a more important secret agent than previously thought, which might explain that the events at Deptford were intended as a rescue attempt.

Once Marlowe is apparently dead Shakespeare emerges into London's theatre land, and is on his own. Later, he writes in conjunction with other playwrights, but never as closely as with Marlowe.

Finally, it is Penry who is buried in St Nicholas' churchyard in Deptford, having been murdered by Marlowe himself. Marlowe is probably buried in Spain under the name he used in Rheims. It may be him who sent a recusant priest to England in 1601, and gave him the name of Christopher Marlowe - a gentle hint to his friends and enemies that he was still alive. As for Shakespeare, he is certainly buried in Stratford, though not necessarily under his own ledger stone, and he as certainly wrote most of the text of the plays which are attributed to him, as well as much of the text of those attributed to Christopher Marlowe. Both men were spies.

AN ENGLYN ON KIT MARLOWE

John Penry lies in Master Marlowe's grave,
In Stratford Will sleeps fast.
Bold Kit lies the deep sea past
Trait'rous priest, in Spain at last.

Appendix I

Some Red Herrings

This appendix examines some events and records which many feel bear on Shakespeare's identity, and whether Marlowe or Shakespeare wrote the works ascribed to them. All but one, though of interest, in the event prove little - except, perhaps the possibility that 'one Morley' written of by the Countess of Shrewsbury, was someone called Christopher Marlowe.

1. Shakespeare's Will

Was it Shakespeare or Marlowe who set off for the continent to spend a life in espionage and hide within the Catholic church after the murder in Deptford? The first contention was that Shakespeare might have died in Deptford and that Marlowe returned to Stratford - resulting in a cold marriage and therefore a disinheriting will. On balance, considering that Shakespeare spent little time in Stratford one might guess that it was Marlowe who remained. This suggestion might also seem to fit with Shakespeare's will, which leaves the largest part of his large fortune to his elder daughter, Susannah, and apparently very little to his widow, Anne. However, this is to misread Elizabethan inheritance law. Anne Hathaway did not need to be left any money, by law she inherited a third of her husband's estate for life, and so

Anne was left extra property when she also got the second best bed, which will have been the marriage bed, rather than the guest bed[1]. There is this, also, in support of William Shakespeare remaining as himself: after 1613 he seems to be quite happy at Stratford and there is no sense of animosity between him and his wife, indeed they are arranging their younger daughter's marriage and Shakespeare leaves her provision in his will as well, though rather less than to her sister, Susannah[2] Marlowe would have had no reason to favour one daughter over the other, since neither was his, whereas Shakespeare might have had several reasons for leaving the elder daughter more property. That Shakespeare left no books is slightly more surprising than leaving more money to an elder child. Books were valuable and are often itemised in wills, like that of the headmaster at the King's

---

1   The bequest is a late insert, it is true. But this may not suggest more than that Shakespeare decided quite late that he wished to leave the bed to his wife, rather than that he had not thought about her.

2   Shakespeare died, or rather was buried, on 23 April 1616. He left the greatest part of his estate in an elaborate fee tail or entail (thus preventing sale of the estate by the current tenant-in-possession) to his elder daughter, Susannah Hall, and her husband, John, and to Susannah's male heirs, followed by her daughter Elizabeth's male heirs. The estate included New Place and two houses on Henley Street, as well as land in and about Stratford. He then added: (all his) "goodes Chattels, Leases, plate, jewles and Household stuffe whatsoever after my dettes and Legasies paied and my funerall expences discharged". This residual estate was left to the Halls as well.

School in Canterbury. But the books may have been given away earlier, or he may have left them in London, with his Dark Lady, and his London property (if this is not the 'Leases;' he mentions among his residual estate in his will), and perhaps other heirs, now unknown to us. Thus, Shakespeare's will provides us with no reason to believe that the testator was not the man born in Stratford. Another point to consider is: where are Marlowe's books? None of his friends mention them, or possess them, and his family leave no books in their wills that might have been Marlowe's. So a playwright lacking books is not so peculiar as it would appear. And if there were books, the obvious candidates for having all Shakespeare's are John Heminges and Henry Condell, who published Shakespeare's plays. It is also possible, too, that Shakespeare's books as well as his plays, had become and remained the property and in the possession of the King's Men acting troupe. Shakespeare would then have no cause to mention them in his will.

In conclusion if it had been Marlowe who had returned to Anne in Stratford either in 1613, or earlier, when New Place was bought, or when there were family funerals, Anne would have realised that he was not her husband, by his behaviour, his knowledge of the town and the house, and his manner in the marriage bed. These things cannot be faked - she would have known, or realised within a short time, that this was not her husband. It would be impossible for Christopher Marlowe to take Shakespeare's place in Stratford. Far simpler for Shakespeare to take his own in London and Stratford, and for Marlowe to correspond with him from abroad[3], sending not only intelligence but also the information that Shakespeare used in his the settings of the plays he set in 'exotic' locations.

2. Evidence of the Grave - and the Skull

Good friend for Iesus sake forbeare,

To digg the dust enclosed heare.

Bleset be ye man yt spares these stones,

And curst be he yt [4]moves my bones.

The famous curse is a fairly standard admonition, a plea that no-one will move the bones either for experiment or to put them in an ossuary rather than leave them in the ground in which they lie. It was not uncommon to disinter bones in order to re-use the grave space. Shakespeare is

---

3   Though Marlowe clearly did not go to Bohemia. Jonson says in *Timber or Discoveries* (1630): 'Shakespeare in a play brought in a number of men saying they had suffered shipwreck in Bohemia, where is no sea near, by some hundred miles.' From *Halleck's New English Literature* by Reuben Post Halleck. New York: American Book Company, 1913.http://www.shakespeare-online.com/biography/benjonson.html (accessed 2018).

4   Notice that 'yt' can stand for : 'that' but also be understood as meaning: 'who' here. See Chapter Eighteen: The Burial Place.

suggesting this will be a bad idea in his case, not that something is buried here that he wished to remain hidden.

In 2014, as part of the celebration of Shakespeare's 400th anniversary in 2016, an investigation was made of the graves in the chancel of Holy Trinity[5] church, Stratford-on-Avon, by Kevin Colls, an archaeologist at Staffordshire University, and Erica Utsi, a geophysicist. The intention was partly to make a Channel 4[6] programme on Shakespeare. They examined the graves using ground penetrating radar (GPR). What they found gave credence to a story published in 1879, in The Argosy [7] magazine, which said that Shakespeare's skull had been stolen in the 1790s, some suggest 1794, by Dr. Frank Chambers, who had returned from abroad in 1791[8] To explain why the skull should have been stolen in the eighteenth century one needs to understand the obsession with collecting at that time, and the interest in famous people's skulls, the morphology of

---

5   The Collegiate Church of the Holy and Undivided Trinity, Stratford-on-Avon.
6   The Channel 4 programme used non-invasive radar techniques to reveal that the head may be missing from the grave lying under Shakespeare's famous curse, and that the bodies lying in the chancel are neither deep nor in caskets, but simply wrapped in shrouds and placed in quite shallow graves.
7   Argosy, Vol. 28,1879.
8   Ibid. p.269.

which was thought to be able to throw light on the abilities of their owner. Phrenology, the study of head bumps, was a popular science that purported to reveal through the examination of the shape of a person's skull, their intelligence and abilities, and has its origins in the work of Aristotle. By the eighteenth century it had become a 'science', through the work of Franz Joseph Gall[9], an Austrian physician, who was one of the first people to consider that the brain, not the heart, was the home of mental activities. He laid the foundations of anatomic characterology, being one of several at the time to link facial physiognomy with character, along with the Swiss author, Lavater.[10] In the nineteenth century phrenology was used, indeed, to differentiate races of humans, but it was also part of the investigation of genius. Owning the skull of a famous person was a collector's dream, with its chance of understanding the origin of the person's life and works, and such items had a high monetary value. So, along with taking fresh corpses for dissection, there was also a market in digging up the famous for sale to collectors. This was reported to have happened to William Shakespeare, and Colls and Utis's investigation showed disturbance at the

---

9   Graham Patrick, (2001) *Phrenology* [video recording (DVD)]: revealing the mysteries of the mind. Richmond Hill, Ont: American Home Treasures.ISBN 0-7792-5135-0
10   The History of Phrenology, https://phrenology.org/intro.html

head end of the grave under Shakespeare's curse. It appeared that the grave had been disturbed and that the head was missing. The disturbance appeared to be caused by repairs, and repairs had been carried out intermittently from the early seventeenth century.

The impetus for the theft is said, in The Argosy, to be a bet by Horace Walpole, that he would pay £300 for the skull of Shakespeare, if it could be had. Details in the story suggest it is based on fact, containing circumstantial details such as inns visited, and the names of Chamber's accomplices.

The 2014 GPR investigation, part of another project to investigate New Place which began in 2010, did indeed suggest that the head was missing from the grave under Shakespeare's curse. While Kevin Colls is convinced that Shakespeare's skull is missing the vicar of Holy Trinity is less sure. "We are not convinced, however, that there is sufficient evidence to conclude that his skull has been taken", says the Rev. Patrick Taylor.

However, as part of the investigation of the graves the team investigated persistent rumours that Shakespeare's skull is now residing in the crypt at St Leonard's, Beorley, in the parish of Redditch. The skull, when examined, turned out to be that of a seventy year old woman.

The floor at Holy Trinity, Stratford, and the chancel have been re-arranged and remodelled since 1644, when Parliament ordered the destruction of 'vestments, organs, fonts, lofts and images'. It was probably during the Commonwealth that the original font, where Shakespeare would have been baptised, was damaged. By 1839 pews, a gallery and a three-decker pulpit (a pulpit with places to stand and preach on three levels) had been installed and in 1887 the choir stalls were moved and in 1890 the high altar was remodelled.[11] In 1799 the old college house was demolished, the charnel house had also gone by that time.

Of even more interest is the information that by 1618 the chancel was described as 'ruinous'[12] and that it was refurbished in 1621-22 (possibly this is the date the monument was erected, as it is built into the chancel wall). Disrepair had returned by the 1800s, as the chancel was boarded off from the main church in the early nineteenth century. Between 1836-1837 and 1839-1841 restoration work was carried out by Harvey Eginton, an architect from Worcester (Holy Trinity is in the diocese of Worcester).[13] Part of the work, according to Historic England's List Entry

---

11 History of Holy Trinity, Stratford,
12 ibid.
13 The 1884-98 restoration was by George Frederick Bodley and Thomas Garner. Ibid.

Summary (Holy Trinity is listed as grade 1), included: 'replacement of the roof coverings of the nave and the chancel, the construction of a new high altar, repaving the chancel and new pews and galleries'. Of particular interest is the repaving of the chancel. Shakespeare's grave is not under his monument, as one would expect, but beyond the grave of his wife, Anne Hathaway. Her grave also has an inscription: "Here lyeth the body of Anne wife of William Shakespeare who departed this life the 6th day of August 1623 being of the age of 67 years."

There are three things of interest concerning the missing skull under Shakespeare's curse, and the skull at Beorley. First, the pavement was relaid between 1836 and 1841, and prior to this the chancel was boarded off from the main church because it was in disrepair, and the last noted repairs were carried out in the 1620s. Secondly, one would expect Shakespeare's monument to be over his grave, but it is his wife's grave marker that is below it, not his (which has no name on it, of course). Thirdly, the skull at Beorley is that of a woman, an old woman. "It was an unknown woman in her 70s," said Colls, as reported by Mark Brown in the Guardian Arts pages, Wednesday 23 March 2016.

Anne Hathaway is described as being sixty-seven when she died.

It is perfectly possible that when the floor was replaced, or re-laid, that the ledger stones were misplaced. It is possible no-one remembered quite where they were by the 1830s, indeed if the floor was damaged then it might well not have been clear in the 1790s either, and paving may have been moved about prior to the nineteenth century replacement - the eighteenth century had no feeling or respect for Gothic architecture until the novels of Horace Walpole appeared, and he built Strawberry Hill, so changing medieval churches to suit modern tastes, or simply tidy up, was not taboo. Thus, in the 1830s the memorials may have been replaced accurately from the point of view of where they were when the floor was unrepaired, but that might not be where they were in 1616. They may also have been re-arranged after the burials of Susannah, in 1649, and her husband John Hall, in 1635, and their son-in-law, Thomas Nash. They may have been moved earlier, to make repairs to the floor any time after 1618, or as part of the general refurbishment in 1621-2, and may also have been damaged during the Commonwealth, whilst removing what were considered papist items and imagery (the medieval font was moved and smashed, for example). It would also have been dark in the chancel in the 1790s, (the removal of the skull would, perforce, be carried out at night) and Frank Chambers and his fellows would have only intermittent light to work from. From this one might extrapolate, with some chance of truth, that the skull at Beorley is Anne Hathaway's, not Shakespeare's, if the legend is true and it comes from Holy Trinity, Stratford, and that Shakespeare is buried under his monument, skeleton intact, in the grave now marked as his wife's. In which case, when Colls and his team reconstructed the facial features of the Beorley skull they showed the world Anne Hathaway. The grave marker for Anne Hathaway contains no interdict on touching the bones. It reads: "Breasts, O mother, milk and life thou didst give. Woe is me - for how great a boon shall I give stones? How much rather would I pray that the good angel should move the stone so that, like Christ's body, thine image might come forth! But my prayers are unavailing. Come quickly, Christ, that my mother, though shut within this tomb may rise again and reach the stars." An investigation of this grave might well prove fruitful, as to the provenance of Shakespeare's skull, but has no bearing on Shakespeare's relationship with Marlowe.

3. 'One Morley'

On 21st September 1592 Elizabeth, Countess of Shrewsbury (better known as Bess of Hardwick), the guardian of her granddaughter, the unfortunate Arbella Stewart, wrote to Burghley that she had dispensed with the services of 'one Morley'[14] who had been employed by her to 'read' to Arbella for the last three and a half years. She speaks of this young man being a university graduate, somewhat suspect in 'forwardness of religion', and as a person who had hoped for some £40 p.a. from Arbella's, and also has tried hard to get back into the countess's favour and retain his job. But this cannot be Christopher Marlowe, as he had appeared in Canterbury and fought with the tailor Corkyne on September 13. Or could it? The picture displayed by Bess of Hardwick, of someone wanting money, a university graduate who cannot take advantage of their degree ('he was so much damnified by leaving of the University' - that is, leaving the university had cost him an income) that I am tempted to think this man was Shakespeare in his role of Marlowe. Shakespeare could take no advantage of his degree from Cambridge, it was in Marlowe's name - he had the education without the substance and leaving Cambridge had thus cost him an income - he could perhaps have continued as a fellow, or in some other position, but Marlowe would go to London. Also, John Aubrey reported that Shakespeare had been a tutor, and he had this information from an actor whose father knew Shakespeare, which suggest it contains some truth, but may also be muddied by time, as memories are, especially

---

14   BL Lansdowne MS71, part 2.

as to when and where. It is possible for Shakespeare to have been 'one Morley' whilst Marlowe worked in London, especially as aristocratic houses were peripatetic, and Arbella is known to have attended court in 1587 and 1588 and spent time at her grandmother's house in London with an extended visit from November 1591 to July 1592.

One of the advantages of Shakespeare and Marlowe's double act, especially to Burghley, if he knew of it and to the protagonists at all times, was that Marlowe could always be proved to be in another place when charged with wrongdoing or suspected of acting as an agent. If 'one Morley' is Shakespeare/Marlowe then he is in Arbella Stuart's household as a spy, set there by the Privy Council (who call Marlowe 'Morley' in their letter to Corpus Christi in 1587). But Bess of Hardwick seems oblivious to the probability her grandchild's tutor is a spy when she writes to her friend Burghley.

However, there are other candidates for this role in the Shrewsbury household. One possibility often put forward is Thomas Morley, an organist at St. Paul's who seems to have been mixed up in Catholic plots. However, it cannot be him as he was definitely employed in London for this period. There is, of course, the possibility it was one of his kinsmen, but they would have to have attended the university (because the countess says Morley has) and who would this be? The only other Morley known at this time is Christopher Morley, who was at Cambridge at about the same time as Marlowe. But it would seem he did not leave Cambridge, but became a fellow and died there - thus he cannot have lost income by leaving the university as 'one Morley' claims.

Which leaves Marlowe or Shakespeare. And Shakespeare - not Marlowe - has attached to him the story told by John Aubrey (admittedly not the most reliable source) who attests that one of the actors in the same company as Shakespeare told the tale to his son, that Shakespeare had been a tutor in the north. The tendency is to assume Lancashire, when Shakespeare was young, but Derbyshire would be equally northern to a Londoner. The money hunting of 'one Morley' also fits with other things we know of Shakespeare. For example, that he was a play broker, the accusation made of him in Ben Jonson's poem *The Poet-Ape*. We also know that he not only bought and sold plays, but had them published for his own theatre company, under his own name, usually as 'revised'. This was done certainly with a play by Robert Greene. Shakespeare was also a buyer of tithes, and land and tenements in Stratford - and possibly also in London. He was also a loan broker, that is, he arranged to put together a loan provider with someone who needed a loan, an arrangement for which he was paid. Proof of this is the letter, written in London from the Bell Inn 25 October 1598 by Richard Quiney (later to be Judith Shakespeare's father-in-law). It is addressed to 'my loving friend and good countryman' William Shakespeare.

'You shall neither lose credit nor money by me, the Lord willing, and now but persuade yourself so as I hope and you shall not need to fear but with all hearty thankfulness I will hold my time and content your friend, and if we Bargain farther you shall be the paymaster yourself'.[15]

This suggests that Quiney is asking Shakespeare to arrange a loan for him and that Shakespeare will lose nothing by doing this, as Quiney will keep the payments up. There is also the suggestion that Shakespeare might lend money himself in the final phrase, 'you shall be the paymaster yourself'. This chimes well with the theatre land activities of the Allen brothers, who were clearly making loans (indeed, operating as money lenders) when Greene and Bradley died (both owing the Allens money) between 1589 and 1592.

It is just possible that Arbella Stuart's tutor was Shakespeare in the guise of Marlowe, and that he was spying on the household, as well as writing plays in London - and there is this. When Marlowe was writing his *Hero and Leander*, he was at Thomas Walsingham's house, not in

---

15   Richard Quiney to William Shakespeare 25 Oct 1598.

London at all. There is no need for either Marlowe or Shakespeare to be continuously in Norton Folgate from 1587 to 1593. They can write anywhere. Certainly, I agree with Nicholls[16] that the story of 'one Morley' would pay investigating.

4. The Massacre at Paris

The Massacre at Paris is occasionally cited as evidence that Marlowe wrote Shakespeare's plays (and poetry). The only surviving version of *The Massacre* appears to be an actors' copy, a playbook (such as Thomas Kyd might have copied out), and it is thought to be both incomplete and corrupt. The basis for suggesting that the writer of *Massacre* is also the writer of Shakespeare's plays is based on the repetition of lines. For example:

Queen Mother: What art thou dead, sweet son? Speak to thy mother.

Massacre at Paris, xiii.16

Compared with:

Queen Margaret: Oh Ned, sweet Ned, speak to thy mother, boy!

---

16   Nicholl, C. *The Reckoning* p.p.428-431.

Henry VI Part III, V.v.49.[17]

And again:

Queen Mother: And he nor hears, nor sees us what we do.

Massacre at Paris, xiii.18

Compared with:

Warwick: And he nor sees, nor hears us, what we say.

Henry VI Part III, II, vi,63.

That is a lot of lines that are very similar. It can be continued. Here is Navarre, in *The Massacre (xviii.2)*: And we are grac'd with wreaths of victory. And King Edward in *Henry VI Part III, V.iii.2:* And we are graced with wreaths of victory.

Such similarities and repeats as these appear throughout *The Massacre*. Now either the writer of *The Massacre* also wrote *Henry VI Part III*, or what we have is a reconstructed copy of *The Massacre*, based on what actors can remember of their parts. Even though currently Marlowe is given status as co-author with Shakespeare for *Henry VI*, these repeated lines seem too close. It may well

---

17   Examples are taken from Andew S. Cairncross (ed) *Henry VI Part III* (Arden Third Series, 1996)

be, and I think it is so, that the writer of one play also wrote the other, but the similarities between them do not prove this. All they prove is that a short, remembered version of *The Massacre of Paris* is what we have - really too short, at 1,250 lines, to be complete - and it is a reconstruction by actors, from memory, with perhaps some help from parts of a play book. The repeated lines have been inserted because either an actor mixed up his plays, or a line was needed and one was found to fit, as Philip Henslowe planned to revive the play (which had been performed ten times between 19th June and 25 September 1594 by the Admiral's Men (as *The Guise or The Massacre at Paris)*, as well as by Lord Strange's Men on 26 January 1593, if it is the play they acted called *The Tragedy of the Guise)* in 1602 - and he may have had it revised.[18] If it had parts missing they would have to be supplied and a little plagiarizing was nothing to seventeenth century dramatists, and certainly not to theatre managers - there was no copyright (and Shakespeare may have added the lines to Marlowe's play himself, since, if my reasoning has been correct, most of it was his anyway).

---

18 Henslowe's diary markes *The Massacre* as 'ne'. This might either mean it was a new play or possibly that it was to be performed at Newington Butts theatre. Henslowe planned a revival in 1602.

One can go further and look beyond *Henry VI*, though, to *Arden of Faversham* in comparing lines:

Duchess of Guise: Sweet Mudgeroun, 'tis he that hath my heart,

>And Guise usurps it, cause I am his wife.

Massacre at Paris, xv, 3-4

Alice: Sweet Mosby is the man that hath my heart,

>And he usurps it, having nought but this -

>That I am tied to him by marriage.

Arden of Faversham, II, 3-4

If anything, this comparison (from Martin White's edition of *Arden of Faversham*) suggests that Shakespeare and Marlowe wrote *Arden* between them. The combination of Shakespeare's mother's surname and the place it was likely Marlowe's family originated also point to this possibility - Shakespeare makes use of his mother's surname (the Forest of Arden, the origin of the Arden surname, still exists outside Stratford) in *As You Like It*, where he also refers to *the reckoning in a small room* and *the passionate shepherd*, likely sly reference to his being Marlowe, just as later, on his monument and tomb.

Of more interest still is *Macbeth* compared to *Tamburlaine*. In *Tamburlaine* Bajazeth is caged in exactly the same way that Macbeth is described as being caged, if he is taken alive at Dunsinane.

Then there is the line spoken by the Duke of Guise, that would appear to come from *Julius Caesar*:

Yet Caesar shall go forth,

Massacre at Paris, xxi, 67,

which, if actually taken from *Julius Caesar*, places the possible reconstruction after 1599 when *Julius Caesar* appeared, fitting with Henslowe having the *Massacre* revised for a new production in 1602 and suggesting the likelihood that Shakespeare, and perhaps others, did the revision. But the repetitions in themselves probably prove nothing. They only show a reconstruction of a play that got partially lost between 1594 and 1602 because acting companies were peripatetic, changed patrons, and therefore repertoires and stages, had members leave (who probably took copies of plays with them) and simply misplaced play books they were not currently using, and an attempt was made to put in the missing parts so it could be performed.

5. *The Taming of the Shrew* and Christopher Sly[19]

The Taming of the Shrew includes an introductory scene, as though it is a framed play, but a frame which is not returned to at the end of the play. The story involves the tricking of one Christopher Sly and owes much to tales from *The Arabian Nights*. The frame of *The Taming of the Shrew* involves the deception of a poor man that he is a rich merchant with a wife. Christopher Sly is duped into believing that he is the focus of a performance of a play which is being put on just for him, and that his wife (who is really a boy dressed as a women, just as Elizabethans played women's parts) from whom he has been estranged because of his strange mental state in which he has believed he is destitute, is coming to join him. This is much the same story as that in *The Arabian Nights* when a beggar is convinced by a group of courtiers (on the order of the Sultan) that he is Sultan. Eventually the beggar, who is shunted back and forth from palace to prison, accidentally kills the hidden Sultan (just as Hamlet stabs Polonius behind the arras) and actually becomes the Sultan. This denouement does not happen to Christopher Sly because the closure of the sequence is omitted from the play. Meanwhile in the play various characters take on other roles. Bianca's suitor

---

19   Gortazar, Isabel, *The Clue in The Shrew (Revised)*

pretends to be a tutor who has studied at Rheims, and a traveller from Mantua is tricked into pretending to be the suitor's father. The references to deceit and Rheims may refer to Marlowe and Shakespeare's swapping of identities, but though Shakespeare may be playing here with the idea of swapping identities and disguises this is not conclusive evidence of anything - they are just hints, without much foundation, as is the suggestion that they reveal that Marlowe wrote the plays of Shakespeare.

Conclusion

These events and records enlighten the picture of Shakespeare, and give some hints that Shakespeare and Marlowe were one and the same person, though two people, until Marlowe disappeared in May 1593. Only the words on Shakespeare's monument and grave, discussed in Chapter Eighteen, give any clue that Shakespeare wrote Marlowe's plays, or that they collaborated in various ways. Once Marlowe was gone, Shakespeare had to take up the banner of being the glover's son from Stratford and distance himself entirely from Kit Marlowe for safety's sake - agents were vulnerable people, as were people inhabiting London's Liberties or ganglands, especially if they had dealings with the Allens as Marlowe had.[20] The various strands, however, of will, monument, grave, tutorship and plays, do support the theory that Shakespeare was Marlowe, and that Marlowe was and continued to be a secret agent, working with Shakespeare as his contact in England, at least until Shakespeare 'drowned his book'[21] in 1610/11, with his last play[22], *The Tempest.* It is Prospero, the magician who drowns his book, a Merlin, after all, so Shakespeare is perhaps saying that he, the magician, the Merlin of his age, has ceased to work or to exist with the ending of his last play. And it may be indeed that Kit Marlowe, who seems, whether when himself or Shakespeare, to have spelled his name Marlin [23] on occasion, died in 1610, and that therefore the association was at an end. It might also be that the life of double agents combined, for Shakespeare, with running part of theatreland with all its corruption, vice, gambling, brothels and protection rackets, along with his Stratford activities and brokering, got too dangerous and onerous and he simply decided that enough was enough. He remained as a manager of the Globe, but wrote no more plays, and ceased

---

20   See Chapter Ten above on Greene's Groat's Worth of Wit.
21   Much as Faustus burns his books at the end of *The Tragedy of Dr. Faustus.*
22   The last he wrote alone, at least.
23   And this is how Greene addresses Marlowe in Groats Worth of Wit.

to act as well (his name stops being on cast lists). In 1613[24] he went home to Stratford, so then, at least, we can assume that contact with Marlowe ceased - unless Shakespeare visited his Dark Lady in London. There is, of course, the possibility that the book Shakespeare drowned had other, darker purposes, that explain some of his great wealth, his ability to buy land and tithes, and to arrange substantial loans. But if Shakespeare was also a blackmailer as well as secret agent, that is another story.

---

24   Perhaps drawn by the scandal and law suit his daughter, Susannah, and her husband, Dr John Hall, were involved in. Also, his brothers Gilbert and Richard had died in 1612, leaving property to be maintained, and William was by then the only surviving son of John and Mary Shakespeare.

GRAVE LINES

John Penry lies in Marlowe's grave,
Will Shakespeare lies in his wife's.
And mighty Kit lies across the sea
In far Valladolid.

Marlowe.

Appendix II

Juliet and Shakespeare's Gangs

Joan Marlowe, Frances Cornwallis and Juliet Capulet
Was Marlowe's Sister, Joan, the Original of Juliet Capulet?

This is an examination of the information we have about the birth, death and marriage of Christopher Marlowe's sister, Joan (or Jane), in order to question whether she, or Frances Cornwallis is the original for Juliet Capulet, and what this might tell us about Marlowe and Shakespeare's lives in Norton Folgate and Shoreditch. First there is a list of Marlowe's siblings, which does not contain Joan, although it contains a brother John who never appears later. What the entries at St. George's and St. Andrew's shows is examined. At the end is a table of months between births. My conclusion is that Joan Marlowe was older than thirteen when she married, and that she was born between 1565 and 1568, not in 1569. She may also have been registered elsewhere than St George's and St Andrew's churches.

Registered at St. George the Martyr's Church, Canterbury. The Marlowe's lived on the corner of St George St and St George Lane:

Births - recorded by baptism

May 21, 1562	Mary, the daughter of John Marlowe
Feb 26, 1563/4	Christofer, the son of John Marlow
Dec 11, 1565	Margarit, the daughter of John Marloe
Oct 31, 1568	-, the son of John Marlow
Aug 20, 1569	John, son of John Marle

July 26, 1570   Thomas, the son of John Marle
July 14, 1571   An, daughter of John Marle
Oct 18, 1573   Daretye, daughter of John Marlye[1]
Deaths - recorded by burial
Aug 28, 1568   daughter of John Marlow (possibly Mary)
Nov 5, 1568   son of John Marlow (possibly child baptised Oct 31 1568)
Aug 7, 1570   Thomas, son of John Marlow
Registered at St Andrew's Church, after the Marlowe's moved out of the parish of St. George.
Births - recorded by baptism
April 8, 1576   Thomas, son of John Marlow's
Discrepancies:
1. Dec 18, 1566   Marget,, daughter of John Marlow
2. Nov 5, 1567   Thomas, son of John Marlow - original entry in the St Andrew's register.

Boas says this entry in St Andrew's register must be wrong (p.3, footnote 3[2]) presumably because this is a transposition error and also that the Marlowe family were not living in the parish of St Andrew in 1567. Since the mistake is a simple transposition of figures that this is an error is entirely possible, and Boas is right. As with the entry for Margrit in 1566, a child is listed, that appears nowhere

---

[1]   Margaret (Margarit), Ann (An) and Dorothy's (Daretye) marriages are recorded, so we know these three daughters survived to adulthood, along with the missing Joan.

[2]   Boas, ibid. p3, described as the archdeacon's transcript, and also used by Tucker Brooke in his *Life of Marlowe,* 1930.

else, but this time it does appear to be an error on the original clerk's part.

Additionally Tucker Brooke suggests in *Life of Marlowe* (1930) that the entry for John, son of John Marlow in 1569 is also a clerical error, this time for Joan or Jane of whom there is no baptismal record, as there is no other reference to a son called John. But the assumption that the clerk registering baptisms made such a complete error is making quite a leap of logic. More likely is actually writing the wrong name for a child, not getting the entry completely wrong as to both name *and* sex. The burial record for John may simply not have survived, or he might have died outside Canterbury.

What is in the record is a substantial gap between the birth of Margaret in December 1565 (or 1566) and the birth of the first Thomas at the end of October 1568. The gap is at the least 22 months (if 1566 is the correct date of Margaret's birth) and 34 months if 1565 is the date of Margaret's birth. There are two issues here. The first is that births occur to John and Catherine Marlowe in 1562, 1563/4, 1565 and then in 1568, 1569, 1570, 1571 and 1573, with another large gap till the birth of the second Thomas in 1576 (this gap may silently record stillbirths or miscarriages, though the true possibility may be a change in Catherine's fertility which might have started to decrease since she was probably around 36 in 1576 and had borne at least 8 children). Such gaps in a record tend to indicate a birth that is not recorded (for example a stillbirth) or births which are recorded elsewhere[3] (as Joan's might be). It is also odd that

---

3   The other, most usual, possibility is that a long gap between

Margaret seems to have been entered twice in the transcript from St. George's, in December 1565 and December 1566. Getting a daughter's name wrong, or confusing it with a previous child is quite possible, baptising the same child twice is unusual. It looks as if Joan or Jane was born between 1565 and late 1567 rather than that she is the boy listed in 1569, born a bare nine months after the previous child in October 1568 (and therefore possibly premature). Indeed, she may well be the child listed as Marget in December 1566, which is a reasonable interval for John and Catherine's next child to be born[4], and the clerk simply mixed up John's daughter, assuming the transcripted record is itself not an error. In any case, she is not the boy baptised in 1569. If this case is what actually happened, when Joan married she was not thirteen (a very young age for a tradesman's daughter to marry, though not impossible in an aristocratic family) but sixteen or seventeen, and died in childbirth aged around eighteen. Convenient as it would be that Joan was Shakespeare's inspiration this revised date of birth makes her much less likely as the original for the play *Romeo and Juliet*, leaving the Cornwallis affair, and the duped daughter, fourteen year old Frances, a much likelier source for the age of Juliet. If Shakespeare, in the role of Marlowe, was participating in the gangs of Norton Folgate, as suggested in Chapter Eleven, then he would know about

---

births indicates a concealed grandchild. This cannot be the case here as none of the children are old enough to have children, and the gap is relatively short, being two and a half years. (It could record the child of another relative perhaps.)

4   Between 1568 and 1571 one child is born roughly every twelve months.

the Cornwallis trick. It is less likely that Marlowe told his alter ego about his sister's marriage, as sisters' marriages were not likely then, as now, a particularly interesting topic to their brothers, especially if there was nothing unusual about it - he may have passed on the fact that Joan had died, though.

Table to show intervals between births to Catherine Marlowe

Date	Year	Months difference
May 21	1562	12 months after marriage on 22/5/61
Feb 26	1564 (1563 OS)	21 months
Dec 11	1565	23 months
(Dec 18)	(1566)	(12 months)
Oct 31	1568	34 months -(22 if 1566 is a birth)
Aug 20	1569	9 months
July 26	1570	11 months
July 14	1571	12 months
Oct 18	1573	15 months
April 8	1576	30 months

In conclusion, Marlowe's sister Joan's marriage and death have little or no bearing on the relationship between Marlowe and Shakespeare. The main interest is in the interpretation of the baptismal records and identifying which of the listed children of John Marlowe Joan actually is. If a child was born in 1566, it is likely Joan. However, identifying Frances Cornwallis as Juliet confirms that Shakespeare was associated with the gangs of theatreland in the late 1580s, and was intimate with details of their scams and quarrels, and was therefore active in London more than two years before his name first appears attached to a publication.

Appendix III

Marlowe's Ancestry

Boas lists the first recorded Marlowe appearing in 1414[1], as a freeman of Canterbury. He is William Morle, a fuller, recorded as paying ten shillings redemption to become a freeman. Simon Morle, is also a fuller paying his redemption as a freeman of Canterbury in 1438. Thomas Morle, son of William is admitted as a freeman free, as the son of a freeman, in 1459. In 1478 there is Thomas Marlow, a roper admitted by paying a redemption and in 1467 a John Marley, tanner also admitted by redemption as a freeman. In 1521 John's son, Richard Marley, a freeman of Canterbury and a tanner, died leaving his estate to his son, Christopher. Christopher died in 1540, leaving a pregnant widow, Joan, and a son, John, whom several researchers have assumed was the playwright Christopher Marlowe's father. However, this unlikely to be John Marlowe, the father of Christopher Marlowe. John Marlowe was not born in Canterbury[2] and as Kuriyama shows there is no evidence of him having received anything from his father.[3]

---

1 Boas, F.S. Christopher Marlowe, a biographical and critical study. p.1 lists possible Marlowe antecedents.
2 Marlowe Society citing William Urry, *Christopher Marlowe and Canterbury*, Faber and Faber, 1988, - see discussion on pp 12-13.
3 Kuriyama, *Christopher Marlowe A Renaissance Life*, p.10.

There is some evidence that John Marlowe was born in near Faversham. That the play, *Arden of Faversham*, has been allotted to Marlowe – and also Shakespeare, since Arden is his maternal family name and the Forest of Arden is a feature of the Stratford area – bears out that this may be true. So, the ancestry set out by Boas is likely to be at best collateral.

Appendix IV

List of William Shakeshaftes in Sixteenth Century Lancashire

Names are taken from the Preston Guild Rolls of Burgesses, surviving parish registers and records of wills.[1]

'Williams' in the Preston Guild Roll Shakeshaftes
1562 William, son of William, glover.
  William son of Thomas, labourer.

1582 William son of William.
  William son of Richard, lead-beater.

These recur:
1602 William son of William.
  William son of Richard, lead-beater.

'Williams' among the Cadley/Fulwood Shakeshaftes
1587 William son of John – named in a will.
1615 William Shakeshafte of Kirkham recorded as dying.

Conclusion
  Shakeshaftes are found all over the Lancashire area in the parishes of Warrington, Stalmine, Wigan, Brindle,

---

1   Hamer, D., *Was William Shakespeare William Shakestaffe?* Review of English Studies, 1970.

Manchester, Garstang and Poulton-le-Fylde (Preston covers other areas, such as Croston and Farnworth).

The Shakeshaftes of Lancashire would appear at first glance to be irrelevant to the identification of William Shakeshaft with William Shakespeare, grandson of Richard Shakespeare or Shakeshafte of Stratford-on-Avon. The number of William Shakeshaftes about Houghton Hall, however, do explain why a clerk might have misspelled the name in the first place, and also why Shakespeare might have used the name Shakeshafte, one of the variants of his surname anyway, in order to conceal his origins as the son of a recusant from Stratford-on-Avon. The numbers are concealing of an arrival and also of a departure of a young man seeking his fortune and forced to take up a possibly unpalatable career in order to succeed. Among so many, one more William Shakeshafte would be practically invisible.

Appendix V

Cited Documents and Texts

1. Sonnet 74

But be contented: when that fell arrest
Without all bail shall carry me away
My life hath in this line some interest,
Which for memorial still with thee shall stay.
When thou reviewest this, thou dost review
The very part was consecrate to thee.
The earth can have but earth, which is his due,
My spirit is thine, the better part of me.
So then thou hast but lost the dregs of life,
The prey of worms, my body being dead,
The coward conquest of a wretch's knife,
Too base of thee to be remembered.
The worth of that, is that which it contains,
And that is this, and this with thee remains.

William Shakespeare

2. William Basse: Elegy upon Mr William Shakespeare
Renowned Spenser, lie a thought more nigh

To learned Chaucer, and rare Beaumont lie

A little nearer Spenser to make room

For Shakespeare in your threefold, fourfold tomb.

To lodge all four in one bed make a shift

Until Doomsday, for hardly will a fifth
Betwixt this day and that by fate be slain
For whom your curtains may be drawn again.
If your precedency in death doth bar
A fourth place in your sacred sepulcher,
Under this carved marble of thine own
Sleep rare tragedian Shakespeare, sleep alone,
Thy unmolested peace, unshared cave,
Possess as lord not tenant of thy grave,
That unto us and others it may be
Honor hereafter to be laid by thee.

3. Jonson: The Poet Ape

Poor Poet-Ape, that would be thought our chief,
Whose works are e'en the frippery of wit,
From brokage is become so bold a thief,
As we, the robb'd, leave rage, and pity it.
At first he made low shifts, would pick and glean,
Buy the reversion of old plays; now grown
To a little wealth, and credit in the scene,
He takes up all, makes each man's wit his own:
And, told of this, he slights it. Tut, such crimes
The sluggish gaping auditor devours;
He marks not whose 'twas first: and after-times
May judge it to be his, as well as ours.
Fool! as if half eyes will not know a fleece
From locks of wool, or shreds from the whole piece?
Ben Jonson (Source poets.org)

4. TO THE MEMORY OF MY BELOVED MASTER WILLIAM SHAKESPEARE, AND WHAT HE HATH LEFT US
by Ben Jonson

To draw no envy, SHAKSPEARE, on thy name,
Am I thus ample to thy book and fame;
While I confess thy writings to be such,
As neither Man nor Muse can praise too much.
'Tis true, and all men's suffrage. But these ways
Were not the paths I meant unto thy praise ;
For seeliest ignorance on these may light,
Which, when it sounds at best, but echoes right ;
Or blind affection, which doth ne'er advance
The truth, but gropes, and urgeth all by chance ;
Or crafty malice might pretend this praise,
And think to ruin where it seemed to raise.
These are, as some infamous bawd or whore
Should praise a matron ; what could hurt her more ?
But thou art proof against them, and, indeed,
Above the ill fortune of them, or the need.
I therefore will begin: Soul of the age!
The applause ! delight ! the wonder of our stage!
My SHAKSPEARE rise ! I will not lodge thee by
Chaucer, or Spenser, or bid Beaumont lie
A little further, to make thee a room :
Thou art a monument without a tomb,
And art alive still while thy book doth live
And we have wits to read, and praise to give.
That I not mix thee so my brain excuses,
I mean with great, but disproportioned Muses :
For if I thought my judgment were of years,

I should commit thee surely with thy peers,
And tell how far thou didst our Lyly outshine,
Or sporting Kyd, or Marlowe's mighty line.
And though thou hadst small Latin and less Greek,
From thence to honour thee, I would not seek
For names : but call forth thund'ring Aeschylus,
Euripides, and Sophocles to us,
Pacuvius, Accius, him of Cordova dead,
To life again, to hear thy buskin tread
And shake a stage : or when thy socks were on,
Leave thee alone for the comparison
Of all that insolent Greece or haughty Rome
Sent forth, or since did from their ashes come.
Triumph, my Britain, thou hast one to show
To whom all Scenes of Europe homage owe.
He was not of an age, but for all time !
And all the Muses still were in their prime,
When, like Apollo, he came forth to warm
Our ears, or like a Mercury to charm !
Nature herself was proud of his designs,
And joyed to wear the dressing of his lines !
Which were so richly spun, and woven so fit,
As, since, she will vouchsafe no other wit.
The merry Greek, tart Aristophanes,
Neat Terence, witty Plautus, now not please ;
But antiquated and deserted lie,
As they were not of Nature's family.
Yet must I not give Nature all ; thy art,
My gentle Shakspeare, must enjoy a part.
For though the poet's matter nature be,
His art doth give the fashion: and, that he
Who casts to write a living line, must sweat,

(Such as thine are) and strike the second heat
Upon the Muses' anvil ; turn the same,
And himself with it, that he thinks to frame ;
Or for the laurel he may gain a scorn ;
For a good poet's made, as well as born.
And such wert thou ! Look how the father's face
Lives in his issue, even so the race
Of Shakspeare's mind and manners brightly shines
In his well torned and true filed lines;
In each of which he seems to shake a lance,
As brandisht at the eyes of ignorance.
Sweet Swan of Avon ! what a sight it were
To see thee in our waters yet appear,
And make those flights upon the banks of Thames,
That so did take Eliza, and our James !
But stay, I see thee in the hemisphere
Advanced, and made a constellation there !
Shine forth, thou Star of Poets, and with rage
Or influence, chide or cheer the drooping stage,
Which, since thy flight from hence, hath mourned like night,
And despairs day, but for thy volume's light.

Source: Jonson, Ben. *The Works of Ben Jonson, vol. 3*.

London: Chatto & Windus, 1910. 287-9.

5. Kyd's Letter to Sir John Puckering

At my last being with your Lordship, to entreate some speaches from yow in my favor to my Lorde, whoe (though

I thinke he rest not doubtfull of myne inocence) hath yet in his discreeter iudgment feared to offende in his reteyning me with out your honors former pryvitie. So is it nowe Right Honourable: that the denyall of that favor to my thought resonable hath movde me to coniecture some suspicion, that your Lp. holds me in, concerning *Atheisme*, a deadlie thing which I was vndeserved chargd withall, & therfore haue I thought it requisite, aswell in duetie to your Lp. & the lawes, as also in the feare of god, & freedom of my conscience, therein to satisfie the world and yow: The first and most (thoughe insufficient surmize) that euer (*illegible*) therein might be raisde of me, grewe thus. When I was first suspected for that Libell that concernd the State, amongst those waste and idle papers (which I carde not for) & which vnaskt I did deliuer vp, were founde some fragments of a disputation toching that opinion, affirmed by Marlowe to be his, and shufld with some of myne vnknown to me by some occasion of our wrytinge in one chamber twoe years synce. My first acquaintance with this Marlowe, rose vpon his bearing name to serve my Lord: although his Lp never knew his service but in writing for his plaiers, For never cold my L. endure his name, or sight, when he had heard of his conditions, nor wold indeed the forme of devyne praier vsed duelie in his Lps house haue quadred with such reprobates. That I shold loue or be familer frend with one so irreligious, were verie rare;when *Tullie* saith *Digni sunt amicitia quibus in ipsis inest causa cur diligantur* (1) which neither was in him, for person, quallities, or honestie, besides he was intemperate & of a cruel hart, the verie contrarie to which my greatest enemies will saie by me. It is not to he nombred amongst the best conditions of men, to taxe or to opbraide the deade *Quia mortui non mordent* (2). But thus muche haue I (with your Lps favor) dared in the greatest cause, which is to cleere my selfe of being thought an *Atheist*, which some will sweare he was. For more assurance that I was not of that vile opinion, lett it but please your Lp to enquire of such as he conversd withall, that is which I am geven to vnderstand with *Harriot, Warner, Royden,* and some stationers in Paules churchyard, whom I in no sort can accuse nor will excuse by reson of his companie, of whose consent if I had been, no question but I also shold haue been of their consort, for *ex minimo vestigio artifex agnoscit artificem.* (3) Of my religion & life I haue alredie geven some instance to the late commissioners & of my reverend meaning to the state, although perhaps my paines and vndeserved tortures felt by some, wold haue ingendred more impatience when lesse by farr hath dryven so manye *imo extra caulas* (4) which it shall never do with me. But whatsoeuer I haue felt R. Ho: this is my request not for reward but in regard of my trewe inocence that it wold please your Lps so (*illegible*) same & me, as I maie still reteyne the favors of my Lord, whom I haue served almost theis vj yeres nowe, in credit vntill nowe, & nowe am vtterlie vndon without herein be somewhat donn for my recoverie. For I do knowe his Lp holdes your honors & the state in that dewe reverence as he wold no waie move the leste suspicion of his Loves and cares both towards hir sacred Ma*j*estie your Lpps and the lawes wherof when tyme shall serve I shall geue greater instances I haue observde. As for the libel laide vnto my chardg I am resolued with receyving of the sacram*ent* to satisfie your Lps & the world that I was neither agent nor consenting thervnto. Howebeit if some outcast *Ismael* for want or of his owne dispose to lewdnes, haue with pretext of duetie or religion, or to reduce himself so to that he was not borne vnto by enie waie incensd your Lps to suspect me, I shall besech in all humillitie & in the feare of god that it will please your Lps but to censure me as I shall prove my self, and to repute them as they ar in deed *Cum totius iniustitae nulla capitalior sit quam eorum, qui tum cum maxime fallunt id agunt vt viri boni esse videantur.* (5) For doubtles even then your Lps shalbe sure to breake *(illegible)* their lewde designes and see into the truthe, when but their lyues that herein haue accused me shal be examined & rypped vp effectually, soe maie I chaunce with *Paul* to liue & shake the vyper of my hand into the fire for which the ignorant suspect me guiltie of the former shipwrack. And thus (for nowe I feare me I growe teadious) assuring your good Lps that if I knewe eny whom I cold iustlie accuse of that damnable offence to the awefull Ma*jes*tie of god or of that other mutinous sedition towrd the state I wold as willinglie reveale them as I wold request your Lps better thoughtes of me that never haue offended yow.

Your Lps most humble in all duties

T. Kydde

(BL Harley MS.6849 f.218^{r,v})

Translation of Latin phrases:

1) They are worthy of friendship in whom resides a cause why they should he esteemed.

(2) Because the dead do not bite.

(3) From the smallest trace the craftsman recognises craft.

(4) Even outside the fold.

(5) With all injustice none is more deadly than that of those who, when they most deeply deceive, would seem to be good men.

Source: http://www.rey.prestel.co.uk/kyd2.htm

8. Marlowe and Thomas Watson were committed to Newgate Prison, 18 September 1589

Thomas Watson late of Norton Folgate in the county of Middlesex,. gentleman and Christopher Marlowe late of the same, yeoman, who wer led to jail the 18th day of September by Stephen Wild Constable of the same on suspicion o murder, namely in the death of (blank) and were committed by Owen Hopton, Knight.

Kuriyama notes that against Thomas Watson's name is the word 'balliatus' (bailed) and againt Christopher Marlowe's name is written 'deliberatus per proclamationem' (released by proclamation).

GLRO MJ/SR 284, No. 12, Newgate Calendar.

Translation from Kuriyama, *Christopher Marlowe, A Renaissance Life*, p. 203

7. Corkyne's complaint against Christopher Marlowe:

City of Canterbury

William Corkine sues Christopher Marlowe, gentleman, on a plea of transgression. And pledges to prosecute viz. John Doo and Richard Roo. And hence the same plaintiff, by Giles Winston his attorney, makes plaint that the foresaid defendant on the fifteenth day France and Ireland, Defender of the Faith etc., in the city of Canterbury aforesaid, in the parish of Saint Andrew and the ward of Westgate of this same city, by force of arms, that is to say with staff and dagger, assaulted this same plaintiff and then and there struck, wounded, and maltreated this same plaintiff. And then and there inflicted other outrages on the said plaintiff to the grave damage of the same plaintiff and against the peace of the said lady the queen, wherefore the same plaintiff says that he has suffered loss and incurred damages to the value of five pounds and hence brings this suit.

Translation from Kuriyama, *Christopher Marlowe, A Renaissance Life*, p. 213

8. THE CONFESSION OF RICHARD BAINES PRIEST AND LATE STVDENT of the Colledge of Rhemes, made after he was remoued out of the common gaile to his chamber.

AS MY MISERIE & WICKEDNES WAS GREATE WHICH I WILL NOW SET downe to the publishing of my ingratitude to God, the Church, and my superiors, so was Gods iustice, mercy and prouidence meruelous towards me to saluation as I verely hope. Of al which to the glory of Christ, and satisfaction of the holy Church and all her children whom I haue offended or scandalized, & to mine owne worthy confusion temporall, I intend to make this my publike confession, that al that stand, may by my example beware of a fall, and such as be fallen may thereby make hast to aryse againe.

The very ground of my fall and of al the wickednes ether committed or intended, was my pride which droue me to a lothsomenes to liue in order and obedience, to conceipts of mine owne worthines and manifold discontentement of the schollarlike condition wherein I liued, to an immoderat desire of more ease, welth, and (which I specially also respected) of more delicacie of diet and carnal delits then this place of banishment was like to yeld vnto me, though (wo vnto me that could not see so fare before) the students state in the Seminarie, where I was in very honest compt and calling is in all points so good and happy, that most wise men wonder at Gods so mercifull and plentifull prouision for the competent maintenance of so many in such a blessed trade of life and education.

Besides this, though I was not onely a student in diuinitie, but also a priest (though many waies I shewed and made my self most vnworthie of that high degree) pretending in dede in the sight of my superiors the study of holy scriptures as dewly required: yet in truth I most delited in prophane writers and the worst sort of them, such as ether wrot against the truth or had least tast of religion, whereby the holy writers of my Christian profession & priesthood, began daily to waxe more and more tedious and lothsome vnto me, in so much that in the doing of such publike exercises as by my course of study or my superiors appointment I often made, I had a delit rather to fil my mouth and the auditors eares with daintie, delicat, nice and ridiculous termes and phrases, then with wholsome sound and sacred doctrine.

Whereby at leinght I had such a liking of my self, that through nouelties of wordes ioyned with pretty prouerbs, termes and mocking taunts, wherevnto by natural inclination and by my said prophane usage I was much giuen, I found meanes to insinuat my self to the familiaritie of some of the yonger sort that me thought might easely be caried into discontentment & to mislike of rule and discipline and of subiection to their maisters and gouernors: for which purpose I vsed ordinarily some prety skoffes against euery of the elders of our howse. Vndermining by art also, but in pretence of great playnnes and holy simplicitie certen very honest men, whom I thought knew somewhat of my superiors secrecie, the knowledge whereof (our lord God forgiue me) I purposed to abuse as occasion afterward should be giuen, to the annoyance and great hurt as wel of the Catholike cause as of the Seminaries, our President and other principal persons, to whom by law of God, nature, and by singular benefits donne to me I owe all duety.

With this I began by litle and litle to the scandal & ruyne of diuers of the youth and other my fellowes, if God had not preserued them by his singuler grace as wel by my example of licentious life, as by wicked words, to shew my mislike of fasting and praying, calling for flesh pies or pasties in my chamber on fry daies at night, and omitting the diuine seruice prescribed to men of my calling, often iesting and skoffing thereat before some of my companions in whose secrecie & loue toward me I had some affiance. And then proceding farther and farther in wickednes I began to mocke at the lesser points of religion, which is the high way to Heresie, Infidelitie & Athisme, as to my great daunger I haue experience in myne owne case, so lamentable. desiring al Christian people to take head by my example. Protesting to al the world, that it is not reason, nor scriptures, nor the spirit of God, which are so much pretended by protestants, that leadeth any man to that damnable sect, by which one countrey is perished, but it is voluptuousnes, sensualitie, pride, ambition singularitie delite and loue of mans selfe, that driueth downe persons laden with sinne to this heresie of the Protestants, and that the next dore, yea the next steape of this staire is atheisme and no beleefe at al. A few wordes wil serue a wise man.

Wel when I had thus entangled my self, & for some daies proued that such as I had vttered my euel heretical speaches vnto kept al things close, I bouldly aduentured vpon their familiaritie and secrecie to vtter diuers horrible blasphemies in plaine termes against the principal points of religion, specially to one person of myne owne calling who afterward (as I must needes confesse to the shame of th'ennemy) godly and trewly for both our good and saluations vttered the whole matter vnto our superior which was Gods great mercy to me, for otherwise I had doubtles perished for euer more.

For a moneth space or there abouts I delt with my said fellow bouldly not only by arguments and often communication to drawe him to heresie, but also vttered to him my intention to goe into England, there to preach heresie: and to annoye the common cause of Christs Church, and specially this Seminary, the President and superiors thereof, as much as I could possibly: discoursing with him and declaring that there was no remedy, but the counsel must needes seeke the dissolution of the Seminary, or els sustaine their state to be ruyned in time by it.

Therevpon I vttered sondry meanes vnto him, how first the president him self might be made away, and if that missed, how the whole company might easely be poysoned or otherwise dispersed further more offering my hand to gage, that the president should not be a liue that daie two yeres that I spake it, one of the yeres being now gone and yet he aliue: as I desire God he may be many. This was often my deuilish communication, and whether I should not haue giuen this ouerture to the counsel when I came into England for dispatch of him and the said Seminarie my derest nurce, my self know not (to say the lest) how farre the deuil would haue driuen me, who now holy occupied my hart in hope of aduauncement in England by these practices. For which purpose I had also fraudulently discouered certaine points of secrecie & set them downe in writing with intent to giue the *note* of the same to the counsel, wherein I rather detected my owne malice then any other thing, for the matters were of no importance in deede.

In breefe this I must needes acknowledge that I would haue done any of these impious iniuries rather then haue fallen from the preferment I hoped & gaped after so inordinatly, our Lord of his infinite mercies forgiue me that detestable treason against him and his Church: and the abhominable periurie dissimulation & fiction, when for a whole moneths space after I had discouered my minde to my fellow, yet I said Masse daily, fought for leaue and viaticum of M. President to goe home to encrease by preaching and al endeuours the Catholick cause, and toke an oth vpon the Euangelists that I beleeued al points of the Catholick faith, and had no other purpose of going into England but for the aduancement of the same. And I desire good M. President & the whole howse euen for the blessed death and woundes of our Sauiour for whose sake they sustaine al this contradiction of me and other sinners, to pardon and healp me by their praiers to true repentance and remission.

And that good Priest my deare louing fellow, whom I would haue had partaker of my wicked and damnable reuoult I cry him mercy euen vpon my knees, and thanke him (though to the carnal wordly [sic] man it might be compted an iniury that he discouered al my counsel vnto his superiors and myne)[1] for els I had been without doute damned for euer more.

---

1   In the original text there is an open bracket and a full stop. Upton's translation reads: 'The latter, to the confounding of the devil, righteously and honestly, and for out benefit and salvation revealed the whole matter to a superior in the seminary, which was, I confess, through God's singular mercy, else I were lost for eternity'.

But al this came of the sweet mercies and dispositions of our Lord God and Sauiour who ouertooke and ouer raught me happely in the very course of my malice and damnable designements, and hath by his vnspeakable wisedom, caused not onely my imprisonment and other my bodely afflictions which he procured for me at the very same time that I had thought to haue been in my ruffe and iolitie amongest his ennemies, but turned my very sinnes and wickednes to the good of his honor and my saluation: at the same time both deliuering his trew and innocent seruaunts of the Seminarie and others whom my malice might haue annoyed, and me also, in most gracious & miraculous sort, his name be blessed therefore for euer more. .

And it is his goodnes that hath deliuered me from the accomplishment of my wicked desires as powrably and miraculously al _____

most as he did Saul persecuting the Christians, but with much more mercie then him, for that he found grace because he did it of ignorance in incredulitie: where I did al against my owne skill and conscience: neuer doubting but the Catholick Romane religion was the onely true, Christian, auncient and Apostolick faith, and worship of God: though I fained my self for the atchiuing of my detestable designement to doubt thereof and to haue some reasonable motiues against the same, and sought by al meanes possible to haue enformed my conscience against that truth which otherwise I in hart beleeued.

Now therefore for the poore amends that lieth in me to make vnto Gods Church. I protest before the blessed Trinitie, and al the glorious company in heauen and by this publike writing which I voluntarily make and subscribe with mine owne hand: That I beleeue in al points the holy, Catholick, Apostolick & Romane Church, submitting my self to her and the cheefe gouernor thereof our Lord and Maister Gregory the xiij. Christs supreme Minister in earth: and do Detest, Accurse, Anathematize and Condemne from the botome of my hart, al Heresies, Schismes and Sectes, and specially the heresies of Luther, Caluin, and al others vnto which I might seeme by my outward wicked behauiour and dissimulation to haue been enclined vnto: Desiring God and our holy mother the Church, no otherwise to haue mercie on me to saluation, then so long & so farre as I keepe, professe and maintaine, to my power the said faith of our holy forefathers, taught & set furth by the See Apostolick.

Giuen in my chamber at Rhemes the xiij. of May 1583. in the presence of M.Thomas Bailly Priest, M.Humphrey Ely Doctor of the Lawes. and M. Seth Foster Priest.

I acknowledge this to be mine owne act,

Richard Baines Priest

Source: The Marlowe Studies, Farey, P.

9. Baines Note on Marlowe
As originally submitted[2]

A note Containing the opinion of one Christopher Marly Concerning his Damnable Judgment of Religion, and scorn of gods word. assuredly writen aboue 16 thousand yeares agone wher as Adam is proued to haue lived within 6 thowsand yeares.

He affirmeth that Moyses was but a Jugler, & that one Heriots being Sir W Raleighs man can do more then he.

That Moyses made the Jewes to travell xl yeares in the wildernes, (which Jorney might haue bin Done in lesse then one yeare) ere they Came to the promised land, to thintent that those who were privy to most of his subtilties might perish and so an everlasting superstition Remain in the harts of the people.

That the first beginning of Religioun was only to keep men in awe.

That it was an easy matter for Moyses being brought vp in all the artes of the Egiptians to abuse the Jewes being a rude & grosse people.

---

2   The Note was later edited, probably by Puckering, for presentation to Elizabeth I. Various parts specific to Marlowe were removed.

That Christ was a bastard and his mother dishonest.

That he was the sonne of a Carpenter, and that if the Jewes among whome he was borne did Crucify him theie best knew him and whence he Came.

That Crist deserved better to Dy then Barrabas and that the Jewes made a good Choise, though Barrabas were both a thief and murtherer.

That if there be any god or any good Religion, then it is in the papistes because the service of god is performed with more Cerimonies, as Elevation of the mass, organs, singing men, Shaven Crownes & cetera. That all protestants are Hypocriticall asses.

That if he were put to write a new Religion, he would vndertake both a more Exellent and Admirable methode and that all the new testament is filthily written.

That the woman of Samaria & her sister were whores & that Christ knew them dishonestly.

That St John the Evangelist was bedfellow to Christ and leaned alwaies in his bosome, that he vsed him as the sinners of **Sodoma**.

That all they that loue not **Tobacco** & Boies were fooles.

That all the apostles were fishermen and base fellowes neyther of wit nor worth, that Paull only had wit but he was a timerous fellow in bidding men to be subiect to magistrates against his Conscience.

That he had as good Right to Coine as the Queene of England, and that he was acquainted with one poole a prisoner in newgate who hath greate Skill in mixture of mettals and hauing learned some things ofhim he ment through help of a Cunninge stamp maker to Coin French Crownes pistolets and English shillinges.

That if Christ would haue instituted the sacrament with more Ceremoniall Reverence it would haue bin had in more admiration, that it would haue bin much better being administred in a **Tobacco** pipe.

That the Angell Gabriell was Baud to the holy ghost, because he brought the salutation to Mary.

That one Ric Cholmley hath Confessed that he was persuaded by Marloe's Reasons to become an **Atheist**.

These thinges, with many other shall by good & honest witnes be aproved to be his opinions and Comon Speeches, and that this Marlow doth not only hould them himself, but almost into every Company he Cometh he perswades men to **Atheism** willing them not to be afeard of bugbeares and hobgoblins, and vtterly scorning both god and his ministers as I Richard Baines will Justify & approue both by mine oth and the testimony of many honest men, and almost al men with whome he hath Conversed any time will testify the same, and as I think all men in Cristianity ought to indevor that the mouth of so dangerous a member may be stopped, he saith likewise that he hath quoted a number of Contrarieties oute of the Scripture which he hath giuen to some great men who in Convenient time shalbe named. When these thinges shalbe Called in question the witnes shalbe produced.

Richard Baines

Source: BL Harley MS.6848 ff.185-6.

10. Pierce's description of the signing of the death warrant for John Penry, and his being taken to St Thomas a Watering to be hanged.

We cannot therefore be surprised to find that the Council was convened very early on Tuesday morning, and the last act in the Penry- tragedy hurried to its close. The warrant for immediate execution was hastily drawn up, and signed by ' John Cant.,' Penry's ancient and sleepless enemy ; also by Sir John Puckering, Keeper of the Great Seal, a creature of Whitgift's ; and Chief Justice Sir John Popham, who had already condemned him. No prefatory warning was sent to ' the Bench.' No intimation was given to the verger at St. George's to be ready to toll his dismal knell and to drive the curious to the place of hanging. All was bustle at the prison. The prisoner had just received his dinner ; it was about eleven in the fore- noon. The smith was hastily summoned, and on his arrival, in the midst of his meal, Penry without ceremony was hurried on to his hurdle and dragged to St. Thomas a Watering, where a gallows stood waiting its next victim. Having arrived there Penry found no friend among the sprinkling of people who saw the grim cortege pass, and were drawn to the scene by their morbid curiosity. It was part of the mean design to have none of the condemned man's friends present ; and, in any case, peremptory orders were issued to deny him the ordinary courtesy of the times, an opportunity at the gallows to bid farewell to the world ; in Penry's case to deny his guilt, to profess his unswerving loyalty to Elizabeth, and his faith towards God. Some chance friend might be present, and if the eloquent young apostle of Wales had any opportunity, he might be trusted to make a touching and memorable dying speech, some more or less authentic version of which would be hawked about Cheapside and St. Paul's the following day by the chapmen. Nearly eighty years later the contemptuous official explanation is given by the chaplain of the first and second Charles, writing in the heyday of the Stuart restoration. Recording that Penry was executed at St. Thomas a Watering, he then says, that he was executed with a very thin company attending on him, for fear the Fellow might have raised some Tumult, either in going to the Gallows, or upon the Ladder.

Pierce, William, John Penry: his life, times and writings, London, 1923

11. Synopsis of Waddington's account of Penry's death (published 1854)

"the instrument was sent immediately to the sheriff, who proceeded on the same day to erect the gallows at St. Thomas a Watering." This place of execution for the county of Surrey was situated close to the second milestone on the Kent road, and near a brook dedicated to St. Thomas a Becket. Canterbury pilgrims stopped to rest there according to Chaucer (Wadd., 203-204).

... in the midst of his meal, Penry without ceremony was hurried on to his hurdle and dragged to St. Thomas a Watering, where a gallows stood waiting its next victim. Having arrived there, Penry found no friend among the sprinkling of people who saw the grim cortege pass, and were drawn to the scene by their morbid curiousity. It was part of [Whitgift's] mean design to have none of the condemned man's friends present; and in any case, peremptory orders were issued to deny him the ordinary courtesy of the times, an opportunity at the gallows to bid farewell to the world, profess his innocence and loyalty
The official version of Penry's sad end was given by the chaplain of King Charles in the heyday of the Stuart restoration. "Penry was executed with a very thin company attending on him, for fear the fellow might have raised some tumult either in going to the gallows, or upon the ladder" (quoted in Pierce, 480).

"Penry would have spoken," says Waddington, "but the sheriff insisted, that neither in protestation of his loyalty, nor in the avowal of his innocence, should he utter a word. His life was taken, and the people were dispersed. The place of his burial is unknown" (204).

Waddington, *Life of Penry*, and Pierce, *John Penry: his life, times and writings*, as above.

12. From the Dictionary of National Biography

Just a week later, on 29 May, he (Penry) was suddenly ordered, while at dinner, to prepare for execution, and at five o'clock in the afternoon he was hanged at St. Thomas-a-Watering, Surrey. A rhyme expressing the satisfaction of the orthodox at his death was current at the time in the north of England. It ran:

The Welchman is hanged
Who at our Kirke flanged,
And at her state banged;
And brened are his buks:
And tho' he be hanged,
Yet he is not wranged:
The deu'l has him fanged
In his kruked kluks.

Dictionary of National Biography, 1885-1900, Volume 44, *Penry, John,* by Sidney Lee

This entry seems to be the source of the idea that the removal from prison was in the late afternoon. The publication of Penry's death would have been an object with those rescuing (or kidnapping him), to allay suspicion

Appendix VI

A Paranoid Society
Too Many Heirs – No Certainty[1]

When Elizabeth I came to the throne in November 1558, on the death of her half-sister Mary, in hindsight we see the beginning of a golden age, celebrated as the reign of Gloriana. But hindsight, as usual, lies. The legend of Gloriana was built up years after her death in March 1603, by men who were rather disappointed in the new King, James I and VI. In 1558 Elizabeth's accession was not seen as a marvellous dawn to a golden age. Rather, there were worries about having another queen regnant, about who she would marry, and about the chances of foreign invasion to secure the throne for a more legitimate heir, for example, Mary Queen of Scots, at that time being brought up in the French court as the future queen of France, Scotland, and as she herself claimed, England. During Elizabeth's life-time the concern about who would succeed her continued, colouring both society and politics. Those who were in power feared constantly what would befall them if the Queen died without an heir, and this fear was heightened in 1562 when Elizabeth contracted smallpox. They, particularly William Cecil, Lord Burghley, urged the Queen either to marry or to name her heir. She would do neither, claiming that she was married to the realm of England and

---

1   de Lisle, L., *After Elizabeth*

clearly stating, in 1561, that she would never name an heir. The statement in 1561 emerged when she had discovered that the Protestant heir, Catherine Grey, had married the Earl of Hertford (Edward Seymour, a descendant of Edward III) in a private, and secret, ceremony, and was about to give birth to a child. Under the terms of Henry VIII's will, the children of Frances Grey, the daughter of his sister Mary with Charles Brandon, were next in line to the throne after his own three children, Edward VI, Mary I and Elizabeth I, if they died without heirs. Thus, the unborn child was indisputably an heir presumptive to Elizabeth.

Elizabeth's solution was to call in question the legality of her cousin's marriage and declare the children of it illegitimate and therefore debarred from the throne (as had been her own ancestors, the Beauforts, illegitimate descendants of John of Gaunt). Unfortunately for Catherine Grey and Edward Seymour their marriage had been very secret indeed, the one witness was dead and the priest who solemnized the marriage had disappeared – Edward Seymour found him in 1608 but by then James I and VI had been crowned king.

Catherine Grey was not the only heir under Henry VIII's will. Her surviving sister Mary (Jane – the nine days' queen – had been executed in 1554, after the Wyatt rebellion and before Mary I's marriage to Philip of Spain) also married and also found herself imprisoned, for Elizabeth feared heirs. She is on record as saying that a prince should fear those who are to succeed him as subjects always look to the rising sun, not the present one. She also feared that naming an heir would trigger an attempt to unthrone her, and also kill her, in favour of a male heir or a Catholic heir. She must

376

have been considerably shaken by the dismissal of Mary Queen of Scots by the Scottish nobles, in favour of her infant son, and this act, underlining as it did that a sovereign could not even trust his own children (James VI was apparently not at all sympathetic to the idea that his mother return to Scotland and rule), may have consolidated her decision not to marry.

This decision has puzzled many, including her contemporaries. Her godson, Sir John Harington, attributed it to an incapacity to have sexual intercourse. (Her vagaries of policy being the result of her being a woman was a not uncommon feeling among her male subjects, including her last favourite, the Earl of Essex.) But the real reasons may be much simpler. Feminists have suggested that she hated her father, who had murdered her mother, and chose to kill off the Tudor line, but there is little evidence Elizabeth hated her father and some that she admired him. Others support Harington's theory, but the most likely is a dual reason. First, Elizabeth's ministers and her subjects all believed that a woman should be ruled by her husband, so marriage might mean giving up her right to rule (Mary Stuart's refusal to give her husband, Lord Darnley, the crown matrimonial had resulted in tragedy and the loss of her throne) and Elizabeth, in fear of her life for much of her childhood, would have been loathe to give up her power. The other reason is even simpler. Childbirth was dangerous. Jane Seymour had died giving birth to Edward VI, and death in childbed was always possible because of the primitive medical practices and the lack of understanding of the need for hygiene. For the safety of the country risking her life in giving birth to an heir could have been seen as irresponsible. Child heirs[2] to the throne had before led to civil war and usurpation – Elizabeth might well have thought of the reigns of Richard II and Henry VI, both children when their predecessors died – and considered that delivering a country only recently released from the horrors of civil war to the dangers of an infant regency was just too dangerous and, indeed, a dereliction of a sovereign's duty (her father's marital problems were caused by just this fear). The logical conclusion to this is that there should be no marriage and no children, because it was too fraught with pitfalls for Elizabeth and the country she had declared she had been married to by her coronation. It is also true that Elizabeth used her unmarried status to make alliance, with her hand in marriage frequently offered but never given, to ensure political stability and to prevent invasion. After the possibility of her marriage had disappeared in the 1580s the country is beset by the worry of who will succeed Elizabeth – and the Queen herself still feared assassination from the machinations of foreign powers wishing to put some other heir on her throne.

However, not all Elizabeth's heirs suffered because of her fears. The descendants of Mary Tudor's second daughter, Eleanor[3], appeared to fare better, perhaps because

---

2   Scotland had three infant heirs in succession through premature death in battle and unthroning, however, not childbirth: James V, Mary and James VI. Many of Mary's problems were probably caused by being taken to France as a child, leaving Scotland to be ruled by others.

3   Though Eleanor's daughter, Margaret, Countess of Derby, found herself in trouble for her apparent activities against Elizabeth, which included an accusation of witchcraft or sorcery (just as the Duchess of

they were not in direct line (and also because they had not attempted to usurp the throne as had Jane Grey), and by 1590 Ferdinando, Lord Strange, Eleanor's grandson, was patron to various theatrical companies, including those for which both Marlowe and Shakespeare wrote. He was at that point sixth in line to succeed Elizabeth, and he died from symptoms suggesting stomach cancer or a stomach ulcer (or, some thought at the time, poison) in 1594, the year after Marlowe's death. He left three daughters, one of whom, Ann, was the legal heir to the throne in 1603, in default of the legitimacy of the four remaining heirs of Catherine Grey.

The person who was not a legal heir under Henry's will was James VI of Scotland, the son of Mary Queen of Scots. He was debarred for three reasons, first that he had been born abroad, which fact an act of Edward III made inadmissible, and second that he was associated with someone who had attempted the life of the sovereign. Mary Queen of Scots had been executed for her links to the Babington plot in 1587 – and she also was debarred from the throne by the act of Edward III, having been born out of the allegiance of England. In a strange coincidence she was executed at Fotheringhay Castle, the place where the last Plantagenet king, Richard III, had been born. The final reason was that after Henry VIII had named his three surviving legitimate children and their heirs as his successors, he named the descendants of his younger sister, Mary Brandon, the Greys. His sister Margaret's children

---

Gloucester is accused in *Henry VI Part II.*. It is a little odd that Shakespeare should bring up this reference to his patron's mother's disgrace.

were thus excluded from succession to the English throne under Henry's will.

By 1590 there was another Stuart heir, equally debarred under Henry VIII's will, but from time to time favoured by Elizabeth: Arbella Stuart, granddaughter of the redoubtable Bess of Hardwick, and daughter of Charles Stuart, Earl of Lennox, and Bess's daughter, Elizabeth Cavendish – and their marriage was well witnessed and entirely legal. There were many questions about Arbella's rights to the throne because she was descended from Henry VIII's elder sister, Margaret, who had married Archibald Douglas, Earl of Angus, after the death of James IV at Flodden. Archibald Douglas apparently had a wife still living at the time of the marriage, making its issue of doubtful legitimacy (James VI's father, Lord Darnley, was also affected by this doubt, but it did not touch James himself as he was the son of a reigning queen and his father's claims had no importance). Nevertheless, Elizabeth had indicated Arbella as her heir in 1587, shortly before the Armada, and kept up this idea for several years, until she felt less threatened by Philip II's Spain. Arbella's story is as sad as those of Catherine and Mary Grey. Her grandmother, by then Countess of Shrewsbury, had given up dynastic ideas about her daughters' lines and was concentrating on her sons'. She abandoned any pretence that Arbella was to be queen, and seems to have kept her a prisoner at Hardwick Hall, until Arbella went on what would now be called a hunger strike. This was the first of several attempts by Arbella to escape her grandmother, and she died in 1613, of starvation[4], in the Tower, where she had been placed by her cousin James, after marrying William Seymour, Duke of Somerset, and trying to escape from England.

Beyond these there was yet another claimant to the throne, and this one had the power and cash to press his right. Philip II of Spain, the son of Charles V, was the descendant through the royal houses of Spain and Portugal, of John of Gaunt, not from the illegitimate Beauforts like the Tudors, but his indisputably legitimate daughters from his marriages to Blanche of Lancaster and Constanza of Castile. Gaunt's daughter Philippa had married the king of Portugal and her descendant was Philip II's mother. Gaunt's other daughter, Catherine, had married Henry III of Castile and Charles V was the son of her great-granddaughter, Joanna the Mad, the daughter of Isabella of Castile and sister of Catherine of Aragon. Philip had become joint sovereign of England when he had married Mary I, but the marriage had been childless. Many Catholics thought that in default of Mary Queen of Scots, Philip was King of England and since Pope Pius V had issued a papal bull excommunicating Elizabeth and releasing her Catholic subjects from their allegiance and obedience to her, many felt free in their conscience to back him, especially as the consequence of the papal bull was the persecution of Catholics. Mary Queen of Scot's death in 1587 may have been the last act that triggered Philip's bid for the English throne in 1588. He now saw himself as the sole Catholic heir. The Armada failed, due to bad weather and the good seamanship of the English sea

---

4   It is possible Arbella Stuart was an anorexic. Her several hunger strikes suggest this.

captains[5] who were well practised in battle at sea as they were mostly licensed privateers, but the claim remained and when Philip died in 1598 it devolved upon his heirs. By 1602 its mantle had fallen on his daughter, the Infanta Isabella of Spain, by then married to Archduke Albert of the Netherlands.

Elizabeth had always supported the Protestants of the Netherlands in their wars to get free of Spanish rule. Some Catholics had committed themselves to fighting on the side of Spain in this particularly nasty war – Guy Fawkes, the Yorkshireman and Gunpowder plot conspirator, was one - but mainly the ordinary English sided with the Protestants. However, the court was divided by the 1590s not only on whether war with Spain was still supportable, but on who Elizabeth, now growing old, should name as her successor. The Earl of Essex favoured James VI and it was unclear who Robert Cecil, younger son of Lord Burghley, favoured but it was feared it was the Spanish succession for he was treating with Spain for peace. By the 1590s England's treasury was empty from foreign wars and propping up the finances of the King of Scots (James had pension of £4000 a year from Elizabeth and was prepared to cause trouble if he did not get it) who was believed to be on the brink of invasion to secure the throne of England for himself. The Scottish borders were subject to raids from both sides which meant that

---

5   This is a moot point as the weather actually prevented the English ships from destroying the Armada. In many ways the bad weather acted in favour of Spain, not England. The English seamanship is not in doubt, however; the heavy Spanish galleons were no match for the light, maneuverable English ships.

England had to spend considerably on their defence at places such as Berwick. There was also famine for the weather had not been kind, and there was the constant fear of plague which broke out most summers in the towns, and especially London. The poor suffered greatly, and though there had been no large rebellion since Kett's in 1549, the prospect of revolt was ever in the minds of those ruling England. Ireland was also in a state of turmoil and costing money to hold on to – the Earl of Essex would have a disastrous campaign there in the 90s which ruined his position as Elizabeth's favourite and led eventually to his abortive attempt at a palace coup in 1601 (which was possibly backed by William Shakespeare, who was paid to put on a performance of Richard II the night before Essex made his bid to force Elizabeth to name an heir – in support of this idea it is notable that Shakespeare was favoured by James as he had not been by Elizabeth).

In all, society and the court felt constantly under threat both from external sources and inside the country. This sense of threat, and the reality of threat both from Spain and from Catholics abroad resulted in the setting up of as secret service to defend Elizabeth. In every sense of the word this secret service made Elizabethan England not the age of gold, but a police state.

***

It was into this maelstrom of fear for the future and courtly intrigue Christopher Marlowe was pitched when he accepted the Parker scholarship to Corpus Christi in 1580, and along with him William Shakespeare of Stratford.

Time Line

1563/4 February Marlowe baptised Canterbury, son of John and Katherine Marlowe.

1564 April Shakespeare baptised Stratford on Avon (Stratford), son of John and Mary Shakespeare. There is no more information about Shakespeare until he marries in 1582.

1568 Richard Baines matriculates at Christ's College, Cambridge. Christ's graduates routinely are ordained as Anglican priests.

1569 John Shakespeare doing well. Attempts in next few years to get a coat of arms but is not granted one.

1570 Watson possibly at Oxford. Baines probably still at Cambridge.

Regnans in excelis - Elizabeth I excommunicated by Pius V. Any Catholics who obeyed Elizabeth's laws would likewise be excommunicated. This put Catholics in an impossible position and also resulted in their being seen as potential traitors.

1572 Ferdinando Stanley matriculates at Oxford, aged 13. He is heir to the throne after his mother (Margaret Clifford, d.1596, a descendant of Henry VIII's sister Mary Tudor,) who is heir presumptive to Elizabeth I.

1573 Ferdinando Stanley called to court by the Queen. Subsequently Member of Parliament before 1579 (when he marries Anne Spencer) as Baron Strange, which is one of his father's titles.

1576 John Shakespeare takes part in his last council meeting. Financial difficulties start.

1579 Marlowe enters the King's School (called the Queen's School at the time). The school holds a copy of the refutation of the Aryan heresy in its library.

1580 Play, *Timon,* written about Drake's circumnavigaton: possibly by   Marlowe.

10 December Marlowe starts at Cambridge. Penry is at Peterhouse.

Greene, Nashe and possibly William Bradley are at St. John's.

Edmund Campion (Jesuit priest and martyr) is in England, goes to Lancashire and Midlands, he also visits Lapworth Park, Warwickshire. 'John Testament' found in Shakespeare house in Stratford may be from him. The Hoghton, Hesketh and Stanley families all have homes in Lancashire.

Shakespeare may be at Hoghton Towers.

Regnans in excelsis modified by Gregory XIII to instruct English Roman

Catholics to obey the Queen in civil matters until a suitable time to overthrower arrived.

1580/7 *Dido Queen of Carthage* and Ovid translations probably written.

1581 John Cottam, teacher at Stratford grammar, returns to Lancashire, his family home. Cottam probably taught Shakespeare. He was also the brother of a Catholic martyr, Thomas Cottam, and probably was aware of Catholic leanings in Stratford, e.g. of Shakespeare family.

Edmund Campion executed.

1582 29 May, Baines in prison in Rheims, having been accused of atheism and also of threatening Dr Allen's life (Allen is the principal of the college at Rheims and later is made a cardinal).

August, Alexander Hoghton's will signed leaving £2 per annum to William Shakeshafte, 'now dwelling with me'. Hoghton dies in August.

August approx Anne Hathaway conceives child with Shakespeare.

28 November Shakespeare marries Anne Hathaway (entry for Anne Whateley the day before).

1583 April Giordano Bruno comes to England and lives with the French ambassador, Michel de Castelnau, in London. (online Britannica).

13 April Baines moved from prison back to a room in seminary at Rheims.

13 May Baines signs his confession (Nicholls pp 147-152).

Late May, Susannah Shakespeare baptised

6 June, Thomas Watson delivers lecture on memory (*Compendium memoriae localis*) in London.

1584 Easter (1st April) approximately Anne Hathaway conceives twins with Shakespeare.

Marlowe gets B.A - but low on list of passes: 199/231

July William the Silent murdered..

1585 Watson probably published *Compendium memoriae localis*, his book on memory, which owes a lot to the work of Bruno on memorization. (Nicholls and online Languages, Literatures, and Cultures Conference, University of Kentucky, Lexington, Kentucky)

February, Shakespeare twins baptised as Judith and Hamnet.

August, Marlowe signs Katherine Benchkin's will in Canterbury with his father and brother-in-law, John Moore.

Marlowe and Benchkin return to Cambridge in September.

October, a mob attacks French embassy. Giordano Bruno leaves England for Paris (online Britannica).

Undeclared Anglo-Spanish war starts.

1586 Babington plot – Poley is involved as a spy and goes to prison with Anthony Babington and other conspirators. Some suggestion Marlowe also involved.

1587 FebruaryMary Queen of Scots executed at Fotheringay.

A Richard Baines becomes rector of Waltham, near Cleethorpes, Lincs. He is described as a Cambridge man (Nicholls ibid).

Marlowe gets M.A. after intervention of Privy Council, after Corpus Christi wish to deny it because he has been absent (35 weeks) and there are rumours he is going to Rheims. Marlowe goes to London.

Tamburlaine I is performed in London.

Penry publishes his petition to have more preaching in Welsh. Whitgift sees this as criticism and Penry is imprisoned for a month.

1588   Spanish Armada attempts invasion of England.

Shakespeare mentioned in a complaints bill in a legal case in Westminster between 1588 and October 1589 (Bate, Jonathan

(2008), The Soul of the Age, London: Penguin, (I can find no other reference for this.)

Regnans in excelis renewed by Sixtus V to support Spanish Armada.

Michaelmas, Penry sets up a printing press which publishes not only his writings but Martin Marprelate. It moves constantly from Surrey to Northamptonshire, then Warwickshire, Coventry, and Manchester.

1589   April the English Armada sets out for Corunna and Lisbon. Returns unsuccessful in July, having been underprovisioned and lacking horses and proper artillery. Leaders of the armada are Francis Drake and John Norris.

August, Penry's printing press seized.

18 Sept (Nicholls p.210) Hog Lane affray. Marlowe fights William Bradley and innkeeper's son, Thomas Watson (who is almost certainly related to Poley by marriage) appeared and joined in. He killed Bradley, who wanted to fight him. Marlowe and Watson (poet) claim self-defence. Marlowe got bail of £40 with sureties Richard Kitchen, attorney at

Clifford's Inn, and Humphrey Rowland, horner (Nicholls p 212). Some suggest sureties produced by Privy Council.

September Penry another Marprelate tract - Job Throckmorton is quite likely Martin Marprelate.

September Valentine Simms, John Hodgkin Arthur Thomlin questioned by the Earl of Derby and then by the Privy Council. Sent to theBridewell. (examination of Simmes etc Lambeth papers).

1590   January Penry escapes to Scotland after Northampton house is searched again.Wife follows, leaving baby daughter with family.

Thomas Watson released from Newgate in March - or earlier, bail notice appended to his name.

Francis Walsingham dies April 6th

Tamburlaine 1 and 2 published.

1591   August Winchester Cathedral burgled by a gang led by Richard Williams and

Edward Bushell (servant to Lord Strange). £1800 of plate stolen to be melted

down for Sir William Stanley's regiment of c.700 men in the Netherlands.

Late in the year Moody goes to Flushing and is picked up by Robert Sydney -

Sydney is reprimanded for interfering with him.

Bruno in Frankfurt-am-Main during the year.

December (probably) Baines, and then Marlowe and Gilbert, leave for Flushing.

1592 January Marlowe is in Flushing with Poole. Richard Baines accuses Marlowe of counterfeiting on behalf of Catholics rebels. Marlowe, Baines and Gilbert taken back to England on 26 January (Nicholls p.278) Marlowe released without charge.

March Bruno goes to Venice. Previously lecturing in Padua - probably from January.

Lord Pembroke's Men first appear in London in the spring.

Jew of Malta performed (pos written 1589-90).

April Hackett conspiracy begins.

May, Bruno arrested in Venice. (online Britannica).

July the Hackett-Copinger plot ends with the hanging of Hackett. Penry returns to Scotland.

Thomas Watson dies in September - buried on 16th.

September Penry returns from Scotland and joins a London separatist church.

September Robert Greene dies aged c.34.

21 September Bess of Hardwick (Elizabeth, Countess of Shrewsbury) writes to Burghley that she has dismissed 'One Morley' who had been reading (tutor) with Arbella Stuart, her grand-daughter, and an heir to the throne. She states he has been tutor for 3 years. (Nicholls).

Marlowe bound over 'to keep the peace' in Shoreditch. (Nicholls)

December, Marlowe has a fight with William Corkyne, probably his tailor, in Canterbury and his father pays 12d surety. Marlowe claims Corkyne was the assailant. Charges dropped. (Nicholls). Corkyne's son (?) sets Marlowe's verse t to music in the early 1600s.

December Greene's *Groat's Worth of Wit* is published, and mentions Marlowe and Shakespeare (?) and refers *to Henry VI part III*. Probably edited, and completed, by Henry Chettle.

During the year:

Roger Manwood dies. Marlowe writes an elegy in Latin. Alleyn puts on a play he may have written, which appears to be a plagiarizedversion of *Tamburlaine - Tamberca*m. This is referred to in one of Greene's comments in Groat's Worth of Wit.

Henry VI - shows signs of collaboration with Marlowe, especially the Jack Cade speeches and character.

Edward II and *Henry VI parts II and III* probably written.

1593 21 March John Penry arrested, having at first escaped his captors, but then been re-captured.

6 April Greenwood (Cambridge friend of Marlowe – he used Marlowe's buttery allowance occasionally) and Barrow finally hanged at Whitgift's orders, following several aborted attempts. Both were friends of Penry. Dutch Church libel

probably fabricated by Richard Baines, Thomas Drury and Chomondley. (Nicholls)

11 May Privy Council meet and decide to arrest people for Dutch Chruch Libel.

12 May Thomas Kyd arrested for Dutch Church Libel. Kyd says Marlowe lodged with him in 1590 and atheist papers in his 'bundle' are Marlowe's.

21 May Marlowe at Thomas Walsingham's (possibly writing Hero and Leander) when asked to report to the Privy Council after Kyd has said atheist papers (Aryan heresy and other heresies) in his possession belong to Marlowe.

21 May John Penry goes on trial. He is said to be about thirty years of age.

May Baines submits his note to Privy Council. It describes Marlowe's atheism and also says he should die. Similar to Baines' own 'confession' in 1583 in Rheims. Unclear if note is seen before 31 May.

28 May Penry appeals to Burghley who cannot stop execution.

29 May Penry taken from his dinner at 11 a.m and hanged at St Thomas-a-Watering around 5 pm. No contemporary account of death, no burial place, no speech nor farewells to his wife and children (as were customary).

30 May someone named as Christopher Marlowe is killed by Ingram Frizer, with Robert Poley and Nicholas Skeres. This happens at Eleanor Bull's house in Deptford. Eleanor Bull is

related to Mistress Parry who had been a confidante of the Queen. She may also be related to Burghley.

31 May inquest held at Deptford on man named as Christopher Marlowe, held

by Queen's coroner, Danby, as 'within the verges' of the Queen's residence at Greenwich. No second coroner sat, which is not illegal but a little odd.

1 June a body identified as Christopher Marlowe buried at St Nicholas' church.

Deptford Register says Marlowe was murdered by 'Francis Frazer'.

July, *Edward II* published.

25 September Earl of Derby dies and Lord Strange succeeds him.

1594 Hesketh plot to put Stanley on throne. Stanley does not co-operate, but reveals the conspiracy and the plot fails (but takes 10 days to reveal plot).

Richard Baines dies (if this is not the Baines who has a living in Lincolnshire) – Baines is apparently framed for stealing a cup – the actual incident is described in *Dr. Faustus*.

16 April Ferdinando Stanley, Lord Strange and Earl of Derby, dies (some suspect poison). His groom disappears the same night.

15 August Kyd dies (online Britanica) as a result of his imprisonment and torture. He is buried at St. Mary Colechurch.

Chomondley disappears, on the accusation of Thomas Drury, who, (according to Nicholls), was involved in the Dutch Church libel plot by Chomondley who wanted to pay Drury back for an earlier betrayal. Chomondley was put in prison and not heard of again.

Pembroke's men sell their play collection including *The Taming of a Shrew,* and cease performing.

Shakespeare starts publishing his plays.

Richard Williams (Winchester Cathedral burglary suspect and William Stanley supporter) hanged.

December Kyd's mother repudiates his estate to avoid paying his debts.

1596 August, Shakespeare's son, Hamnet, dies in Stratford.

October, Shakespeare's father granted coat of arms by Garter King of Arms. (New York Times 30/6/16, No Sweat Shakespeare, www.literarygenius.info).

1597 Shakespeare a partner in building a theatre.

Shakespeare buys New Place in Stratford, a substantial house.

1598 Shakespeare was holding 10 quarters of barley in a time of famine and so is l isted by the Privy Council. He owned no farmland, but he was selling grain. He may have bought the barley cheaply locally in order to sell it on at a profit later.

1599 *The Passionate Pilgrim* published by William Jaggard under t the authorship of William Shakespeare. It contains, among other works, Marlowe's *The Passionate Shepherd.*

1601   *Richard II* performed on eve of Essex rebellion. Shakespeare and Burbage sucessfully plead that they were paid £2 per actor to put it on, and therefore did so for the money.

A seminary priest calling himself Christopher Marlowe comes from Valladolid in c.1601. His real name is apparently Matthews. Two years later a man called Matthews is executed   as a recusant priest.

1603   24 March Queen Elizabeth dies. James I and VI succeeds, despite respective claims of Lady Anne Stanley, and the children of Catherine Grey. The Lord Chamberlain's Men, Shakespeare's company, become the King's Men.

1604   *All's Well that Ends Well* possibly written (the possible date ranges from 1598-1608). Shakespeare was living with the Mountjoys in Shoreditch at the time he wrote *Alls Well,* and seems to have acted as broker in their daughter's marriage, as evidenced by his statement in a legal case brought in 1612, which was a marriage dispute in Shoreditch. His evidence is recorded but not his words (Greenblatt ibid).

Shakespeare sues Philip Rogers for 35s and 10d, plus 10s damages, to recover a loan and the remaining cost of the sale of 20 bushels of grain. (A 3.1 Shakspere as a broker, London University 'Who was Shakespeare' course).

1605   Shakespeare not on cast list for Ben Jonson's *Volpone,* suggesting he has given up acting. (Wells, Stanley; *Taylor, Gary; Jowett, John; Montgomery, William, eds. (2005), The Oxford Shakespeare: The Complete Works (2nd ed.), Oxford: Oxford University Press*)

1610	*The Tempest* probably written between 1610 and 1611, with line 'I have drowned my book' – frequently interpreted as Shakespeare saying he has stopped writing. It also contains Medea's speech from Ovid's Metamorphosis (Vaughan and Vaughan, pp. 26, 58–59, 66, for *Medea* speech. Arden Shakespeare).
1612	Shakespeare tells Thomas Heywood he knew nothing about the publication of Heywood's poems under his name, in 1599 in *The Passionate Pilgrim*.
	Shakespeare is in London and involved in the Bellott v Mountjoy case as a witness.
1613	*The Tempest* performed for wedding of Frederick of Bohemia and Princess Elizabeth, daughter of James I and VI.
	Shakespeare has retired to Stratford, though it is not clear when he did so and it may have been as early as 1610.
1616	April Shakespeare dies after a 'merry meeting' with his friends Drayton and Jonson (according to John Ward, vicar in Stratford, writing some fifty years later, source: Schoenbaum, Samuel. *Shakespeare's Lives*, Oxford University Press. 1991, Page 78.), and is buried in Stratford, in the chancel of Holy Trinity church. He leaves a large fortune and property, and an apparently cryptic message on his tomb, as well as two married daughters and his wife. His will contains no mention of the property he was associated with in London, and no books. He has no direct descendants.
1623	At some point between 1616 and 1623 Shakespeare's monument is erected. Jonson mentions the bust as being a good likeness in the First Folio.

First Folio published by Shakespeare's colleagues John Heminges and Henry Condell as well as Edward Blount (publisher) and William Jaggard (source online Britanica), who had published *The Passionate Pilgrim* in 1599. Jaggard's inclusion suggests that Shakespeare was being economical with the truth when he told Heywood he knew nothing of the publication of *Pilgrim* – he may also be concealing that he had forgotten that *The Passionate Shepherd* had been 'written' by Marlowe.

6 August, Anne Hathaway dies and is buried next to her husband in Holy Trinity Church, Stratford.

1925 Leslie Hotson finds the cornoner's record of Christopher Marlowe's death.

Refences

Printed Works

Books

Alfrord, S., Burghley, *William Cecil at the Court of Elizabeth I,* Yale University Press, New York and London, 2011
Bate, J., *The Soul of the Age, London: Penguin, 2008*
Bakeless, J. E., *Christopher Marlowe,* Jonathan Cape, 1938
Bakeless, J. E., *The Tragicall History of Christopher Marlowe,* Modern Language Association of America,Harvard University Press, 1942
Bakeless, J. E., *The Tragicall History of Christopher Marlowe,* Greenwood Press, Dramatists, English, 1970
Baker, O., *In Shakespeare's Warwickshire and the Unknown Years,* Simpkin
Marshall Ltd, 1937
Boas, F.S., *Christopher Marlowe, A Biographical and Critical Study,* O.U.P., Clarendon Press, 1964
Brook, B, *The Lives of the Puritans,* 1813
Chambers, E.K., *The Elizabethan Stage,* Oxford, Clarendon Press, 1923
Chambers, E.K. *William Shakespeare: A Study of Facts and Problems ,* Oxford, Clarenden Press, 1930
Chambers, E.K., *William Shakeshafte,* in *Shakespearian Gleanings,* London, O.U.P., 1944
Cooper, J., *The Queen's Agent, Francis Walsingham at the Court of Elizabeth I: Francis Walsingham and and the rise of espionage in Elizabethan England,* Faber and Faber, 2011, New York and London, 2012
Cooper, Tanya, *Searching for Shakespeare,* National Portrait Gallery, 2006,
Duncan-Jones, Katherine, and H. R. Woudhuysen, eds., *Shakespeare's Poems* London: Arden Shakespeare, Thomson Learning, 2007
Greenblatt, S., *Will in the World, How Shakespeare Became Shakespeare,* Jonathan Cape, 2004

Halleck, Reuben Post, *Halleck's New English Literature*, New York: American Book Company, 1913

Hess, W. Ron, *The Dark Side of Shakespeare*, Writers Club Press, 2002

Holden, A., *William Shakespeare*, Little, Brown and Company, 1999

Honan, P., *Christopher Marlowe, Poet and Spy*, Oxford University Press, 2007

Honigmann, E.A., *Shakespeare: the lost years*, Manchester University Press, 1985

Hopkins, Lisa, *A Christopher Marlowe Chronology*, Palgrave, Macmillan, 2005

Horne, C. Silvester. "*A Popular History of the Free Churches*", Fifth Edition, James Clarke & Co., London, 1903

Hotson, J. L. *The Death of Christopher Marlowe*, London: The Nonsuch Press, Cambridge: Harvard University Press, 1925

Kendall, Roy, Christopher Marlowe, Journeys Through the Elizabethan Underground, Rosemont Publishing and Printing Corp, 2003

Kuriyama, Constance Brown, *Christopher Marlowe, A Renaissance Life*, Cornell University Press, 2010

Lisle, L. de, *After Elizabeth: How James King of Scots Won the Crown of England in 1603*, Ballantyne, 2005

Lyons, M., *The Favourite, Sir Walter Raleigh at the Court of Elizabeth I*, Constable, London, 2011

Martineau, Jane. *Shakespeare in Art*, Merrell, 2003

Nicholl, C., *The Reckoning,.The Murder of Christopher Marlowe*, Vintage, 2002

Pierce, William, John Penry: his life, times and writings, London, 1923

Riggs, D., *The World of Christopher Marlowe*, Faber and Faber, 2004

Rubinstein, William D., *Who Wrote Shakespeare's Plays?* Amberley Publishing, 2003

Tucker Brooke, *The Works of Christopher Marlowe* (1910), Marlowe Canon read on line at The Christopher Marlowe Library (most recent edition: Kessinger Publishing, LLC (September 10, 2010), facsimile)

Tucker Brooke, *The Life of Marlowe and the Tragedy of Dido, Queen of Carthage*, Methuen, 1930

Urry, William, *Christopher Marlowe and Canterbury*, Faber and Faber, 1988

Warner, Charles Dudley, ed, Giordano Bruno, Library of the World's Best Literature Ancient and Modern, 2015

Williams, David Rhys, *Shakespeare, Thy Name is Marlowe*, Philosophica Library, 2007 (original publication 1966)

Wilson, A.N.,*The Elizabethans*, Arrow Books, 2012

Waddington, John, *John Penry the Pilgrim Martyr*, 1854

Wraight A.D. P. *Shakespeare, New Evidence*, The Christopher Marlowe Library, 2017

Articles

Alhiyari, Ibrahim. *"Thomas Watson: New Birth Year and Privileged Ancestry.*" Notes and Queries? 53, no. 1, 2006

Born, Hanspeter, *Why Greene was angry with Shakespeare*, in Medieval and Renaissance Drama in England, 2012.

Downie, J.A., *Marlowe Fact and Fiction* in *'Constructing Christopher Marlowe'*, Downie, J.A. and Parnell, J.T eds., Cambridge University Press, 2000

Barker, N. *Shake-scene and that Upstart Crow*, The Marlowe Society Journal, 36, Spring 2011

Bearman, R.,Appendix: Excerpts from the will of Alexander Houghton, 3 August 1581 adapted from Records of Early English Drama: Lancashire, ed. David George, University of Toronto, 1991

Bearman, R., *'Was William Shakespeare William Shakestaffe?' Revisited*, Shakespeare Quarterly, 2002

Chatterly, A, Marlowe Society Newsletter no. 23, 2003

Daugherty, L., *Ferdinando Stanley, Richard Hesketh, and Jane Halsall: Was the Foster Mother of Shakespeare's Patron also the Biological Mother of the Plotter who Offered him the English Throne in 1593?* Notes and Queries? Volume 60, Issue 3, September 2013

Farey, P. *The Deptford Jury,* Peter Farey's Marlowe Page, 2008

Farey, Peter, *Hoffman and the Authorship Question,* © 2008 All Rights Reserved, The Marlowe Society Research Journal - Volume 06 - 2009

Farey, Peter. *The Stratford Monument*: A Riddle and Its Solution, 1999-2004

Fisher, T. *The Grafton Portrait*, The Marlowe Society Journal, 44, Spring 2015

Freeman, Arthur, *'Marlowe, Kyd, and the Dutch Church Libel'*, English Literary Renaissance 3, 1973

Gortazar, Isabel, *The Clue in The Shrew (Revised)*, Online Research Journal Article, 2009

Hamer, D., *'Was William Shakespeare William Shakestaffe?'* Review of English Studies, 1970

Hieatt, A. Kent, Hieatt, Charles W., and Anne Lake Prescott. "When Did Shakespeare Write 'Sonnets 1609'?" Studies in Philology, Vol. 88, No. 1 Winter, 1991

Joseph, L. B, ed, *The Martin Marprelate Tracts: A Modernized and Annotated Edition,*. Cambridge University Press, 2011

Krüger, Joachim; Winkler, Peter; Lüderitz, Eberhard; Lück, Manfred;

Manley, Lawrence, "From Strange's Men to Pembroke's Men: 2 "Henry VI" and "The First Part of the Contention", Shakespeare Quarterly, vol. 54, No. 3 Autumn, 2003

Martineau, Jane. *Shakespeare in Art*, Merrell, 2003

Melan, Igor, *Sassetti, Tommaso*, in the Dizionario Biografico degli Italiani - Volume 90, 2017

Pinksen, Daryl, *Was Robert Greene's 'Upstart Crow' the actor Edward Alleyn?* Marlowe Society Research Journal, Vol 6, 2009

Prior, Roger, "Shakespeare's Visit to Italy," The Journal of Anglo-Italian Studies, Vol. 9, 2008, The University of Malta

Roberts, P. *Christopher Marlowe at Corpus, 1580-87*, in Pelican - The Magazine of Corpus Christi College, Cambridge - Easter Review,

Read, Charles, ed., *Thomas Kyd, Theatre History.com* Article from *Elizabethan and Stuart Plays*. Baskerville. New York: Henry Holt and Company, 1934

Salkeld, Duncan, *Shakespeare among the Courtesans: Prostitution, Literature, and Drama, 1500-1650*, Anglo-Italian Renaissance Studies. Farnham: Ashgate, 2012

Scott, Mark W.; Schoenbaum, S. Shakespearean Criticism. 5. Detroit: Gale Research Inc, 198

Tedeschi, J., *Tomaso. Sassatti's account of the St. Bartholomew's day massacre*, in The massacre of St. Bartholomew. Reappraisals and documents, ed. Soman, The Hague 1974

Tedeschi, J., ed., *Introduzione*, in T. Sassetti, *Il massacro di San Bartolomeo,*
Rome, 1995

Wernham, R.B., *Christopher Marlowe at Flushing, 1592*, English History Review, Vol XCII, Issue CCCLIX, 1976

Winship, Michael P. (Univ of Georgia) *'Puritans, Politics and Lunacy.' The Coppinger-Hackett Conspiracy as the Apotheosis of Elizabethan Presbyterianism.* The Sixteenth Century Journal: The Journal of Early Modern Studies, Vol. 28, 2007/2 (Summer)

Questier, M. *English clerical converts to Protestantism,* Recusant History 2, 1991

Scientific and Technical Texts

Elks, Ken., *Mestrelle's Coins*, in Borden, D.G. and Brown, I.D., eds,, *The Milled Coinage of Elizabethan England,* The Coinage of Britain: 7 Early Milled Coins, 2001

Greenwood, N. N. & Earnshaw, A., Chemistry of the Elements (2nd ed.). Oxford: Butterworth-Heinemann, 1997

Matson, John, *Fact or Fiction? Lead Can Be Changed into Gold. Particle accelerators make possible the ancient alchemist's dream – but at a steep cost,* in Scientific American, January 31, 2014

Krüger, Joachim; Winkler, Peter; Lüderitz, Eberhard; Lück, Manfred; Wolf, Hans Uwe, "Bismuth, Bismuth Alloys, and Bismuth Compounds". Ullmann's Encyclopedia of Industrial Chemistry. Wiley-VCII, Weinheim, Suzuki, Hitomi, 2001

Seaby's Standard Cataloge of British Coins, parts 1 and 2: Coins of England and the United Kingdom, 14th ed. B.A. Seaby Ltd, 1975

Suzuki, Hitomi, Organobismuth Chemistry, Elsevier, 2001

Wiberg, Egon, Holleman, A. F.; Wiberg, Nils, Inorganic chemistry. Academic Press, 2001

Magazines and Newspapers
Argosy, Vol. 28,1879

History Today, August, 2005
Mail Online: *Was Bard's lady a woman of ill repute?* 'Dark Lady' of Shakespeare's sonnets 'may have been London prostitute called Lucy Negro', Dalya Alberge and Claire Ellicott, 27 August, 2012
Roberts, P. *Christopher Marlowe at Corpus*, 1580-87, in Pelican - The Magazine of Corpus Christi College, Cambridge: Easter Review, 2014
The Guardian, *Shakespeare first folio found in French Library,* Kim Willsher, 25 Nov 2014

Online Sources

Online sites
Ashworth, Elizabeth, *The Lost Years of William Shakespeare*, Elizabeth Ashworth, 29 October, 2014
Alex Jack's list of Literary Similarities Between Marlowe and Shakespeare – The Marlowe Studies, The Christopher Marlowe Library
Archaeologia Cantiana Vol. 31, 1915, *Extracts from some lost Kentish registers,* by Leland Duncan William Shakespeare. Online blog 2014
Ayres, R. *Evidence that Christopher Marlowe was the 'Ghost' of William Shakespeare,* Ayres on Environment, Exergy, Economy and Growth
Church of England apologize for the death of John Penry. BBC Online News, 15.05.2008
How We Know That Shakespeare Wrote Shakespeare: The Historical Facts by Tom Reedy and David Kathman
Duff, M., *Marlowe and the Dark Lady*, in P. Farey's marlowe-shakespeare.blogspot.co.uk, 2011
Farey, P, *Deptford and M. le Doux*, Farey.P and Caveney, G., Peter Farey's Marlowe Page
Farey, P, *A Deception in Deptford,* Christopher Marlowe's alleged death, (www.prst17z1.demon.co.uk/title.htm) 1997-2000
Farey, P, *Shakespeare and Cambridge,* Marlowe Shakespeare Blogspot, 2013
Farey, P., *Review of Donna Murphy's The Marlowe Shakespeare Continuum,* Peter Farey's Marlowe Page, c.2009

Herbermann, Charles, ed. *"Douai"*. Catholic Encyclopedia. New York: Robert Appleton, 1913
Luce, Morton, ed. *The Works of Shakespeare: Twelfth Night or What You Will*. Ed. Morton. London: Methuen and Co., 1906 in http://www.theatrehistory.com/british/twelfth_night002.html
Marlovian theory of Shakespeare authorship – Wikipedia, ed. 29 September 2019
More, David A,. *Drunken Sailor or Imprisoned Writer?*, The Marlowe Studies, 1996
Patrick, Graham, *Phrenology* [video recording (DVD)]: revealing the mysteries of the mind. Richmond Hill, Ont: American Home
Shakespeare Institute Library, Mason Croft, Church Street Stratford-upon-Avon Warwickshire
Thomas Watson (poet), Wikipedia, ed. 11 January 2019

Online History Sources and Projects
English College, Douai: *An English College,* Wikipedia, January 2014
History of Holy Trinity, Stratford-on-Avon
List of Catholic martyrs of the English Reformation, Wikipedia, January 2012
Llangammarch Wells web page
Old Lea Hall, a hint of Preston's Past, ashtonribble.com, Ashton-on-Ribble's community web, 2016
The Martin Marprelate Press: A Documentary History. UMASS, Amherst
Powys Digital History Project
Shakespeare Documented: Manuscript copy of William Basse's elegy on William Shakespeare, https://shakespearedocumented.folger.edu/exhibition/document/manuscript-copy-william-basses-elegy-william-shakespeare
Sixteenth Century Europe, blog of Bromley Adult Education College, created by Dr. Anne Stott
Thought Co, Lifelong Learning: *Transmutation Definition and Examples,* February 2019
University of London: Introduction to who wrote Shakespeare. Course tutor: Dr. Ros Barber

Websites

https://www.britannica.com/topic/Globe-Theatre
https://christophermarlowe221.weebly.com/
http://dailbach-welldigger.blogspot.com/2014/07/the-prophet-martyr-from-epynt.html, John Penry the martyred prophet
https://davidgreenports.weebly.com/blog/lost-copy-of-shakespeares-first-folio-discovered
https://elizabethashworth.com
https://great-harwood.org.uk/about/people/Families/hesketh.htm
https://www.poemhunter.com/poem/elegy-on-mr-william-shakespeare/
https://thehistoryjar.com/tag/the-hesketh-plot/
http://internetshakespeare.uvic.ca/Library/SLT/drama/reputation/jonson 1 html. Accessed 13/9/18
https://phrenology.org/intro.html,The History of Phrenology
https://poets.org/poem/poet-ape
https://www.nosweatshakespeare.com, No Sweat Shakespeare, *As You Like It*, ActV.sc.1.
https://www.william-shakespeare.info/william-shakespeare-globe-theatre.htm
https://shakespeareauthorship.com/
http://www.shakespeare-online.com/biography/benjonson.html
https://sililibrary1.wordpress.com/2015/12/21sing-lousy-lucy-shakespeare-and-the-roes-of-charlecote,
Betterton, Conversations with the people of Stratford-upon-Avon (1715), Shakespeare Institute Library.
https://thehistoryjar.com/tag/the-hesketh-plot/
http://www.treccani.it/enciclopedia/tommaso-sassetti_(Dizionario-Biografico)/http://www.theatrehistory.com/british/

Contemporary Sources

Plays and poetry
Basse, William, *Elegy on William Shakespeare*, Poem Hunter
Dutch Church Libel: Bodleian Library, MS.Don.d.152 f.4v
Jonson, Ben, *The Poet Ape,* Poets.org

Jonson, Ben. *The Works of Ben Jonson, vol. 3,* London: Chatto & Windus, 1910

Marlowe, Christopher, *The Complete Plays*, ed. J. B. Steane, Penguin Classics, 1986

Marlowe, Christopher, *The Complete Poems and Translations*, ed. Stephen Orgel, Penguin Classics, 2007

Shakespeare, W, *Complete Works*, introduced by Henry Glassford Bell, William Collins and Son, &Co, Ltd, 1902

Shakespeare, W, *Complete Works*, Vol. IV, *The Tragedies and the Poems*, Heron Books, London (no date of publication)

Shakespeare,W., *The Sonnets*, in *William Shakespeare, Complete Works*, ed. Richard Proudfoot, Ann Thompson and David Scott Kastan, Arden Shakespeare, 1998, revised 2011

Shakespeare, W., *As You Like It*, The Plain Text Shakespeare, Blackie and Sons Ltd, (no date of publication)

Shakespeare, W., *As You Like It* with *The Tale of Gamelyn (anon)*, introduced by Henry Morley, Cassell and Co., Ltd. (no date of publication)

Shakespeare, W., *As You Like It*, ed. Alan Brissenden, Oxford World Classics, O.U.P., 1998

Shakespeare, W., *Henry VI Part III*, ed. Andrew S. Cairncross, Arden Third Series, 1996

Shakespeare, W., *Henry VI Part 1, 2 and 3,* New Oxford Shakespeare, 2016

Shakespeare, W, *Julius Caesar,* ed. Norman Sanders, with introduction by Martin Wiggins, Penguin Books, revised edition 2005 (orig. 1967

Shakespeare, W, *Macbeth*, T. J. B. Spencer, New Penguin Shakespeare, 1988

Shakespeare, W, *Macbeth*, ed. Frank Green, with additional material by Rick Lee and Victor Juszkiewicz, Heinemann, 1994

Shakespeare, W, *The Comedy of Errors,* ed. T.S. Dorsch, revised with new introduction by Ros King, C.U.P., 2004

Shakespeare., W., *The Merchant of Venice*, ed. John Russell Brown in Shakespeare, W., *Othello,* ed E.A.J. Honigmann, in *William Shakespeare, Complete Works*, ed. Richard Proudfoot, Ann Thompson and David Scott Kastan, Arden Shakespeare, 1998, revised 2011

William Shakespeare, Complete Works, ed. Richard Proudfoot, Ann Thompson and David Scott Kastan, Arden Shakespeare, 1998, revised 2011
Shakespeare., W., *The Tempest,* ed. Virginia Mason Vaughan and Alden T. Vaughan, The Arden Shakespeare, Third Series, 2006
Shakespeare, W., *Twelth Night,* ed. Guy Boas, The Touchstone Shakespeare, Edward Arnold &Co (no date of publication)
Shakespeare, W., *Twelth Night,* with original 1623 text and modern version, ed Nick de Somogyi, Nick Hern Books, reprinted 2004
Shakespeare, W, *Romeo and Juliet,* ed. T. J. B. Spencer, New Penguin Shakespeare, 1967
Shakespeare, W., *Romeo and Juliet,* ed Jonathan Bate and Eric Rasmussen, Macmillan, 2009
The Norton Anthology of English Literature, gen.ed. M. H. Abrams, Vol. I, Fifth edition, W.W. Norton & Co, 1986
Unknown, *Arden of Faversham,* ed. White, M,, Lockwood, T., New Mermaids, 2007

Contemporary letters and diaries
Baines Note, BL Harley MS.6848 ff.185-6, 1593
Countess of Shrewsbury's letter to Lord Burghley, concerning'one Morley', 1592, BL Lansdowne MS71, part 2
Kyd's Letter to Puckering, 1593, CA. June 1593, BL Harleian MSS 6848, F. 154
Henslowe, Philip, *Diary,* ed.R.A. Foakes and R.T. Rickert, Cambridge, 1961
Richard Quiney's Letter to William Shakespeare, 25 Oct 1598, University of London: Introduction to who wrote Shakespeare. Course tutor: Dr. Ros Barber
Sir Robert Sydneys's Letter to Lord Burghley, 1592, PRO SP 84/44/60
Parker Correspondence, Parker Society
Timber, or Discoveries (1630). Jonson on Shakespeare, Internet Shakespeare Editions, Treasures, 2001

Contemporary Publications
Allen, William, publisher, *A True Representation of the Late Apprehension and Imprisonment of John Nichols:* Includes: *The Confession of Richard Baines*
Bacon, Richard, *Solon, his Folie*, 1594
Barber, R., ed., *John Aubrey, Brief Lives, A Selection*, Folio Society, 1975
Chettle, Henry, *Kind Heart's Dream, 1592*
Dick, O.L. (ed) *Aubrey's Brief Lives*, with an introduction by Ruth Scurr, Vintage (Penguin Random House), 2016
Davenant's I*n Remembrance of Master Shakespeare* in *Madagascar with other poems*, 1638
Dugdale, Sir William, *Antiquities of Warwickshire*, published in 1656
Gascoigne, George, *The Steel Glas and Compalynte of Phylomene*, 1576
Greene's *Groats-werth of Witte*[1], Harrison, ed, Andesite Press, 2017 (original publication 1592)
Heylin, Peter, *Aerius Redivivus : A History of the Presbyterians*, Oxford, 1670. (Published posthumously)
Meres, Francis, *Palladis Tamia*, 1598
Vaughan, *Golden Grove*, 1600

Reference

Registers and archives
A Cambridge Alumni Database. University of Cambridge
Archaeologia Cantiana Vol. 31, 1915, *Extracts from some lost Kentish registers*, Leland Duncan
Archives Internationales D'histoire des Idees / International Archives of the History of Ideas, The Massacre of St. Bartholomew, Volume 75 *Collectania Topographica Et Genealogica*, Frederick Madden, Bulkeley Bandinel and John Gough Nichols

---

1   In the body of the text the modern spelling, *Greene's Groat's Worth of Wit,* is used to refer to Greene's testament, in order to avoid confusion between various contemporary spellings.

Corpus Christi Audit Books, 1580-85,1586-87 (1585-86 missing)
Corpus Christi Buttery Books, 1580-87 (1586-87 missing)
Masters, R, *Corpus Christi*, ed. Lamb, 337. Ref Volumes: 1558-1603
PCC 39 Pyckering; Add. 48018, f. 294v
Strype, *Parker, HMC 7th Rep.* 630, 642
Strype, *Whitgift*, i. 46; *CSP Dom.* 1598-1601
Strype, *Whitgift p. 413, C3/284/39*
The Mayden's Holaday, Lansdowne MS 807, British Library, John Warburton's MS plays (list): *no. 13*

Reference Works
British Library, Lansdowne MS71, part 2
British Library, Lansdowne MSS.78, No.67
Cambridge History of English and American Literature, Vol III, *Renascence and Reformation*, Ward, A.W. and Waller, A.R. eds., 1911
Dictionary of National Biography, 1885-1900, Volume 44
Dictionary of National Biography, (Parker, Matthew); Lansdowne MS. 97, f. 177
Dictionary of National Biography, White, Adam. *Johnson (Janssen) family (per c.1570-c.1630)* Oxford, Oxford University Press, 2004
Dictionary of Welsh Biography Down to 1940, National Library of Wales, online source, original publication 1959, digital version 2004.
Dictionary of National Biography, 1885-1900 , Volume 60, Sidney Lee, *Thomas Watson (1557?-1592)*
Dizionario Biografico degli Italiani - Volume 90, 2017
Encyclopedia Britannica, 11th Ed. Vol IV. Cambridge: Cambridge University Press, 1910
Encyclopedia Britannica, 11th Ed. Vol XX. Cambridge: Cambridge University Press, 1910
The Oxford Companion to English Literature 7th ed., ed. Dinah Birch, Oxford, O.U.P., 2009
Wells, Stanley; *Taylor, Gary; Jowett, John; Montgomery, William, eds., The Oxford Shakespeare: The Complete Works (2nd ed.), Oxford: Oxford University Press, 2005*

Other Works Consulted
Gardner, H., ed. *The Metaphysical Poets,* The Penguin Poets, Penguin, 1968
Jonson, Ben, *Volpone,* in *Four English Comedies,* Penguin Books, 1969
Lucie-Smith, E., ed. *The Penguin Book of Elizabethan Verse,* The Penguin Poets, Penguin, 1968
The Norton Anthology of Poetry, Third Edition, Allison, A.W., Barrows, H., Blake, C.R., Carr, A.J., Eastman, A.M., English, H.M., eds. W.W. Norton & Co. 1983

Other Reference

Background information
Austen, J., *Mansfield Park,* ed. Katherine Sullivan, with Penguin Classics Note by Tony Tanner, Penguin Books, re-issue of 1996 edition, 2003
Cornwell, Patricia, *Portrait of a Killer,* A Little Brown Book, 2002
Chisholm, Kate, *Fanny Burney, Her Life,* Chatto and Windus, 1998
Holland, Clive, *Things Seen in Shakespeare's Country,* Seely, Service & Co, Ltd, 1927
Didau, David, *The Learning Spy*, Wordpress
Jerry Springer, the Opera, Richard Thomas and Stewart Lee, BBC version, Broadcast Monday 8 January, 2005
The Diaries of Samuel Pepys – A Selection, by Samuel Pepys and Robert Latham, Penguin Classics, 2003

Quotations to Introduction, and front matter
Christie, A. *The Mysterious Mr Quin: At the 'Bells and Motley',* Harper, 2003
The Monthly Review, or Literary Journal, 1819, quoted in Boas, F.S., *Christopher Marlowe, A Biographical and Critical Study*, p. 300. O.U.P., Clarendon Press, 1964

About the author

Jenny Clarke has been a teacher of English as a second language in Leicestershire and London. She has also taught history and English , qualifying as a teacher at Reading University's Bulmershe College, studying history and linguistics at the University of Leicester, and history and philosophy at Keele. She is also a member of the Marlowe Society. She lives in Leicester and Blackpool with her second husband and is currently working on a collection of otherworldy poems, and further investigation of the mysteries surround Christopher Marlowe and William Shakespeare. Her other work includes research on the 1930s campaign for the right of married women to work, and a study of errors in cohesion among second language learners. Her interests include bell ringing, writing poetry, amateur dramatics, and writing fiction.

If you have enjoyed this Daybreak Publication you may also enjoy these:

The Brotherhood – a novel of Shakespeare and Marlowe – James Clarke

The Ratscape Chronicles – and autobiography of Shetland life - James W. Clarke

Songs of the Simmerdim – poems – Jennifer Clarke

Lady Shounagan Plucks Her Eyebrows – poems – Joanne Byrne

The Book of Order – a philosophical fantasy – Jonathan Byrne